GW00792393

Alison's

Animal Lovers' Guide

to SUSSEX

2006/2007 Edition

May 2006

This book is dedicated to:
Brian Arnett

A close friend of the family, such a
lovely man, who was always the life and
soul of the party, lost so suddenly.

The loss of Brian made me put my life back into
perspective (does it really matter that I didn't wash
the dishes before I came out?) and made me realise that
we should enjoy life, our health, friends and family,
because you never know what's round the corner.

Alison's

Animal
Lovers'
Guide
to
SUSSEX

2006/2007 Edition

by Alison Frost

JASPER MAVERICK PUBLISHING CO
Bexhill-on-Sea, England

Copyright 2006 © Alison Frost

All rights reserved

No part of this publication may be reproduced, stored in a retrieval
system or transmitted, in any form or by any means: electronic,
mechanical, photocopying, recording, or otherwise, without
prior written permission of the publisher.

The author understands, to the best of her ability, that the information
contained in this book was accurate at the time of going to press.

Author: Alison Frost

Editor: Caroline Knight

Design and layout: Kirsty Doherty
Artwork: Mike Fitt
Illustrator: Helen Yeo
Picture research: Rob Willard and Rebecca Kerton
Web design: Wicked Kippers

Printed in Latvia. EU

ISBN 0-9553157-0-0
ISBN 978-0-9553157-0-1

Published by Jasper Maverick Publishing Co,
Fortune House, 13 Sackville Road,
Bexhill-on-Sea, East Sussex, TN39 3JD

www.jaspermaverickpublishing.co.uk

Contents

7	The team who helped make this guide possible
8	Acknowledgments
9	Charity animal helpline
10	A few words from Alison
11	Our illustrator
12	Contacts page; Talks
13	Our website; advertising on website
14	Submit an article
15-16	Submit an entry
17-18	Calendar of events
19-24	How to buy a copy
25-26	Pet names
27	Dating agency
28-29	How to use this book
30-31	Map - West Sussex
32-33	Map - Brighton
34-35	Map - East Sussex
37-108	Places to visit in Sussex
109-190	Informative features
191-281	Directory of services in Sussex
282	Crossword solution
283-303	Index
304	Photo acknowledgments

The team who made this book possible:

By Alison Frost

Glenda: who helped secure the website name.

Sue Crisford: my first member of staff, who tried to decipher my writing and helped set up the first office at home. She always wanted to make the text "flowery" and I wanted basic and simple language, but we always managed to compromise.

Mike Fitt: endlessly patient, who designed all the artwork, and somehow produced work that was what I imagined it needed to be and felt right.

Rob Willard: my second member to come on board, who was so tenacious when sourcing entries and was constantly reassuring people that it really was a FREE entry. He also proved to be superb at finding appropriate photos.

Bob and Craig at Wicked Kippers (best web company ever): who, with their patience, expertise and great communication, created the superb website we have today. They showed me ways to do things which I thought were impossible.

Ann Hood: a researcher who helped show us the way with our spreadsheets.

Tanya Vice: marvellous with web page write-up and superb contribution to meetings.

Fiona Bauval: who saw the job advert in Spain and quickly managed to grasp researching the Brighton and Hove areas.

Rosie Finey: admin office lass, who created her own role and was invaluable in keeping the whole project together; liaising with all the team and always knowing everything that was going on.

Kirsty Doherty: freelance graphic designer whose creativity, skill, expertise and vision implemented a great book layout and design – all exceeding my original expectations.

Caroline Knight: editor, whose expertise has helped me confound the sceptics who sneered at the Animal Lovers' Guide being a self-published book.

Helen Yeo: illustrator, talented and humorous.

Rebecca Kerton: who keeps me organised. As my office manager, she is multi-skilled, fun to have on board and nothing seems to faze her.

Sarah Shearer: our junior member.

Patrick Morgan and **Jane Utting:** our diligent proof readers.

Christine Boylan: our indexer, who seemed unfazed by the tight deadline!

Acknowledgments By Alison Frost

Please skip this page if you hate soppiness

Those of you who have not gone through really bad times in order to achieve a vision and dream won't understand the need for the following thanks. My advice for others who also have vision and ambition: keep at it and sod the others. Who knows if this may be the only book I self-publish? Only time and my inner strength will tell.

It was a long and hard 16 months that preceded the publication of this book. Along the way, many people dismissed my vision for a guidebook as a silly idea and far too costly. But some supported, encouraged and helped me in lots of different ways when I was down – and for them I will always be truly grateful. Especially the whole team of ALG whose passion, enthusiasm and drive spurred me on to finish it so that they could all feel and touch the BOOK!

So thanks go firstly to my mother and Jim, who just wanted me to have a proper job but still fed me and Jasper, lent me money and gave me love unconditionally. Pat Rogers, who was always at the end of the phone and constantly offered tea at the right time. Sheila Woolcott, my old neighbour, who was so positive about the concept. Mike, who showed endless patience when creating the artwork and never lost his temper. Rosie, whose belief, kindness, food parcels and supply of shortbread will be embedded in me for life. Bert Mepham for his physical and practical help and his moral support while selling the houses – always believing in me even though I owed him money.

Carole and Denise Barnes, who encouraged me and sent cash at such desperately needy times. Jackie Hammond who made me laugh and helped me feel strong, along with the cheese scones and hot chocolates we shared. Bill Shearer from the E-biz centre, who was enthusiastic and had belief in the ALG from our first meeting at the Broadband centre in Bexhill during April 2005. He was always there for me unceasingly, for every revised business plan that was needed, research, ideas and financial projections along the way. His unwavering enthusiasm, suggestions and input helped to make the book what it is now. Bill's love of figures and ensuing spreadsheets helped clinch the GRIST loan from Brighton University. For that I will be eternally grateful.

For Jasper's aunties Jo and Alison, who looked after him and fed him, gave him TLC and took the worry away while working on the book, especially when I was late, a million thanks. Jane and Mike, who always supported and believed. Jim Christy, Lu and Ellin from the Hastings and Bexhill hub, thanks for input, cups of tea and chocolate. Edward Clarke from the E-biz centre for his expertise and support on the technical intricacies of the world wide web.

The Creative Media Centre in Hastings, whose intangible support helped in many ways.

Thanks

Future plans: Charity Animal Helpline

As we researched for the book, one aspect became very apparent: that there appears to be no central number for people to call with any queries, night or day.

The RSPCA is perhaps the best known national charity but its resources are stretched and it hasn't always got the manpower to answer calls.

So from the sale of each book I am allocating £0.25 towards setting up a call centre, firstly for South East England, then covering more parts of UK once the other counties have been researched.

The idea of the Helpline is that it could help with the following scenarios, and more:

? If you are out late at night and come across an injured deer, fox or dog, what do you do?

? If you want to buy a hamster, where do you get it from?

? Who's your local breeder for a dog or cat?

? Just moved to the area? Where's the nearest specialist vet for your African grey parrot?

? Need a good, reliable person to mind your pet while you are away?

? Found a stray dog but don't know the nearest place that can scan the animal in order to see if it's chipped?

A dedicated Charity Animal Helpline formed by co-ordinating resources and attracting co-operation and support from relevant people could prove invaluable for those seeking animal-related information, advice, guidance and emergency information.

A few words from Alison

For those interested: The idea for Alison's Animal Lovers' Guide first came to me after I scoured many bookshops, including Ottakar's, Waterstone's, Borders and Sussex Stationers, asking for a book on animal attractions that I could visit.

Alas, none of them stocked it or could find such a thing on their vast databases. So I decided to write it!

I already knew of Raystede, an animal sanctuary near Ringmer in Sussex, as I had my dog, Lucy, there in quarantine when I returned from Cyprus. It was free to visit, with just a donation for car parking. The many birds, small animals, horses, donkeys and other animals that visitors could see were fabulous. I wondered how many other places existed that offered either free or reasonably priced entry.

In order to offer even better value for money, I decided to add features to my book. I wanted them to be informative, fun, humorous, highbrow and educational. My team of five researchers and myself also discovered that there were over 111 categories with a connection to animals and 1,750 establishments or places to visit in Sussex alone.

We included all those that sent the forms back, ranging from vets, alternative therapies, pet shops and equine to catteries, crematoriums, kennels, pet minders, rescue groups, wildlife sanctuaries and many more.

Hence the book as it is now. I know we are scraping the surface. So many aspects should be included – for instance breeders; specialist dog/cat rehoming centres; listing of pet names – which at present will be recorded on the website until the next edition in 2007. I am hoping that readers will fill us in on missing bits and help this book become the ultimate Animal Lovers' Guide.

Our illustrator ... Helen Yeo

Helen Yeo has been illustrating and drawing cartoons professionally for two years. She first hit upon the idea when drawing animals as a hobby in her spare time. When the time came to buy her first horse, selling her work was the ideal way of raising much needed cash, and so it blossomed.

Helen's skill with the pencil is equally as good as her vivid imagination. She has a special ability to turn an animal's expressions into something comical. And it's not just animals but people too. Working around animals all day, Helen has the perfect environment to see the sometimes hilarious situations animals get themselves into. Incredibly, she manages to convey this through her illustrations and paintings to capture that precise moment.

The process starts with a sketch outline of the scene, usually in pencil. She follows this with water colours (if it is a colour painting), or with shades of pencil on a sketch. She will then draw over the detail with fine-tipped pen, and add in more specific detail.

Helen sometimes feels that working to a brief enables her to have the freedom to be creative within set parameters. For example, when creating cartoons to work alongside a magazine article, it is clear what needs to be illustrated, however it also offers the chance to use the imagination to create an image around a topic.

When Helen takes on a commission, on the order form she asks her customers to state something funny or quirky about their pet, something that makes them unique. This helps create a brief for Helen to work around, and helps to create a caricature or cartoon that the customer can relate to, and that sums up the character of their pet.

As well as illustrating the Animal Lovers' Guides and concentrating on completing private commissions, Helen has been successful in winning the contract to draw cartoons and illustrations for Carriage Driving Magazine, and has had work published in the West Sussex Gazette. She is also in the process of creating a set of greeting cards to be available for sale in summer '06.

Contact details

Please don't hesitate to give us your feedback, ideas, complaints, input or just an observation.

Phone: 01424 205380

E-mail: alison@animalloversguides.co.uk

Web: www.animalloversguides.co.uk

Write: Alison's Animal Lovers' Guides
             Creative Media Centre
             17 & 45 Robertson Street
             Hastings
             East Sussex
             TN34 1HL

I am happy to come and give a talk, chat and answer questions about the book free of charge.

If you are a member of a club or group and need a speaker, please contact me at any of the above.

Alison Frost

Our website and how to advertise

www.animalloversguides.co.uk

As I started this book, I was paying lip service to having a website but now the site has evolved to provide such a wealth of information and is indispensable.

Apart from me, Alison (!), it has been our best advert as the guide was being created. Wicked Kippers our website company based in Bexhill, have excelled themselves in the creation of it, working in such harmony with me to show what can be done if one has a can-do attitude and imagination.

You can browse the site for:
- ✓ Ordering the hardcopy version.
- ✓ Buying the e-book of Animal Lovers' Guide to Sussex – updated quarterly.
- ✓ Subscription – getting all of the contents of current book and updates as they happen in real-time. Free invite to talks and subsidised trips out.
- ✓ Dating agency to meet like-minded pet owners, animal lovers and/or conservation enthusiast.
- ✓ Join the forums and discuss animal issues close to your heart.
- ✓ Enter competitions.
- ✓ Submit your establishment's photograph for display on website and maybe inclusion in next guide.
- ✓ The only place in Sussex to provide a comprehensive list of animal events.
- ✓ Jasper's diary (Alison's dog). All about his antics and behind the scenes at ALG
- ✓ Pet names and why they were named.
- ✓ Any animal place to visit or service can enter details and get a **FREE** entry in our e-book, next printed edition and view real time via a subscription.
- ✓ Locating a stockist near you to buy a copy or five of the guide.

ADVERTISING ON OUR WEBSITE

The prices are very competitive and are good value for money.

Ideal for those with animal businesses to promote and target their customers directly.

To advertise on the website contact **adverts@animalloversguides.co.uk** for rates and booking an advert.

Submit an article

Would you like to see your own name in print?

If you are enjoying reading and using Alison's Animal Lovers' Guide to Sussex, you may feel inspired to contribute to a future edition. Coming soon are Animal Lovers' Guides to Kent, Surrey and Hampshire – and articles from readers are welcomed.

This is a chance to share your animal-related knowledge in the form of a short article (up to 750 words). You will see that we have already covered topics such as indigenous species; phobias; training your pet; pets for children; equestrian pursuits and many others. Perhaps you have your own 'pet' subject that you would like to see in print, alongside a credit to you, the author.

Articles should be original and impartial. All facts should be carefully checked before submission. Copyright of any entry submitted to Alison's Animal Lovers' Guides (ALG) automatically passes to the guide and ALG reserves the right to edit articles where deemed necessary.

Good-quality photographs, preferably in a high-resolution digital format, could also be incorporated within your article, with credits to photographers on request.

Entries should be submitted:
via e-mail: **info@animalloversguides.co.uk**;
via the website: **www.animalloversguides.co.uk**;
or by post to:
Alison's Animal Lovers' Guides,
Creative Media Centre,
17 & 45 Robertson Street,
Hastings, East Sussex, TN34 1HL

Submit an entry for our forthcoming guides:
Kent, Surrey and Hampshire

Want your animal-related business or 'place to visit' to be included in the next guide?

Alison's Animal Lovers' Guides 'Directory' and 'Places to Visit' sections are being continually updated and expanded ready for the next edition of the guide. If your own business has an animal connection, perhaps you would like it to appear in print within the forthcoming **Kent, Surrey** or **Hampshire** guides, or in the **next edition of the Sussex** guide. This service is offered completely free of charge and entries will be included, space permitting, providing they are considered to be suitable.

Please complete the form overleaf and submit as soon as possible.

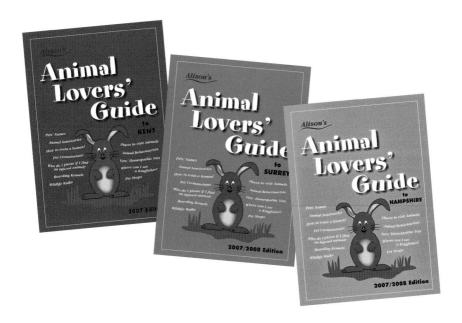

Free entry form

	FIELD		FIELD
Name of establishment:	1	Name of founder and date founded:	14
Type of establishment:	2	Public parking (Y/N; Free?):	15
Address: Postcode:	3	Public transport (nearest train station/bus stop):	16
Telephone:	4	Dogs allowed/walked:	17
Fax:	5		
Web:	6	Facilities (refreshments/toilets etc.):	18
E-mail:	7		
Nearest Town/Village:	8	Principal attraction/Human aspect:	19
Location/Directions:	9	Special events (eg open days):	20
Hours of opening to public:	10	Special aspects/specialise in a particular animal:	21
Disabled access/facilities:	11	Contact Name: Signed:	
Admission charges/details:	12		
Would you stock the book? (sale or return)	13	Tel: E-Mail:	

Send form by post to: **Alison's Animal Lovers' Guides, Creative Media Centre, 17 & 45 Robertson Street, Hastings, East Sussex, TN34 1HL** you can also submit online by visiting **www.animalloversguides.co.uk**

Free entry in our calendar of events:

As an event co-ordinator we would like to include yours in our calendar of events for Sussex at **www.animalloversguides.co.uk**

This is a free, regularly updated, one-of-a-kind, service where your event(s) can be viewed by everyone looking for a great day out in Sussex.

Below is an example of how the events will appear when viewed on our website.

Brownbread Highland Pony Open Day

Brownbread Street, Ashburnham, Battle
East Sussex
Highland Pony ride by owners in morning. 2pm open to the public, free entry (you may bring a picnic and eat on the lawn). At about 3pm there will be a conducted tour around the stud to see the stallions, mares and foals; about 1 hour. On return there will be tea and cakes on the lawn, croquet, bowls and possible swimming.
http://brownbread_rescue.250free.com/brownbread.html
tony.brownbread@tesco.net
01424 892381
Free entry, donation to Horse Rescue Charity for tea and cakes.
2pm + for public (HPEC & HPS riders in morning)
☺

Start Date» 13 August 2006
End Date» 13 August 2006

Screenshot © 2006 Wicked Kippers

To be included, please:
1. Send us a copy of any leaflets/booklets detailing your events; or
2. Complete the form overleaf and return to:
   Alison's Animal Lovers' Guides, 17 & 45 Robertson Street,
   Hastings, East Sussex, TN34 1HL; or
3. E-mail: events@animalloversguides.co.uk; or
4. Add an event online at **www.animalloversguides.co.uk**

For more than one entry, please photocopy the form.

All at the Animal Lovers' Guides look forward to hearing about your events.

Calendar of events entry form

PLEASE WRITE IN BLOCK CAPITALS	
Name of event:	
Town:	
County:	
Description:	
E-Mail:	
Phone:	
Price:	
Date/Time:	

CONTACT DETAILS (FOR OFFICE REFERENCE ONLY)	
Contact Name:	
Contact Telephone:	
Contact Address:	
Any other information:	

Send form by post to: **Alison's Animal Lovers' Guides, Creative Media Centre, 17 & 45 Robertson Street, Hastings, East Sussex, TN34 1HL** you can also submit online by visiting **www.animalloversguides.co.uk**

How to buy a copy

Are you reading this book in an animal establishment, book shop, friend's/neighbour's house? Or in a library? Why not treat yourself to your own copy?

Recommended retail price is £11.99 for the 2006/07 edition.

Also available from our website as well as an e-book updated quarterly (priced at £5.99).

The stockists' list is updated regularly on the website. Alternatively, view the stockists' list in the next few pages to find your nearest town. We advise you phone first to check stock levels.

See also in the directory section those establishments marked **S** denoting stockists.

If you would like to be a stockist, please phone us 01424 205430.

ARLINGTON
Arlington Bluebell Walk & Farm Trail
Bates Green Farm, Tyehill Road, Arlington, Polegate, East Sussex, BN26 6SH.
01323 485152

ARUNDEL
Arundel Boatyard and Riverside Tea Gardens
Arundel Boatyard Mill Road, Arundel, West Sussex, BN18 9PA.
01903 882609

The Wildfowl and Wetlands Centre
WWT Wetlands Centre Mill Road, Arundel, West Sussex, BN18 9PB.
01903 883355

ASHINGTON
Vickathea Animal Grooming
London Road, Ashington, West Sussex, RH20 3JR.
01903 893790

BATTLE
Senlac Vets
Mount Street, Battle, East Sussex, TN33 0EG.
01424 772148

BECKLEY
Manor House Cattery
Manor House, Whitbread Lane, Beckley, East Sussex, TN31 6TY.
01797 260253

BEXHILL-ON-SEA
Naturally Pets
Sunnylea, Watermill Lane, Bexhill-on-Sea, East Sussex, TN39 5JB.
01424 830551

Pebsham Riding School
Pebsham Lane, Bexhill-on-Sea, East Sussex, TN40 2RZ.
01424 732637

The Stable Door
3 Collington Mansions, Collington Avenue, Bexhill-on-Sea, East Sussex, TN39 3PU.
01424 216657

The Studio
31 Sackville Road, Bexhill-on-Sea, East Sussex, TN39 3JD.
01424 212301

BILLINGSHURST
Little Brockhurst Farm Canine Centre
Little Brockhurst Farm, Lordings Road, Billingshurst, West Sussex, RH14 9JE.
01403 784516

BOGNOR REGIS
Aldwick Pets
87 Aldwick Road, Bognor Regis, West Sussex, PO21 2NW.
01243 869444

BRIGHTON
A Pets Life
128 Whitehawk Way, Brighton, East Sussex, BN2 5QJ.
07932 239508

Booth Museum of Natural History
194 Dyke Road, Brighton, East Sussex, BN1 5AA.
01273 292777

Brighton Peace and Environment Centre
39-41 Surrey Street, Brighton, East Sussex, BN1 3PB.
01273 766610

Diamond Edge Ltd
126 Gloucester Road,
Brighton, East Sussex,
BN1 4BU.
01273 605922

Pampermepet
16 Imperial Arcade, Brighton,
East Sussex, BN1 3EA.
01273 746273

Repco Herpetological Supply
132 Preston Drove, Brighton,
East Sussex, BN1 6FJ.
01273 553303

BROAD OAK, BREDE
Beacon House
Boarding Cattery
Beacon House, Udimore
Road, Broad Oak, Brede, Rye,
East Sussex, TN31 6BX.
01424 882326

Rohese Cattery
Rosewood Furnace Lane,
Broad Oak, Rye,
East Sussex, TN31 6ES.
01424 882129

BURGESS HILL
T C Tack and Things
3 Valebridge Road, Burgess
Hill, West Sussex, RH15 0RA.
01444 230709

BUXTED
Sian Saddlery
Vulcan House, Farm Coopers
Green, Buxted, Uckfield,
East Sussex, TN22 4AT.
01825 732636

CROWBOROUGH
Ashdown Cattery
2 Spring Cats, London Road,
Crowborough,
East Sussex, TN6 1NT.
01892 662197

Karen's Dog Parlour
Sunrise Cottage, Queens
Road, Crowborough,
East Sussex, TN6 1PT.
01892 663210

Orchid Riding Centre
Walshes Road, Crowborough,
East Sussex, TN6 3RE.
01892 652020

The Pet Food Shop
Croft Road, Crowborough,
East Sussex, TN6 1DL.
01892 662961

DITCHLING
Dragonfly Saddlery
2 South Street, Ditchling,
East Sussex, BN6 8UQ.
01273 844606

Garden Pride
Garden Centre
Common Lane, Ditchling,
Hassocks, East Sussex,
BN6 8TP.
01273 846844

Stoneywish Nature Reserve
Spatham Lane, Ditchling,
East Sussex, BN6 8XH.
01273 843498

DURRINGTON
Pet Sitting Service
68 Greenland Road,
Durrington, Worthing,
West Sussex, BN13 2RN.
01903 260851

EAST DEAN
St Anne's Veterinary Group
15 Downland Way, East Dean,
East Sussex, BN20 0HR.
01323 422062

Seven Sisters Sheep Centre
Birling Gap Road, East Dean,
Nr Eastbourne,
East Sussex, BN20 0AA.
01323 423302

EAST GRINSTEAD
East Grinstead
Veterinary Hospital
Maypole Road, East Grinstead,
West Sussex, RH19 1HL.
01342 323072

Goughs
34 Railway Approach,
East Grinstead, West Sussex,
RH19 1BP.
01342 322255

Hayden Feeds
Orchard Farm, Holty Road,
East Grinstead,
West Sussex, RH19 3PP.
01342 323113

Portland Road
Veterinary Surgery
27 Portland Road,
East Grinstead, West Sussex,
RH19 4EB.
01342 327799

EAST PRESTON
Sally's Dog Grooming
2 South Strand Parade,
East Preston, West Sussex,
BN16 1NR.
01903 776800

EAST WITTERING
Canine Clips
4 Stocks Lane, East Wittering,
Chichester, West Sussex,
PO20 8BS.
01243 671444

EASTBOURNE
Champooch Studios
27 Firle Road, Eastbourne,
East Sussex, BN22 8EE.
01323 438999

Enterprise Centre
Station Parade, Eastbourne,
East Sussex, BN21 1BD.
01323 725593

St Anne's
Veterinary Group
6 St Anne's Road,
Eastbourne,
East Sussex, BN21 2DJ.
01323 640011

EASTERGATE
SPR Centre
Greenfields Farm, Fontwell,
Avenue, Eastergate,
Chichester, West Sussex,
PO20 3RU.
01243 542815

FELPHAM
Bognor Regis and District
Dog Training Club
Felpham Village Hall, Vicarage
Lane, Felpham, Bognor Regis,
West Sussex, PO22 7DZ.
01243 860083

Colour Therapy Healing
High Banks, 108 Limmer
Lane, Felpham, Nr Bognor
Regis, West Sussex, PO22 7LP.
01243 585609

FITTLEWORTH
Farthings
Wyncombe Close, Fittleworth,
Pulborough, West Sussex,
RH20 1HW.
01798 865495

FORD
New Carlton
Boarding Kennels
Ford Road, Ford, Arundel,
West Sussex, BN18 0BH.
01903 883116

FOREST ROW
Ashdown Forest Llama Park
Wych Cross, Forest Row,
East Sussex, RH18 5JN.
01825 712040

GORING-BY-SEA
Shoreline Pet Supplies
278 Goring Road,
Goring-by-Sea, Worthing,
West Sussex, BN12 4PE.
01903 243100

HADLOW DOWN
Kit Wilson Trust for
Animal Welfare
Stonehurst Lane,
Hadlow Down, Nr Uckfield,
East Sussex, TN22 4ED.
01825 830444

HAILSHAM
Dicker Aquatics
Wyevale Garden Centre,
Lower Dicker, Hailsham,
East Sussex, BN27 4BJ.
01323 844655

Lindey Lodge
Hempsted Lane West,
Hailsham, East Sussex,
BN27 3PR.
01323 842049

Marshfoot Cattery
145 Marshfoot Lane,
Hailsham,
East Sussex, BN27 2RD.
01323 841204

HAMBROOK
Amberley Boarding
Kennels
Woodmancote Lane,
Hambrook, West Sussex,
PO18 8UL.
01243 573671

HAYWARDS HEALTH
Mid Sussex Badger
Protection Group
Centenary Hall,
St Wilfrid's Way,
Haywards Heath,
West Sussex.
07910 198720

Oathall Veterinary Group
30 Oathall Road,
Haywards Heath,
West Sussex, RH16 3EQ.
01444 440224

Supreme Pet Care
43a Haywards Road,
Haywards Heath,
West Sussex, RH16 4HX.
01444 410661

The Dog Scene
6 Climping Close,
Haywards Health,
West Sussex, RH16 4DY.
01444 454398

The Pet and Garden
Warehouse
Unit 1, 30 Bridge Road,
Haywards Heath,
West Sussex, RH16 1TX.
01444 474019

HEATHFIELD
J & J Pets
23 Ridgeway Close,
Heathfield,
East Sussex, TN21 8NS.
01435 866544

HEYSHOTT
Canine Partners
Mill Lane, Heyshott,
Nr Midhurst, West Sussex,
GU29 0ED.
08456 580480

HOLLINGTON
Tammy's Pet Store
113 Battle Road, Hollington,
East Sussex, TN37 7AN.
01424 424988

HORAM
Downwood
Veterinary Centre
High Street, Horam,
Heathfield,
East Sussex, TN21 0EJ.
01435 812152

HORSHAM
A Cut Above
27 Swann Way, Horsham,
West Sussex, RH12 3NQ.
01403 272184

Farthings Veterinary Group
Farthings, Guildford Road,
Horsham,
West Sussex, RH12 1TS.
01403 252900

Holmbush Farm World
Faygate, Nr Horsham,
West Sussex, RH12 4SE.
01293 851700

**Oak Leaves Pet
Crematorium**
Brooks Green, Horsham,
West Sussex, RH13 0JW.
01403 741112

St Andrews Farm Kennels
Brooks Green, Horsham,
West Sussex, RH13 0JW.
01403 741248

HOVE
Avon's Dog Grooming
Unit 1, Lion Mews,
Richardson Road, Hove,
East Sussex, BN3 5RA.
01273 771779

Acorn
177 Hangleton Way, Hove,
East Sussex, BN3 8EY.
01273 430301

Pet Pet Pet
5 West Way, Hove,
East Sussex, BN3 8LD.
01273 884949

HURSTPIERPOINT
Pierpoint Pet Supplies
97 High Street, Hurstpierpoint,
West Sussex, BN6 9RE.
01273 832368

Washbrooks Farm
Brighton Road, Hurstpierpoint,
West Sussex, BN6 9EH.
01273 832201

IDEN
Grove Farm Riding School
Grove Farm, Grove Lane,
Iden, Nr Rye,
East Sussex, TN31 7PY.
01797 280362

IFIELD
**Ifield Park Animal &
Country Centre**
Bonnetts Lane, Ifield, Crawley,
West Sussex, RH11 0NY.
01293 511832

LANGNEY
St Anne's Veterinary Group
1 Anstrim Court,
Pembury Road, Langney,
East Sussex, BN23 7LU.
01323 763949

LEWES
Small Pets Hotel
35 Evelyn Road, Lewes,
East Sussex, BN7 2SS.
01273 476559

The Equine Warehouse
The Depot Spring Gardens,
Lewes, East Sussex, BN7 2PT.
01273 483399

LITTLEHAMPTON
**Fitzalan House
Veterinary Group**
31 Fitzalan Road,
Littlehampton,
West Sussex, BN17 5ET.
01903 713806

LOWER WILLINGDON
St Anne's Veterinary Group
9 Gorringe Valley Road,
Lower Willingdon, Eastbourne,
East Sussex, BN20 9SX.
01323 487655

LOXWOOD
**The Wey and Arun
Canal Trust**
The Granary, Flitchfold Farm,
Loxwood, Billingshurst,
Sussex, RH14 0RH.
01403 752403

MIDHURST
Cowdray Leisure
The Estate Office,
Easebourne, Midhurst,
West Sussex, GU29 0AQ.
01730 812423

Posh Dogs
Cocking Causeway,
Midhurst,
West Sussex,
01730 816167

NEWHAVEN
Guinea Pig Rescue Centre
6 Northdown Road,
Newhaven,
East Sussex, BN9 9JB.
01273 512248

**Sussex Amphibian and
Reptile Group**
c/o 7 Gibbon Road,
Newhaven, East Sussex,
BN9 9EW.
01273 515762

NORTHIAM
Northiam DIY & Garden
Main Street, Northiam,
East Sussex, TN31 6NB.
01797 252162

NUTBOURNE
Priors Leaze Veterinary Clinic
Priors Leaze Lane, Nutbourne,
Nr Chichester, West Sussex,
PO18 8RH.
01243 376000

PETWORTH
The Stag Inn
The Stag Inn Balls Cross,
Petworth, West Sussex,
GU28 9JP.
01403 820241

PULBOROUGH
Arun Veterinary Group
121 Lower Street, Pulborough,
West Sussex, RH20 2BP.
01798 872089

PUNNETTS TOWN
Farthing Saddlery
South West View, Punnetts
Town, Nr Heathfield,
East Sussex, TN21 9DE.
01435 830440

RINGMER
The Raystede Centre for Animal Welfare
Raystede, Ringmer,
East Sussex, BN8 5AT.
01825 840252

RUSSELLS GREEN
Happy Hunting Grounds
Little Park Farm, Hooe Road
(B2095), Russells Green,
Ninfield, East Sussex,
TN33 9EH.
01424 892396

RYE
Alfie Greys
Units 20-23 Ropewalk
Shopping Centre, Ropewalk,
Rye, East Sussex, TN31 7NA.
01797 227495

Cinque Ports Veterinary Associates
Cinque Port Square, Rye,
East Sussex, TN31 7AN.
01797 222265

SEAFORD
Pet Love
9 Talland Parade, Saxon Lane,
Seaford, East Sussex.
01323 897929

Seaford Aquatics
14 Sutton Road, Seaford,
Sussex, BN25 1RU.
01323 897623

Seaford and District Dog Training Club
4 Kingsmead Close, Seaford,
East Sussex, BN25 2EY.
01323 899032

Seven Sisters Country Park
Sussex Downs Conservation,
BD Seven Sisters Country,
Park, Exceat, Seaford,
East Sussex, BN25 4AD.
01323 870280

SHOREHAM-BY-SEA
Taking The Lead
16 Mill Hill Close,
Shoreham-by-Sea,
West Sussex, BN43 5TP.
01273 463554

Living World
28 Kingston Broadway,
Shoreham-by-Sea,
West Sussex.
01273 595779

TTL Shop
16 Mill Hill Close,
Shoreham-by-Sea,
West Sussex, BN43 5TP.
01273 440949

SIDLEY
Barby Keel Animal Sanctuary
Freezeland Lane, Sidley, Bexhill,
East Sussex, TN39 5JD.
01424 222032

SOMPTING
Four Paws Dog Grooming
34 Sedbury Road, Sompting,
West Sussex, BN15 0LL.
01903 521499

ST LEONARDS ON SEA
Hastings Badger Protection Society
304 Bexhill Road, St Leonards
on Sea, East Sussex, TN38 8AL.
01424 439168

Internal Arts
61 Westfield Lane,
St Leonards on Sea,
East Sussex, TN37 7NF.
07950 264204

Keith Bing MBIPDT
4 Sandwich Drive,
St Leonards on Sea,
East Sussex, TN38 0XJ.
01424 720475

The Dawg's Biscuits
65 Norman Road,
St Leonards on Sea,
East Sussex, TN38 0EG.
01424 424682

STEYNING
Steyning Pet Shop
46 High Street, Steyning,
West Sussex, BN43 3RD.
01903 814455

TWINEHAM
Groomingdales
Hillmans Farm,
Bolney Chapel Road,
Twineham, West Sussex,
RH17 5NN.
01444 881810

UCKFIELD
Heaven Farm
Furners Green, Uckfield,
East Sussex, TN22 3RG.
01825 790226

Hurstwood Feeds Ltd
Vulcan House Farm,
Coopers Green, Nr Uckfield,
East Sussex, TN22 4AT.
01825 733073

Meadowside Boarding Kennels
High Cross Farm,
Eastbourne Road, Uckfield,
East Sussex, TN22 5QW.
01825 840674

Sussex Horse Rescue Trust
Hempstead Farm,
Hempstead Lane, Uckfield,
East Sussex, TN22 3DL.
01825 762010

Wilderness Wood
Hadlow Down,
Nr Uckfield, East Sussex.
01825 830509

UPPER BEEDING
Handsome Hounds
4 Hyde Square,
Upper Beeding,
West Sussex, BN44 3JE.
01903 810061

WARNHAM
**Mayes & Scrine Equine
Veterinary Practice**
Dawes Farm, Bognor Road,
Warnham, West Sussex,
RH12 3SH.
01306 628222

WEST CHILTINGTON
West Chiltington Cavaliers
Kelmscott, The Hawthorns,
West Chiltington,
West Sussex, RH20 2QH.
01798 813474

The White Orchid
Harbolets Road,
West Chiltington,
West Sussex, RH20 2LG.
01798 815191

WILMINGTON
**Josie Tipler Animal
Portraits**
Magpie Cottage, Hayreed
Lane (off Thornwell Road),
Wilmington, Polegate,
East Sussex, BN26 6RR.
01323 485153

WORTH
A K Jones Bird Vet
The Cottage, Turners Hill
Road, Worth, Crawley,
West Sussex, RH10 4LY.
01293 884629

WORTHING
Manor Guest House
100 Broadwater Road,
Worthing,
West Sussex, BN14 8AN
01903 236028

Worthing Animal Clinic
30/32 Newland Road,
Worthing,
West Sussex, BN11 1JR.
01903 202248

As we go to press we are also approaching Tourist Information Centres and Independent Bookshops to become stockists. Please see our website **www.animalloversguides.co.uk** for up to date information.

Pet name questionnaire

We are carrying out research for Animal Lovers' Guides to find out the various names that people give their pets, and the reasons behind those names.

To be included, simply complete and return the questionnaire overleaf. For more than one entry, please photocopy the form.

Alternatively you may e-mail to:
petnames@animalloversguides.co.uk

You and your pet could soon be appearing on our website www.animalloversguides.co.uk and in the next edition of Animal Lovers' Guides.

Some results so far:

Type	Name	Reason	Owner
Cat	Mouse	Very nervous ex-lab rescue	Felix, Winchelsea
Siamese cat	Kareltje	Dutch name, 'little carl' and the name of the only cat that the neighbours' dog had ever known	Jan Vermaat
Cat	Griffin	Named after sign on side of a van seen opposite rescue centre	Loni Mayhew, Hailsham
Dog	Archie Moo	'mou' is greek for my and he is black and white like a cow, so spelt 'mou' as Moo! - My Archie	K. Williams, Brighton

Pet names questionnaire

PLEASE WRITE IN BLOCK CAPITALS	
Pet's Name:	
Type of pet: (cat, dog, horse, rabbit, rat, tarantula, etc.)	
Reason for choosing pet's name:	
Name of owner:	
Address:	
Contact Number:	

Send form by post to: **Alison's Animal Lovers' Guides, Creative Media Centre, 17 & 45 Robertson Street, Hastings, East Sussex, TN34 1HL** you can also submit online by visiting **www.animalloversguides.co.uk**

Dating Agency ♡

What better way to meet a lovely person who has a pet or loves animals, than through the Animal Lovers' dating agency?

Love tarantulas? There maybe someone else out there who shares the same passion.

People who like animals are generally a great type, having kind and caring natures. That, in itself, enhances the chance of meeting a partner via the Animal Lovers' Dating Agency.

The service will be available to subscribers via the website, initially for the Sussex region, followed by Kent, late 2006.

How to use this book

We have tried to make this book as easy to use as possible.
However, sample entries below make this even easier to follow.

COWDRAY LEISURE

By appointment badger
watching, guided wildlife
awareness. School trips catered for

The Estate Office, Easebourne, Midhurst,
West Sussex, GU29 0AQ.
Tel: 01730 812423.
Fax: 01730 817962.
e-mail: leisure@cowdray.co.uk
web: www.cowdray.co.uk
Contact: Darron Carver.
Opening hours: By appointment only.
Admission: £70 for an outing. Maximum
of 4 in group.

Directions: 1 mile north of Midhurst on
the A272.
Map Reference: WS44
Information:
• Guided walks and badger watching.
• Toilets and refreshments in golf club.
• Most indigenous mammals and birds,
  flora and fauna.

SECTION ONE
Places to visit in Sussex for animal lovers.
• Organised alphabetically by town,
  then by attraction.

• Colour coded to depict the type of
  establishment.
  ▨ Animal Sanctuary
  ▨ Aquatic and Sealife
  ▨ Country Parks and Walks
  ■ Equestrian Centre
  ▨ Nature Reserve
  ■ Visitor Attraction
  ▨ Working Animal Centre

• Animals likely to be seen at establishment:

Symbol	Represents	Symbol	Represents
🐕	Dogs	🐦	Birds
🐈	Cats	🐒	Zoo animals
🐸	Amphibians and reptiles	🐬	Aquatic
		🐿	Small mammals
🐐	Farm animals	🦙	Exotic animals
🐎	Equestrian	🕷	Insects

• Contact details and opening hours.

• Facilities at establishment (from left to right):

Dogs allowed; Disabled access; Restrooms;
Refreshments; Parking; Stock this book.
• Directions.
• Map Reference Number.
• Other information.

**Please note that not all establishments will allow dogs entry, although most places accept
guide dogs. Please check the place to visit beforehand.**

SECTION TWO
A series of informative articles for pet owners and animal lovers.

WHERE CAN I SEE ... ?

Helpful tips for Sussex wildlife hunters

You've got the book, bought the tee shirt, now all you need is a glimpse of a particular animal in order to make your wildlife hunt complete. But where can you see our wonderful British wildlife in its natural state? Here are a few tips to help you on your journey:

Water vole

Ratty in Wind of the Willows is really our beloved water vole, a shy creature who has declined in numbers by over 90% in the last 20 years. If you are a casual wildlife watcher it's doubtful that you will have ever seen one – you need to know where to look and then you need lots of patience! Water voles need good clean water, they won't tolerate pollution and can't survive in dry areas, as their name suggests. The East Sussex Coastal Plain has a couple of strongholds for the endangered water vole in this county – including Pett Levels nature reserve in Rye. The good news is that this animal responds quickly when water management improves, so it is possible that you will find Ratty in areas that are well managed, with good levels of water and little pollution.

Otters

We all love this cheeky little chappie, with his playful nature and semi-amphibious lifestyle. But where can we see one in Sussex? Back in the 1950s, otters were numerous, particularly around the Arun, Adur and Western Rother areas. But hunting, combined with the poisoning of

fish and eels by chemicals that were once widely used on crops and farm stock, saw the rapid decline of this beautiful animal. No evidence of them was found from the mid 1970s onwards. Recently, however, otters are reappearing in both East and West Sussex, some due to re-introductions. An otter road-kill victim on the Sussex/Hampshire borders in 2001 confirmed that the animals were crossing through the Western Rother region into Sussex from Hampshire, where there are already established breeding otters. Further evidence has also suggested that otters are present at Wallers Haven in Pevensey, Rye Harbour and Rustington. Sightings have also recently been recorded around the Pulborough Brooks area on the river Arun.

Wading birds

Mud, glorious mud, is what is loved most by many waders such as oystercatchers, godwits, turnstones, dunlins and avocets. There are about 200 species of wading birds that love to feed in soft mud and sand at the water's edge. Those with short beaks such as ringed plover, knot, sanderling, turnstone and dunlin pick food from the

Otters can now be seen in both East and West Sussex

surface, whilst longer-beaked birds such as redshank oystercatcher, snipe, avocet and curlew dig down deeper for worms and shellfish. Pagham Harbour in West Sussex together with Chichester and Langstone Harbours form the largest area of mud in the south. Birdwatchers should be armed with a good pair of binoculars and be prepared to sit and watch for at least a couple of hours – just a few minutes is not enough to see the wealth of wading birds that will appear.

Birds of prey

The sparrowhawk is now one of the most commonly seen birds of prey. It loves set-aside land and even visits garden bird tables ... not to feed in a picturesque manner from nuts and seeds, but to snatch other birds such as blue tits whilst they feast! The female sparrowhawk is larger than the male, preying on bigger birds including

pigeons, doves and thrushes. Kestrels are also quite common in Sussex – usually seen hovering above roadways, in open countryside and even along motorway verges. The hobby is an uncommon visitor from Africa, whilst the buzzard is gradually making its way up from the west country and there have been recent sightings in Sussex. The latter can often be identified by the mewing 'kiew' sound as it soars effortlessly on thermal winds. It prefers open hillsides and wooded valleys and likes to nest in trees and on cliff ledges. Other Sussex visitors include Montagu's harrier, hen harrier and marsh harrier.

Nightingale

Beachy Head in Sussex may not be the first place you would associate with nightingales, but in fact they breed here very successfully. They love the dense clipped scrub that is hidden away in

148   www.animalloversguides.co.uk   Calendar of events visit www.animalloversguides.co.uk   149

LANGNEY

St Annes Veterinary Group
Veterinary care for small animals
1 Anstrim Court, Pembury Road, Langney,
East Sussex, BN23 7LU
Tel: 01323 763949 **Fax:** 01323 73896
web: www.eastbournevet.co
Contact: Jim Dash.
Opening Hours: ... ay to Friday 9am to
11am and 5p... to 7... Saturday 9am to 11am.

Directions: Off Langney Rise near Langney
Shopping Centre.

SECTION THREE
Directory of professional animal services.

- Colour coded to depict the type of service (contents listing on page 191).
- Organised alphabetically by town, then by service, then by name.
- Contact details.
- Opening hours.
- Admission charges.
- Facilities at service (see opposite for key).
- Directions.
- Specialist information about service.

West Sussex

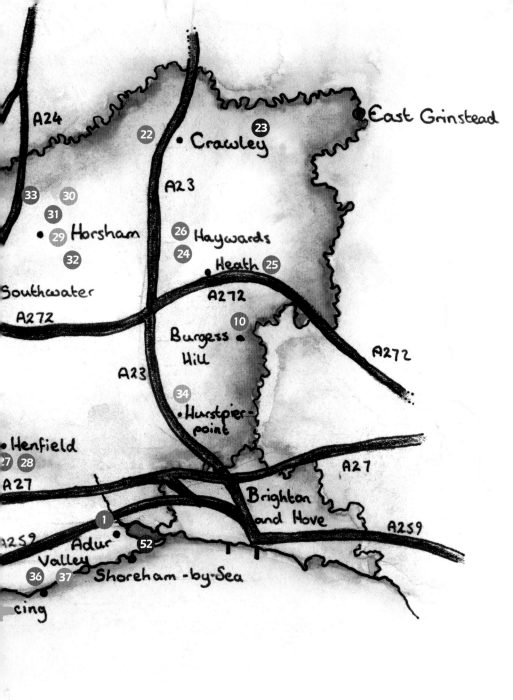

Map not to scale

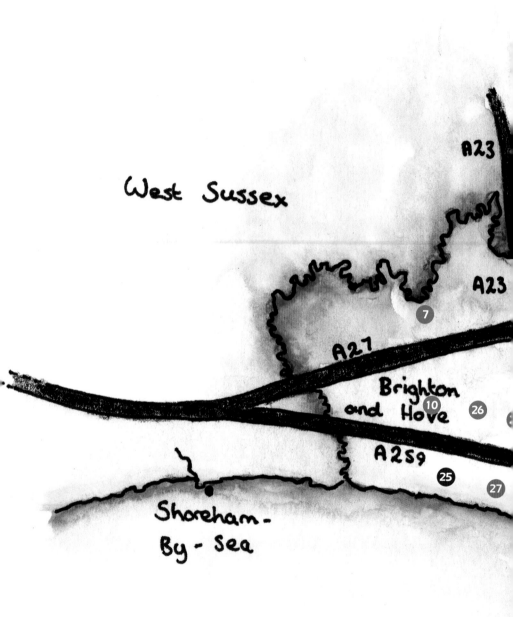

West Sussex

A23

A23

7

A27

Brighton
and Hove

10

26

A259

25

27

Shoreham-
By-Sea

Map not to scale

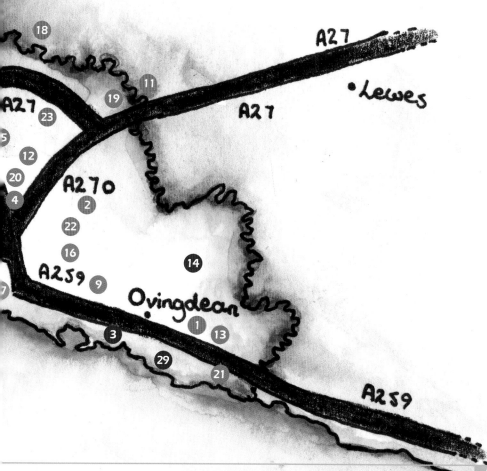

Brighton & Hove

East Sussex

A27

•Lewes

A27

A27

A270

A259

Ovingdean

A259

A26

A26

A22

A26

A22

A26

19 Forest
24 Row
25

21 22

23 Eridge

Fair
warp

16 15

Crowbor-
oug

A

53

51

A22

54

49

South
Chailey

Uckfield

52

Black boys

13

East

Hoathle

Chiddina

20

A272

17 18

14

Ditchling

A26

A22

A23

34 33

South
Malling

50

Ringmer

41

39

35

A27

Lewes

36 38

37

3

2

Arlingt

A27

1

A259

Alfriston

A259

A259

40

Newhaven

47

48

Seaford

Birli

East Sussex

hurst •
55

265

A21

A28

A21

hfield

7

271

42 •

Hailsham

A27

22

Battle •

5 4

6

Russell's
Green
7
11 A259 9
8 10
Bexhill

Iden •
32

A28

Rye •

45

46

44

43

A259

27
28
29 30

Hastings

A259

Map not to scale

Places to visit in...

38	Adur Valley
38	Alfriston
39	Amberley
39-40	Arlington
41-42	Arundel
42-43	Battle
44-46	Bexhill
47	Billingshurst
48	Birling Gap
48	Blackboys
49	Bognor Regis
50-61	Brighton
62	Burgess Hill
63-68	Chichester
68	Chiddingly
69	Crawley
70	Crowborough
71	Ditchling
72	East Grinstead
72	East Hoathly
73	Eridge
74	Fairwarp
74-75	Forest Row
75	Hailsham
76-77	Hastings
78-79	Haywards Heath
79	Heathfield
80	Henfield
81-83	Horsham
84-85	Hove
86	Hurstpierpoint
86	Iden
87-88	Lancing
88-91	Lewes
92-94	Littlehampton
95	Midhurst
96	Newhaven
96	Ovingdean
97-98	Petworth
99	Pulborough
100	Ringmer
100	Russell's Green
101-102	Rye
103	Seaford
104	Shoreham
104	South Chailey
105	South Malling
105	Southwater
106-107	Uckfield
108	Wadhurst
108	Wannock

MILL HILL

DRUSILLAS PARK

Nature reserve with beautiful
scenery and wildlife

Mill Hill, West Sussex.
Tel: 01273 625242.
web: www.adur.gov.uk
Opening hours: Open reserve.

Map Reference: WS1
Information:
• Views across the Adur Valley.
• Wild flowers and butterflies.
• Rare Adonis Blue Butterfly.
• 500 metres of easy access trail for
  the disabled.

Zoo and leisure attractions with
playground and shops

East Sussex, BN26 5QS.
Tel: 01323 874100.
Fax: 01323 874101.
e-mail: info@drusillas.co.uk
web: www.drusillas.co.uk
Opening hours: Winter, 10am to 4pm.
Summer, 10am to 5pm. Closed Christmas
Eve, Christmas Day and Boxing Day.
Admission: Phone first as prices change.

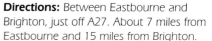

Directions: Between Eastbourne and
Brighton, just off A27. About 7 miles from
Eastbourne and 15 miles from Brighton.
Map Reference: ES1
Information:
• Zoo, leisure attractions, train, and
  playground.
• Two restaurants, five shops and five
  toilet blocks.
• See www.drusillas.co.uk or
  www.animalloversguides.co.uk for
  events throughout the year.
• Lar gibbons are new at the Zoo.
• Guide dogs welcome.

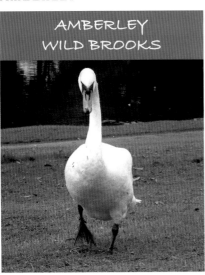

AMBERLEY WILD BROOKS

Country walk and nature reserve

Amberley, West Sussex. Nearest postcode BN18 9NT.
Tel: 01273 494777.
web: www.sussexwt.org.uk

Map Reference: WS2
Information:
- Lovely country walks with the possibility of sighting Bewicks swans, dragonflies and wetland wildlife.
- Access from Wey South path only, which is located through the middle of the Brooks Farm from Hog Lane in Amberley village.
- Bewicks swans.
- Dogs must be on leads.

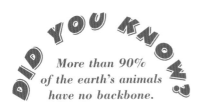

More than 90% of the earth's animals have no backbone.

ARLINGTON BLUEBELL WALK & FARM TRAIL

Many species of birds and wildlife. Lovely nature park

Bates Green Farm, Tye Hill Road, Arlington, Polegate, East Sussex, BN26 6SH.
Tel: 01323 485152.
e-mail: jmccutchan@nlconnect.co.uk
web: www.bluebellwalk.co.uk
Contact: Carolyn and John.
Opening hours: Daily, 10am to 5pm.
Please ring to check season opening times.
Admission: Adults £2.50. Children £1.00. Seniors £2.00. Family £6.00.

Directions: 5 miles north west of Polegate, midway between A22 and A27.
Map Reference: ES2
Information:
- Wildlife, insects, flora and fauna.
- Many species of birds to see.
- Dogs must be on leads.

ARLINGTON RESERVOIR

*Conservation area
with dog walking park*

Berwick, Nr Polegate, East Sussex.
Tel: 01323 870810.
e-mail: contactcentre@southeastwater.co.uk
web: www.southeastwater.co.uk
Opening hours: Open reservoir.

Directions: Approximately half a mile off the A27 Lewes to Eastbourne Road. Signposted to Berwick.
Map Reference: ES3
Information:
• Beautiful setting with nature trail.
• Toilets, car park and several picnic areas.

A group of rhinos is called a crash.

ARUNDEL BOATYARD AND RIVERSIDE TEA GARDENS

*Boatyard with boats for hire.
Cruises along the River Arun*

Arundel Boatyard, Mill Road, Arundel, West Sussex, BN18 9PA.
Tel: 01903 882609.
e-mail: arundelboats@hotmail.com
web: http://carol-buller.tripod.com
Contact: Carol Buller.
Opening hours: Seasonal, March to October: Boats 10am to 4pm, Tea garden 9am to 5pm.

Directions: On A27 between Chichester and Brighton. Mill Road is by old bridge next to Post Office. Boatyard is via Mill Road.
Map Reference: WS3
Information:
• Boat hire, cruises.
• Tea gardens, water for dogs and gift shop.
• Arundel Festival at the end of August.

DENMANS GARDEN

Walled garden, gravel stream, ponds and wildlife

Denmans Lane, Fontwell, Nr Arundel, West Sussex, BN18 0SU.
Tel: 01243 542808.
Fax: 01243 544064.
e-mail: denmans@denmans-garden.co.uk
web: www.denmans-garden.co.uk
Opening hours: 9am to 5pm.
Admission: Adults £3.95. Children (4-16) £2.25. Seniors £3.45.

Directions: Situated off the A27 (westbound) between Chichester and Arundel. Adjacent to Fontwell Racecourse.
Map Reference: WS4
Information:
• Garden café and plant centre (entry free).
• Toilets.
• Courses, functions and evening visits.
• Guide dogs welcome.

THE WILDFOWL AND WETLANDS CENTRE

A must-see! Fabulous place. Almost certainly see Kingfishers

WWT Wetlands Centre, Mill Road, Arundel, West Sussex, BN18 9PB.
Tel: 01903 883355.
Fax: 01903 884834.
e-mail: info@arundel.wwt.org.uk
web: www.wwt.org.uk/visit/arundel/
Contact: Geoff Squire.
Opening hours: Summer, 9.30am to 5.30pm. Winter, 9.30am to 4.30pm.
Admission: Adults £5.95. Children £3.75. Concessions £4.75.

Directions: On the A27 between Chichester and Worthing. The WWT Centre is three-quarters of a mile outside of town, next to river and clearly signposted.
Map Reference: WS5
Information:
• Wild and captive birds.
• Restaurant, gift shop, toilets and disabled toilets.
• Regular programmes – ask for leaflet.
• Birds, wildfowl, Kingfishers and New Zealand Blue Ducks.
• Guide dogs welcome.

PLACES TO VISIT

1066 COUNTRY WALK

Country walk and nature trail

Battle Tourist Information Centre,
Battle Abbey Gatehouse, High Street,
Battle, East Sussex, TN33 0AD.
Tel: 01424 773721.
Fax: 01424 773436.
e-mail: battletic@rother.gov.uk
web: www.1066country.com
Opening hours: Open country.

Directions: Just off junction of A2100
and Marley Lane.
Map Reference: ES4
Information:
• Stunning countryside between Rye
  and Battle.
• Information centres at Rye and Battle.
• Many events throughout the year. See
  website for details.
• Many species of plants and wildlife.
• Dogs must be on leads.

BUCKWELL FARM

*Country walk with views
of the High Weald landscape*

Buckwell Farm, Nr Battle, East Sussex.
Opening hours: Open park.

Map Reference: ES5
Information:
• The circular 2km walk connects with a
  public right of way to take you through
  a characteristic High Weald landscape
  which is being sensitively managed for
  the benefit of wildlife.
• Hedgerows are being restored through
  a programme of copicing and
  replanting and arable land is being
  reverted to species rich grassland using
  seed from neighbouring flower-rich
  meadows.
• Please keep to the marked path.
• Dogs must be on leads.

POWDERMILL WOOD

Nature reserve with wildlife walks

Powdermill Wood, Battle, East Sussex.
Nearest postcode TN33 0SY.
Tel: 01273 494777.
web: www.sussexwt.org.uk
Opening hours: Open park.

Map Reference: ES6
Information:
- Cycle network nearby.
- Circular nature trail winds through whole of Powdermill Wood.
- Wildlife and beautiful setting.
- Plants such as Marsh Marigold, Tussock Sedge, Golden Saxifrage can be found here.
- The best time to visit is Spring. No stiles or gates, but steep slope.

DID YOU KNOW?
Greenfly give birth to 25 babies.

PLACES TO VISIT

BEXHILL

BROAD OAK PARK

Open park with allotments

Broad Oak Lane, Bexhill, East Sussex.
Tel/Contact: Rother District Council.
web: www.rother.gov.uk
Opening hours: Open park.

Directions: See website for directions
Map Reference: ES7
Information:
• Allotments, open space and woodland.
• Horse rides available.

EGERTON PARK

Lovely park with pretty lakes

Egerton Road, Bexhill, East Sussex.
Tel/Contact: Rother District Council.
web: www.rother.gov.uk
Opening hours: Open park.

Directions: Start at Sackville Road in
town centre and head towards seafront.
Egerton Road is on the right-hand side
but Egerton Park is on the left.
Map Reference: ES8
Information:
• Play area, bowls, five-a-side football,
  tennis, putting, boating lake, yacht
  pond, swans and ducks.

GALLEY HILL PARK

Take your dog and children –
wonderful views across the sea

East Parade, Bexhill, East Sussex.
Tel/Contact: Rother District Council.
web: www.rother.gov.uk
Opening hours: Open park.

Directions: Along the seafront towards Hastings, up on the hill.
Map Reference: ES9
Information:
• Play area.
• Basketball hoop.
• Skateboard ramps.
• Cafe a short walk from park.

GILLHAM WOOD

Small but beautiful woodland

Withyham Road, Bexhill on Sea,
East Sussex, Nearest postcode TN39 3BA.
Tel: 01273 494777.
web: www.sussexwt.org.uk
Opening hours: Open park.

Directions: Accessible via the B2182 (Cooden Drive). Many access points, the easiest being Withyham Road which runs across the Southern Border.
Map Reference: ES10
Information:
• Many woodland birds.
• Dogs must be on leads.

It takes 12 honeybees
working together their
entire lifetimes to make
about a teaspoon of honey.

HOOE COMMON

Nature reserve with wildlife walks

Bexhill, East Sussex.
Nearest postcode TN33 9HT.
web: www.sussexwt.org.uk
Opening hours: Open park.

Directions: Public footpaths begin in Hooe village opposite the telephone kiosk and cross a field to enter the reserve.
Map Reference: ES11
Information:
• Variety of Warblers.
• Many plant species.
• Dogs must be on leads.

DID YOU KNOW?
A female chicken less than a year old is called a 'pullet'.

FISHERS FARM PARK

A unique place to visit - a wonderful day out for the family

Newpound Lane, Wisborough Green, Billingshurst, West Sussex, RH14 0EG.
Tel: 01403 700063.
e-mail: info@fishersfarmpark.co.uk
web: www.fishersfarmpark.co.uk
Opening hours: From 10am to 5pm every day except Christmas and Boxing Day.
Admission: Adults £7.75-£10.75. Children (3-16) £7.25-£10.25. Children (to 2 yrs.) £4.00-£7.00. Seniors £6.25-£9.25.

Directions: Signposted from all main roads approaching Wisborough Green. Off the A272.
Map Reference: WS6
Information:
- Giant Spiders Web frame, pony rides, Shire Horse and pony demonstrations.
- Adventure play equipment, quad bikes, trampolines, electric cars and tractors. Diggers, kites, outside games, table football and garden machinery.
- Restaurant, tuck shop, Farmers Grill in the park, hot food, snacks, drinks and ice creams.
- Animal adoption, family visits, birthday parties, group visits and membership schemes.

THE WEY AND ARUN CANAL TRUST

Canal restoration and wildlife walk

The Granary, Flitchfold Farm, Loxwood, Billingshurst, West Sussex, RH14 0RJ.
Tel: 01403 752403.
Fax: 01403 753991.
e-mail: pr@wact.org.uk
web: www.weyandarun.co.uk
Contact: Sally Schupke.
Opening hours: 9am to 9pm.

Directions: The public trip boat operates from the landing stage at the Onslow Arms on the B2133 in Loxwood.
Map Reference: WS7
Information:
- Scenic towpath along the Surrey/Sussex border.
- Refreshments available at the canal-side pub.
- Small boats rally in May. Heritage open days in September and special boat trips Christmas, Boxing Day and Easter.
- Dogs and horses are very welcome to use the wide and restored towpath.
- Boat trips cost £4 per person.

Largest collection of sheep breeds
in the world – 47

Birling Gap Road, East Dean,
Nr Eastbourne, East Sussex, BN20 0AA.
Tel: 01323 423302.
Fax: 01323 423302.
e-mail: sevensisters.sheepcentre@talk21.com
web: www.sheepcentre.co.uk
Contact: Terry Wigmore.
Opening hours: July to September, 2pm to
5pm, weekdays, 11am to 5pm, weekends
and school holidays. March to May, 2pm to
5pm on weekdays. Closed at weekend.
Admission: Adults £3.50. Seniors and
concessions £3.00. Children (2-15) £2.50.
Family £11.00 (2 adults and 2 children).

Directions: 3 miles west of Eastbourne
on the A259. In the village of East Dean,
turn left towards sea and Birling Gap.
The centre is half a mile on the left.
Map Reference: ES12
Information:
• Tea room, picnic area and toilets. No
  disabled toilets.
• Sheep, horses, calves, goats, pigs, geese,
  ducks, chickens, rabbits, guinea pigs,
  chinchillas and ferrets.

Wildlife Walk!

Blackboys, East Sussex.
Tel: 020 7238 6907.
web: www.defra.gov.uk
Opening hours: Open park but best to
visit Spring, Summer and Autumn.

Directions: Accessible off the B2102
towards Blackboys. East of Hollow Lane.
Map Reference: ES13
Information:
• Picnic areas and linking paths.
• Range of birds, mammals and insects.
• Dogs must be on leads.

There's no language without a word for butterfly.

HOTHAM PARK

See all the fish in the pond

Hotham Way, Bognor Regis, West Sussex.
Opening hours: Open park.

Map Reference: WS8
Information:
- Picnic area, play area, mini railway, tennis courts, boating lake, putting green and pond.
- Cafe and toilets.
- Crows and wood pigeons, blackbirds, tits, sparrows, starlings, robins and wrens. Squirrels by the hundreds, rabbits, foxes and fish in the pond.
- Many Sweet Pea trees in the park and a rose garden.

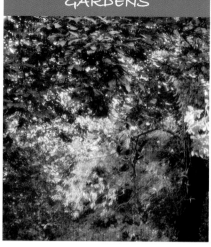

MARINE PARK GARDENS

Lovely park to walk your dog and take the children

Marine Drive West, Bognor Regis, West Sussex.
Tel: 01243 820245.
web: http://bognor-regis.co.uk
Opening hours: Open park.

Directions: On the seafront.
Map Reference: WS9
Information:
- Road train from pier will take you to the park.
- Bedding displays, 18-hole putting green and fountain.

BEACON HILL

Nature reserve with park
for all the family

Brighton, East Sussex.
Opening hours: Open park.

Directions: Longhill Road (Ovingdean) or
Nevill Road (Rottingdean). Between
Rottingdean and Ovingdean about half a
mile north of A259 coast road.
Map Reference: BH1
Information:
• Old dry dew pond.
• Chalk grassland, Skylark Butterflies (The
  Pride of Sussex Cowslip and Marbled
  White and Common Blue Butterflies).

BEVENDEAN DOWN

Nature reserve with park
for all the family

Brighton, East Sussex.
Opening hours: Open park.

Directions: Accessed by footpaths off the
Avenue and Heath Hill Avenue.
Map Reference: BH2
Information:
• Rich in invertebrate fauna, dew pond
  and horse paddocks.
• Chalk grassland.

BLACK ROCK LIDO

A place to visit for solace

Marine Drive, Brighton, East Sussex.
web: http://www.mybrightonandhove.
org.uk/black_rock_lido_personal.htm
Opening hours: Open beach.

Map Reference: BH3
Information:
- Exposed section of famous "elephant beds". Full of bones of Mammoth, Woolly Rhino and the Age Horse).
- All facilities at the Marina.
- Birdwatching and sealife.

BLAKERS PARK

Lovely park for all the family

Cleveland Road, Preston Drove and
Southdown Road, Brighton, East Sussex.
Tel: 01273 293080.
Opening hours: Open park.

Directions: Follow directions to Fiveways, Ditchling Road, then down to Preston Drove.
Map Reference: BH4
Information:
- Clocktower (miniature copy of Big Ben).
- Cafe, toilets, tennis courts, playground and clocktower.

DID YOU KNOW?
Ladybirds can fly backwards on take-off.

BOOTH MUSEUM OF NATURAL HISTORY

Fascinating place. A must! Over 525,000 insects and other animals - all dead! Free entry

194 Dyke Road, Brighton,
East Sussex, BN1 5AA.
Tel: 01273 292777.
Fax: 01273 292778.
e-mail:
boothmuseum@brighton-hove.gov.uk
web: www.virtualmuseum.info
Opening hours:
Monday, Tuesday, Wednesday, Friday and Saturday, 10am to 5pm. Thursday, closed. Sunday, 2pm to 5pm.
Admission: Free.

Directions: See website.
Map Reference: BH5
Information:
• Events throughout the year.
• Specialises in birds, insects, skeletons and geology.

CHATTRI DOWNS WAR MEMORIAL

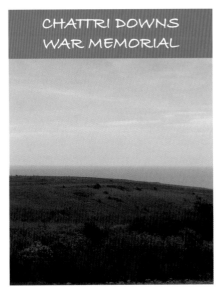

Nature reserve with park for all the family

Chattri Downs, Brighton, East Sussex.
Opening hours: Open park.

Directions: North of Brighton, between Patcham and Pyecombe. Take Braypool Lane turnoff from A27, near the junction with the A23. Turn right onto the lane to Lower Standean Farm.
Map Reference: BH6
Information:
• Popular local beauty spot, visit the Chattri Memorial (dedicated to the Indian solders who died in WW1).
• Sparrowhawk, little owl, green woodpecker, hen harrier and long-eared owl.
• Sussex Border Path and North Brighton Countryside Trail pass through.

DEVIL'S DYKE

DYKE ROAD PARK

National Trust open space

Devil's Dyke Road, Brighton,
East Sussex, BN6 9DY.
Tel: 01273 834830.
Opening hours: Open park.

Map Reference: BH7
Information:
• Deepest dry valley in the world.
• Horse riding trails.
• Facilities are in the local pub.

*Park with lots to do as well
as walk your dog*

Dyke Road, Brighton,
East Sussex, BN3 6EH.
Opening hours: Open park.

Directions: Opposite the Booth
Museum.
Map Reference: BH8
Information:
• Bowling, tennis, playground and
football pitch.
• Cafe and toilets.

A giraffe's spots fade with age.

PLACES TO VISIT

EAST BRIGHTON PARK

Fun for all the family park

Wilson Avenue, Brighton, East Sussex.
Tel: 01273 292059.
Opening hours: Open park.

Directions: Behind Brighton Marina.
Map Reference: BH9
Information:
• Wide open space to contemplate wildlife.
• Cafe, tennis, football, cricket, playground, small dog-free area, caravan grounds.
• Local wildlife.

EASTHILL PARK

Green Flag awarded park

Easthill Way, Brighton, East Sussex.
Tel: 01273 292216.
Opening hours: Open park.

Directions: Between Easthill Way and Locks Hill.
Map Reference: BH10
Information:
• On the edge of Portslade village.
• Cafe, toilet and picnic area.
• Green Flag Award.
• Green woodpecker and swift.

FALMER CONSERVATION AREA

HOLLINGBURY PARK

Conservation/farm area

Park with lots to do

Falmer, Nr Brighton, East Sussex.
Opening hours: Open conservation area.

Ditchling Road, Brighton, East Sussex, BN1 7HS.
Opening hours: Open park.

Directions: Follow A27 eastwards from Brighton.
Map Reference: BH11
Information:
• Pond located within the Sussex Downs Area.

Directions: Between A23 and A27.
Map Reference: BH12
Information:
• Golf club, toilets and cafe.

DID YOU KNOW?
A typical tuna swims 100 miles a day.

KIPLING GARDENS

Park with rose garden,
herb garden and wild garden

The Elms, Rottingdean,
Brighton, East Sussex.
Tel: 01273 292059.
Opening hours: Open park.

Directions: Opposite North End House.
Map Reference: BH13
Information:
• Replica of a Victorian walled garden.
• Birds.

NEWMARKET HILL

A place to visit

Woodingdean, Brighton, East Sussex.
Opening hours: Open nature reserve.

Directions: Follow Warren Road then
Falmer Road to Woodingdean.
Map Reference: BH14
Information:
• Facilities in Woodingdean only.
• Nature Reserve – Special Site of
  Scientific Interest.
• Red footed Falcons and rare insects.

DID YOU KNOW?
Hippos can
get sunburned.

PRESTON PARK

QUEEN'S PARK

Brighton's first and largest planned park

Preston Road (A23), Brighton, East Sussex.
Tel: 01273 292060.
Opening hours: Open park.

Directions: On eastern side of the London to Brighton Road (A23). Preston Drove to the north and Preston Park Avenue to the east.
Map Reference: BH15
Information:
* Two cafes, children's playground, toilet, lawn bowls, tennis, cricket, football, skating, cycle track and skateboarding.
* Opposite the western side is the Rock Garden. Phone for details.
* Green Flag Award.

Family fun park

Between West Drive and East Drive, Brighton, East Sussex.
Tel: 01273 293193.
Opening hours: Open park.

Directions: Signposted from seafront and junction of Eastern Road and Egremont Place.
Map Reference: BH16
Information:
* Lake with cascades, ducks and a fountain.
* Cafe, toilet, disabled toilet, scented garden, tennis, bowls and lake.
* Wildlife garden with workshops run by Council.

Calendar of events visit www.animalloversguides.co.uk

SEALIFE CENTRE

Wonderful place to visit with
new Tropical Reef complete
with underwater tunnel

Marine Parade, Brighton,
East Sussex, BN2 1TB.
Tel: 01273 604234.
Fax: 01273 681840.
web: www.sealifeeurope.com
Contact: Danielle Crane.
Opening hours: Daily, 10am to 5pm
Admission: Adults £9.95. Children (3-14)
£7.50. Seniors £8.50. Students £8.50.
Family £32.90. Disabled children £6.50.

Directions: On Marine Parade near
Brighton Pier. See website for more details.
Map Reference: BH17
Information:
• Concentrates on conservation,
education and entertainment.
• Over 150 species and 50 displays.
• Giant turtles, sharks, rays, tropical reef
and seahorses.
• Toilets, Victorian tea rooms and gift
shop.
• Guide dogs welcome.

THE SOUTH DOWNS

Nature reserve with beautiful
scenery and wildlife

Brighton, East Sussex.
Opening hours: Open reserve.

Directions: Off the A286 onto local
roads. The South Down's Trail is 160km
long.
Map Reference: BH18
Information:
• National park and area of outstanding
natural beauty.
• Prehistoric ridge with layers of chalk.
• Grazing sheep, farmland, chalkland and
local wildlife.

PLACES TO VISIT

STANMER PARK

Recreation and wildlife facility.
English Heritage
(Grade II-Listed site)

Brighton, East Sussex.
Tel: 01273 292060.
Opening hours: Open park.

Directions: West of Sussex University Campus, off A27 Lewes Road.
Map Reference: BH19
Information:
• Grade II-listed stable complex.
• Pasture land.
• Pond.

THE LEVEL

Fun for all the family park

Ditchling Road, Brighton, East Sussex.
Opening hours: Open park.

Directions: Between Ditchling Road and Lewes Road, near St Peter's Church.
Centre of town by the Open Market.
Map Reference: BH20
Information:
• Cafe.
• Playground, sand pit and paddling pool.
• Skateboard run.
• Cycling.

Sharks have no bones except their teeth and jaws.

UNDERCLIFF WALK

Wonderful walk with rock pools

Undercliff Walk, Saltdean, Brighton, East Sussex.
Opening hours: Open walkway.

Directions: Follow the path from Brighton Marina towards Saltdean.
Map Reference: BH21
Information:
- The rock pools are alive with various sea creatures.
- Cafe and toilet.

WHITEHAWK HILL

Whitehawk Camp (a Neolithic enclosure and ancient monument)

Brighton, East Sussex.
Opening hours: Open park.

Directions: Access via Warren Road, at top of Manor Hill. Off Donald Road to the south. Brighton Racecourse to the west, Whitehawk housing estate to the east and Kemp Town to the south.
Map Reference: BH22
Information:
- Adonis and chalkhill butterfies and Whitehawk soldier beetle.

DID YOU KNOW...

Birds Nest Soup is made from the nests of cave swiftlets in Asia.

WILD PARK

Woodland, dew pond, largest
nature reserve in Brighton

Ditchling Road, Brighton, East Sussex.
Opening hours: Open park.

Directions: Access via Lewes Road
(Moulsecoomb area). Just off A27 Lewes
Road or off Ditchling Road towards
London junction.
Map Reference: BH23
Information:
• Woodland, dew pond.
• Cafe, toilets, sports grounds, golf
  course and mountain bike tracks.
• Arable and grazing fields attract seed-
  eating birds, chalk grassland fauna.

WITHDEAN WOODS

Woodland surrounded by
urban development along
London/Brighton railway line

Withdean Road, Brighton, East Sussex.
Opening hours: Open park.

Directions: Access from Withdean Road
and Eldred Avenue. South of Withdean
Stadium and west of the Deneway
Local nature reserve.
Map Reference: BH24
Information:
• Diverse woodland bird community
  and native fauna and flora.
• Great spotted woodpecker, tawny owl
  and goldcrest.

BEDELANDS FARM NATURE RESERVE

Nature reserve with
pond wildlife including
wildfowl, plants and insects

Off Maple Drive, Burgess Hill,
West Sussex.
web: www.burgesshill.gov.uk
Opening hours: Open reserve.

Directions: Bedelands Farm Nature
Reserve is situated on the northern edge
of Burgess Hill and access is from the
playing fields next to Burgess Hill Town
Football Club, off Maple Drive, and from
Coopers Close. Other entry points are
from a footpath near Valeb.
Map Reference: WS10
Information:
• The site is owned by Mid Sussex District
  Council and the Friends of Bedelands
  Farm Nature Reserve help maintain it.
• The Nature Reserve consists of ancient
  meadows, woodland, hedgerows and
  ponds, covering 80 acres.

CHICHESTER CANAL

Canal with very interesting sights along its banks

Chichester, West Sussex.
Opening hours: Open waterway.

Map Reference: WS11
Information:
• Narrowboat rides, rowing boats, canoeing, angling, strolling.
• Wild flowers.
• Painting.
• Bird watching.
• Cycling.

Gorillas have fingerprints.

CHICHESTER HARBOUR

Dog walking harbour with wildlife

Harbour Office, Itchenor, Chichester, West Sussex, PO20 7AW.
Tel: 01243 512301.
e-mail: harbourmaster@conservancy.co.uk
web: www.conservancy.co.uk
Opening hours: Open harbour.
Admission: Some facilities will charge.

Directions: Located north of B2179 towards West Worthing.
Map Reference: WS12
Information:
• Area of outstanding natural beauty, nature walks, boating, wildlife.
• Visitor information, toilets, shop and cafe.
• See website for details of events.
• Wading birds, mud creatures, sea wildlife, herons and gulls.

PLACES TO VISIT

COOKSBRIDGE MEADOW

Country walk and nature reserve

Nr Henley Common, Chichester, West Sussex.
Tel: 01273 492630.
Fax: 01273 494500.
web: www.sussexwt.org.uk

Directions: North of Henley Common, near to Courts Furniture Store.
Map Reference: WS13
Information:
• Woodland birds, peace and quiet.
• Dogs must be on leads.

EARNLEY BUTTERFLIES AND GARDENS

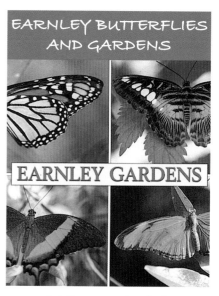

Walk among tropical butterflies and exotic birds

133 Almodington Lane, Earnley, Chichester, West Sussex, PO20 7JR.
Tel: 01243 512637.
Opening hours: March to October, 10am to 6pm.
Admission: Call to enquire.

Directions: Off the A27 Chichester.
Map Reference: WS14
Information:
• Wander through a maze of 17 covered theme gardens, with a free competition for kids.
• See the artefacts from the shipwrecked HMS Hazardous sunk in 1706.
• Refreshments, picnic and play area, crazy golf and gift shop.

DID YOU KNOW?
Zebras don't howl they bark.

GOODWOOD RACECOURSE

Horse racing

Goodwood, Chichester, West Sussex,
PO18 0PS.
Tel: 01243 755022.
Fax: 01243 755025.
e-mail: racing@goodwood.co.uk
web: www.goodwood.co.uk/horseracing
Opening hours: 11.30 mornings, 4.30
afternoons.

Directions: A3 from London and A27
from Brighton and Southampton. Look for
tourist signs towards racecourse.
Map Reference: WS15
Information:
• Horse racing.
• Bars, eateries and toilets.
• Many events throughout the year. See
  website for more details
• Family days.

KINGLEY VALE

Fabulous nature reserve
and yew forest

Game Keepers Lodge, West Stoke
House Farm, West Stoke, Chichester,
West Sussex, PO18 9BN.
Tel: 01243 557353.
Fax: 01243 557353.
e-mail: dave.mercer@english-nature.org.uk
web: www.english-nature.org.uk
Contact: Dave Mercer.
Opening hours: Open nature reserve.
Admission: Free.

Directions: Take the A286 out of
Chichester at mid Lavant take the left turn
to West Stoke, the carpark is sign posted
National Nature Reserve.
Map Reference: WS16
Information:
• Check website for details of events
  throughout the year.
• Fallow deer, roe deer, badgers, stoats,
  rabbits, mice, buzzards.
• Dogs must be on leads.

PLACES TO VISIT

LEVIN DOWN

Nature reserve with wildlife walks

Nr Charlton, Chichester, West Sussex.
Nearest postcode PO18 0JG.
web: www.sussexwt.org.uk
Opening hours: Open park.

Directions: Chichester is accessible via the A285, A27, A259 and the B2166. There is a parking layby at the crossroads in Charlton and a footpath leading across the field to the reserve.
Map Reference: WS17
Information:
- Many butterfly species, including Duke of Burgundy, brown and green hairstreaks.
- Chalkland scenery and plants.
- Warblers and finches.
- Dogs must be on leads.

NOAH'S ARK

Get close to many small animals and reptiles that have been rescued

133 Almodington Lane, Chichester, West Sussex, PO20 7JR (based at Earnley Butterflies and Gardens, see page 64).
Tel: 07961 516731.
web: www.noahs-ark.freeuk.com
Opening hours: Open all year around except Christmas Eve, Christmas Day and Boxing Day. Call to enquire.

Directions: Off the A27 Chichester bypass.
Map Reference: WS18
Information:
- Learn about the reptiles' needs at the education centre. Help the animals by sponsorships or donations. Boarding facilities available.
- Picnic area, refreshments, crazy golf and gift shop.
- Call to enquire about events throughout the year.
- Farmyard animals, chinchillas, chipmunks and rabbits. Lizards, snakes and tortoises.

PAGHAM HARBOUR

Nature reserve with wildlife walks

The Ferry Selsey Road, Sidlesham,
Chichester, West Sussex, PO20 7NE.
Tel: 01243 641508.
web: www.sussexwt.org.uk
Opening hours: Open park.

Map Reference: WS19
Information:
• Huge variety of wildfowl and waders.
• Wildlife hospital to the east.
• Visitor centre.
• Saltmarsh, mudflats, copses, farmland, lagoons, reedbeds and shingle beaches.
• Southern Marsh Orchid can be seen here.
• Most of the 1450-acre reserve is a site of special Scientific Interest.
• Dogs must be on leads.

WEALD & DOWNLAND OPEN AIR MUSEUM

Traditional breed farm animals

Singleton, Chichester, West Sussex, PO18 0EU.
Tel: 01243 811348.
Fax: 01243 811475.
e-mail: office@wealddown.co.uk
web: www.wealddown.co.uk
Contact: Cathy Clark.
Opening hours:
April to October, daily 10.30am to 6pm.
November to 21 December, daily 10.30am to 4pm. Plus daily for 'A Sussex Christmas' 26 December to 1 January 2007 10.30am to 4pm. 3 January to 18 February 2007, Wednesday, Saturday and Sunday only 10.30am to 4pm. 19 February to 31 March, daily 10.30am to 4pm.
Admission: Adults £7.95. Seniors £6.95.
Children £4.25. Family (2 plus 3) £21.95.
Under 5s free.

Directions: Midway between Chichester and Midhurst on A286.
Map Reference: WS20
Information:
• 45 rescued historic buildings in a Downland setting.
• Rural craft demonstrations.
• Lakeside cafe, picnic areas, shop and toilets, including disabled.
• Traditional breed farm animals and working Shire Horses.
• Limited access to some buildings and site for the disabled.

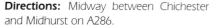

WEST DEAN GARDENS

MOHAIR CENTRE

Beautiful gardens and open landscape with wildlife

Nature trail with working farm

West Dean, Chichester, West Sussex.
Tel: 01243 811301.
Fax: 01243 811342.
e-mail: gardens@westdean.org.uk
web: www.westdean.org.uk/site/gardens
Opening hours: March to October, 10.30am to 5pm, daily. November to February, 10.30am to 4pm, Wednesday to Sunday. Christmas and New Year: Closed 24th December to 3rd January.
Admission: March to October, Adults £6.00. Children £2.50. November to February, Adults £3.00. Children £1.25.

Directions: Accessible from the A286 southwards to Chichester. Take the A27 from the West.
Map Reference: WS21
Information:
• Visitor centre.
• Licensed restaurant.
• Several events hosted annually.
• Victorian glasshouses.
• Walled kitchen garden.
• Guide dogs allowed.

Brickfield Farm, Laughton Road, Chiddingly, East Sussex, BN8 6JG.
Tel: 01825 872457.
Fax: 01825 872460.
Opening hours: March to October. Please call for times.

Directions: Situated on the B2124 off the A22 between Hailsham and Lewes.
Map Reference: ES14
Information:
• Children's farm with angora goats and other farm animals. Courses available.
• Toilets, educational facilities.
• Lambing in the Spring and other events. Please call for details.
• Nature trail and spinning and weaving demonstrations.

BUCHAN COUNTRY PARK

Wide variety of birds, reptiles, deer and foxes

Horsham Road, Crawley,
West Sussex, RH11 9HQ.
Tel: 01293 542088.
Fax: 01293 513811.
e-mail: buchanpark@westsussex.gov.uk
web: www.westsussex.gov.uk
Contact: Simon Rowledge.
Opening hours: Summer, 8am to 8pm.
Winter, 8am to 6pm.

Directions: Access from westbound
A2220 Horsham Road from Crawley.
Map Reference: WS22
Information:
- Haven for quiet recreation and nature study. Also has a visitor centre.
- Events throughout the year, see website or park itself for details.

TULLEYS FARM

Adventure park with working farm

Turners Hill Road, Turners Hill, Crawley,
West Sussex, RH10 4PE.
Tel: 01342 718472.
Fax: 01342 718473.
e-mail: shop@tulleysfarm.com
web: www.tulleysfarm.com
Opening hours: 9am to 5pm.

Directions: Located between East
Grinstead and Crawley. Accessible from the
B2110.
Map Reference: WS23
Information:
- Many family activities available, festivals, parties and Christmas specials.
- Farm shop and tea room.
- Seasonal events throughout the year. Please call for more information.
- Goats, rabbits, pigs and other farm animals.
- Dogs must be on leads, call before visiting.

THE CUCKOO TRAIL

Nature trail

Crowborough, East Sussex, TN6 1BR.
Tel: 01273 481637.
e-mail: countryside.management@
eastsussex.gov.uk
web: www.eastsussex.gov.uk
Opening hours: Open trail.

Directions: Situated from Eridge to
Polegate, passing through Heathfield,
Horam, Hellingly and Hailsham
Map Reference: ES15
Information:
• Dog walking, horse riding, cycling
and wildlife.
• Accommodation, toilets, information
centre, shops, cafe and pubs.
• Wildlife in beautiful setting.

OLD LODGE

Nature reserve with beautiful
scenery and wildlife

Nr Kings Standing, Crowborough,
East Sussex. Nearest postcode TN22 3JD.
web: www.sussexwt.org.uk
Opening hours: Open park.

Directions: Located east of Kings
Standing, accessible off the B2026.
There is a small car park.
Map Reference: ES16
Information:
• Set in the Ashdown Forest.
• Nightjar, redstart, woodcock,
tree pipit, stonechat and alder.

DITCHLING BEACON

STONEYWISH NATURE RESERVE

Country walk and nature reserve

Lovely nature walk with farm animals, gardens and ponds

Access from National Trust Car Park, Westmeston, East Sussex, BN6 8XG.
Tel: 01273 494777.
web: www.sussexwt.org.uk
Opening hours: Open reserve.

Directions: See website for details.
Map Reference: ES17
Information:
• Chalkhill Blue butterflies.
• Beautiful grassland flowers.
• The road through the reserve is too dangerous for pedestrians on foot.

Spatham Lane, Ditchling,
East Sussex, BN6 8XH.
Tel: 01273 843498.
web: www.stoneywish.com
Contact: Rosemary Alford
Opening hours: March to November, daily 9.30am to 5pm. November to March,daily 9.30am to 4pm.
Admission: Adults £3.75. Children £2.75. Seniors £2.75. Under 3s free.
Wheelchair concessions.

Directions: Quarter of a mile off the B2116 on the east side of Ditchling.
Map Reference: ES18
Information:
• Nature walk, play and picnic area, farm animals, gardens and exhibitions.
• Tea room, garden gift shop and toilets.
• Farm animals, herons, woodpeckers and wild birds.
• Guide dogs welcome.

In a pack of wolves, only one pair breeds.

FOREST WAY COUNTRY PARK

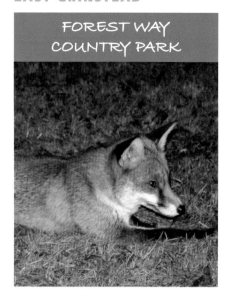

CROUCHES FARM

30 acres of beautiful countryside

Network of bridle paths and a vast range of countryside and insects to view

Nr East Grinstead, East Sussex.
Tel: 01273 481000.
Fax: 01273 481261.
web: www.eastsussex.gov.uk
Opening hours: Open park.

Crouches Farm, East Hoathly, East Sussex.
Tel: 01825 840242.
web: www.defra.gov.uk
Opening hours: Open access.

Directions: Near the B2110 between Forest Row in the east.
Map Reference: ES19
Information:
• Horse riding and cycling allowed.
• Swallows, badgers and foxes.

Directions: Call for specific locations of bridle paths.
Map Reference: ES20
Information:
• Bridle paths and views of countryside.

DID YOU KNOW?
Puffins are the only birds that moult their beaks.

ERIDGE PARK

Walk along the edge of
Eridge Old Park - views of
deer and other wildlife

Eridge, Nr Frant, East Sussex.
Tel: 020 7238 5909.
web: www.defra.gov.uk
Opening hours: Open park.

Map Reference: ES21
Information:
• Lovely walks.
• Small circular route available through
  Whitehill Wood and Saxonbury Wood.
• Eridge Old Park is reputed to be one of
  the oldest and largest deer parks in
  England.
• Dogs must be on leads.

ERIDGE ROCKS

Beautiful location and scenery.
Peaceful and tranquil

North-east of Eridge train station,
East Sussex. Nearest postcode TN3 9JU.
web: www.sussexwt.org.uk
Opening hours: Open park.

Directions: Entrance to private road off
the A26 situated next to church and small
printing works.
Map Reference: ES22
Information:
• Rare wildlife and plants.

PLACES TO VISIT

BRICKFIELD MEADOW

ASHDOWN FOREST

Country walk and nature reserve

Outstanding natural beauty

Fairwarp, East Sussex. Nearest postcode
TN22 3BT.
Tel: 01273 494777.
web: www.sussexwt.org.uk
Opening hours: Open nature reserve.

Directions: Located 400 metres from
Fairwarp. Cars may be parked in the
village.
Map Reference: ES23
Information:
• Large variety of flowers and
  ancient fauna.
• Ancient natural setting.
• Dogs must be on leads.

The Ashdown Forest Centre, Wych Cross,
Forest Row, East Sussex, RH18 5JP.
Tel: 01342 823583.
e-mail: conservators@ashdownforest.org
web: www.ashdownforest.org
Opening hours: Open park.

Directions: 3 miles south-east of East
Grinstead. Just south of Forest Row.
The forest is on both sides of A22.
Map Reference: ES24
Information:
• Rich in wildlife with many activities
  all year.
• Rare wildlife, including Marsh gentian,
  Dartford warbler, Silver Studded blue
  butterfly and nightjar.
• Winnie the Pooh walk route and Pooh
  Bridge.

A glowworm is
NOT a worm.

ASHDOWN FOREST LLAMA PARK

KNOCKHATCH ADVENTURE PARK

A fabulous Llama place in a great setting with award-winning Llamas and Alpacas. Treat yourself in the lovely shop

Wych Cross, Forest Row, East Sussex, RH18 5JN.
Tel: 01825 712040.
Fax: 01825 713698.
e-mail: info@llamapark.co.uk
web: www.llamapark.co.uk
Contact: Linda Johnson.
Opening hours: Daily, 10am to 5pm
Admission: Adults £4.50.
Concessions £3.75.

Directions: On A22, 3 miles south of Forest Row.
Map Reference: ES25
Information:
• Llamas and Alpacas.
• Alpaca knitwear and South American crafts.
• Walking with the llamas for adults only.
• Coffee shop and toilets.
• Events throughout the year – see website for more details.

Birds of prey and other fabulous animals

Hempstead Lane, Hailsham, East Sussex, BN27 3PR.
Tel: 01323 442051.
Fax: 01323 863035.
e-mail: knockhatch@aol.com
web: www.knockhatch.com
Contact: Colin Jaggers.
Opening hours: Daily, 10am to 5.30pm
Admission: Adults £7.25. Children £6.25.
Family £25.00. Concessions £5.25.

Directions: Off A22 west of Hailsham.
Map Reference: ES26
Information:
• Adventure park.
• Animals include birds of prey, rabbits, goats, chipmunks, donkeys and pigs.
• All facilities available.
• Displays every day.
• Specialises in birds of prey.
• Guide dogs allowed.

ALEXANDRA PARK

FILSHAM REEDBED

109-acre park with wildlife, trees and duck pond

Nature reserve with wildlife walks

Lower Park Road, Hastings,
East Sussex.
Tel: 01424 781066.
Fax: 01424 781769.
e-mail: hbc@hastings.gov.uk
web: www.hastings.gov.uk
Opening hours: Open park.

Directions: From Hastings train station, turn left into Devonshire Road, left into South Terrace Road and then Queens Road and at the roundabout, the park is directly opposite.
Map Reference: ES27
Information:
• Beautiful park which will take forever to walk around, but absolutely worth it.
• Cafe, toilets, tennis courts, bandstand, fishery and boating lake.
• See website for details of events.
• Ducks, bird species, squirrels and fish.
• The best burger and chips overlooking a lovely park.

Hastings, East Sussex. Nearest postcode TN38 8DY.
web: www.sussexwt.org.uk
Opening hours: Open park.

Directions: Footpath runs alongside Combe Haven River, from the Bulverhythe Recreation Ground, just off A259 in St Leonards. Footbridge located over the river.
Map Reference: ES28
Information:
• Reed warblers, water rail, teal, reed bunting and other bird species.
• Variety of amphibians and specialist moths.
• Dogs must be on leads.

DID YOU KNOW? The bee has 12,000 eyes.

MARLINE VALLEY

Nature reserve with wildlife walks

Near High Beech, Hastings, East Sussex.
Nearest postcode TN38 9NY.
web: www.sussexwt.org.uk
Opening hours: Open park.

Directions: Located east of Hollington off the B2092. The easiest way to the park is via Napier Road or nearby and cross over Queensway to access one of the footpaths.
Map Reference: ES29
Information:
• Many species of plants, including coppice, bluebell, wild garlic, mosses and ferns.
• Nightingales and Warblers.
• Dogs must be on leads.

UNDERWATER WORLD

Variety of marine life for all the family to enjoy

Rock-a-nore Road, Hastings, East Sussex, TN34 3DW.
Tel: 01424 718776.
Fax: 01424 718757.
e-mail: tracey@discoverhastings.co.uk
web: www.discoverhastings.co.uk
Opening hours: Easter to October, 10am to 5.30pm. October to Easter, 11am to 4pm.
Admission: Adults £6.20. Children £4.20. Seniors £5.20.

Directions: A259 links Hastings to Channel Ports and the Channel Tunnel to the East and Brighton to the West. The A21 links Hastings to the M25. In Hastings, head towards fishing huts by cliff railway and follow signposts.
Map Reference: ES30
Information:
• Mammals to sea creatures. Fish of all types. Very educational.
• Gift shop, coffee shop and toilets.
• See website for details of events.
• Sharks, seahorses, crabs, coral reefs, 70 species to view and enjoy.
• Guide dogs allowed.

PLACES TO VISIT

BORDE HILL GARDEN

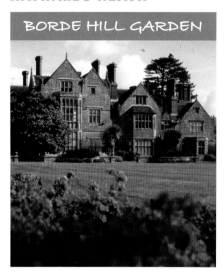

NEWBURY POND

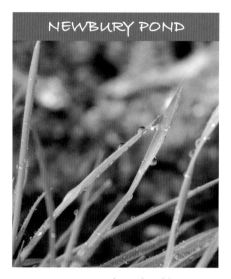

Fabulous heritage garden with lots going on, including sculptures

Balcombe Road, Haywards Heath, West Sussex, RH16 1XP.
Tel: 01444 450326.
Fax: 01444 440427.
e-mail: info@bordehill.co.uk
web: www.bordehill.co.uk
Contact: Sarah Brook.
Opening hours: 1st April to 31st October, daily, 10am to 6pm.
Admission: Adults £6.00. Children £5.00. Concessions £3.50.

Directions: Leave the A23 at Junction 10a, follow the B2036 to Cuckfield and turn left into Ardingly Road. At the T-Junction, turn left and Borde Hill is 300 metres on the left.
Map Reference: WS24
Information:
- Botannical collection of plants.
- Tea room, restaurant and toilets.
- 200 acres of spectacular parkland.
- Stunning views, magical woodland and lakeside walks.
- Dogs must be on leads.
- Adventure playgrounds.

Nature reserve with wildlife walks

Nr Cuckfield, Haywards Heath, West Sussex. Nearest postcode RH17 5LL.
web: www.sussexwt.org.uk
Opening hours: Open park.

Directions: Accessible from the A272 and the B2184. Possible to park at the end of Newbury Land, close to the pond. Parking also available by the church.
Map Reference: WS25
Information:
- Delightful pond and area of marshy woodland.
- Many pondlife species and recently planted meadow.
- Dogs must be on leads.

NYMANS GARDEN

SELWYNS WOOD

Rare, beautiful plants, rose garden and woodland walks

Staplefield Road, Handcross, Nr Haywards Heath, West Sussex, RH17 6EB.
Tel: 01444 405250.
Fax: 01444 400253.
e-mail: nymans@nationaltrust.org.uk
web: www.nationaltrust.org.uk
Opening hours: February to October, Wednesday to Sunday, 11am to 6pm and bank holidays.
Admission: Adults £7.00. Children £3.50. Family £17.50.

Map Reference: WS26
Information:
• Restaurant, shop and plant sales area.
• See website for details of events.
• Local wildlife.
• Rock garden, sunken garden, topiary, lakes and cascades.

Country walk and nature reserve

Heathfield, East Sussex. Nearest postcode TN21 0LY.
Tel: 01273 494777.
web: www.sussexwt.org.uk

Directions: Access point marked with the Trust sign at entrance to a track near Fir Grove, next to White Lodge House.
Map Reference: ES31
Information:
• Woodpeckers and other birds.
• Woodland species include cuckoo,
• Heather, rowan, wood ant and bluebells.
• Dogs must be on leads.

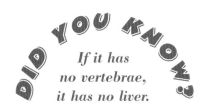

DID YOU KNOW? *If it has no vertebrae, it has no liver.*

PLACES TO VISIT

SUSSEX WILDLIFE TRUST

All native wildlife

Woodsmill, Henfield, West Sussex,
BN5 9SD.
Tel: 01273 492630.
Fax: 01273 494500.
e-mail: enquiries@sussexwt.org.uk
web: www.sussexwt.org.uk
Contact: Sarah Hince.
Opening hours: Open all year except
Christmas week.
Admission: Free.

Directions: 1 mile south of Henfield and
half a mile north of Small Dole.
Map Reference: WS27
Information:
• Nature reserve with woods, lake
  and meadow.
• Events throughout the year. See
  website for details or phone for
  enquiries.
• All native wildlife.

WOODS MILL

Nature reserve with
lake and waterbed

Horn Lane, Henfield, West Sussex.
Opening hours: Open nature reserve.

Directions: A2037 north of Small Dole.
Map Reference: WS28
Information:
• Lake and waterbed.
• Main building is in water mill.
• School visits and education
  programmes.
• Nightingales, woodpeckers, turtle
  doves, warblers and grey wagtail.

A group of owls is called a parliament.

CHESWORTH FARM

Working farm and nature trail

Chesworth Lane, Horsham, West Sussex.
Tel: 01403 731218.
e-mail: leisure@horsham.gov.uk
web: www.horsham.gov.uk
Opening hours: Open farm.

Directions: 10 to 15-minute walk from town centre to the north east. Following the A281 off Queensway.
Map Reference: WS29
Information:
• Woodland, bridlepath, natural beauty and coppice woodland.
• Farm animals can be seen.
• Dogs must be on leads.

HOLMBUSH FARM WORLD

Farm animals, tractor rides and much more

Faygate, Nr Horsham, West Sussex, RH12 4SE.
Tel: 01293 851700.
e-mail: info@holmbushfarm.co.uk
web: www.holmbushfarm.co.uk
Opening hours: 10am to 5.30pm. Seven days a week, March to November.
Admission: Adults £4.50. Children £4.00.

Directions: Situated between Crawley and Horsham off the A264.
Map Reference: WS30
Information:
• Cow and goat milking, goat races and tractor rides.
• Tea room, toilets and gift shop.
• Events throughout the year. See website.
• Farm animals with lambing in Spring.
• Guide dogs allowed.

HORSHAM PARK

LEECHPOOL AND OWLBEECH WOODS

Lovely park for all the family, with wildlife too

Park House, North Street, Horsham, West Sussex.
Tel: 01403 215256.
e-mail: leisure@horsham.gov.uk
web: www.horsham.gov.uk
Opening hours: Open park.

Directions: North of the town's main shopping area, on the way to the train station.
Map Reference: WS31
Information:
• Lakes, trees and colourful flowerbeds.
• Cafe, tennis courts, children's play area and bowls green.
• Family fun days and concerts. See website for more details.
• Wildlife in a beautiful setting.

Ancient woodland of 53 acres

Harwood Road, Horsham, West Sussex.
Tel: 01403 731218.
e-mail: leisure@horsham.gov.uk
web: www.horsham.gov.uk
Opening hours: Open woodland.

Directions: To the east of Horsham off the Harwood Road (B2195).
Map Reference: WS32
Information:
• Rare selection of flora and fauna.

Some birds do indeed sing for pure pleasure.

WARNHAM NATURE RESERVE

Nature reserve with wildlife walks

Warnham Road, Horsham, West Sussex, RH12 2RA.
Tel: 01403 256890.
e-mail: leisure@horsham.gov.uk
web: www.horsham.gov.uk
Opening hours: Daily. 10am to 6pm.
Admission: A low-cost fee allows access to reserve features.

Directions: North-west of Horsham on the B2237 (just off A24). Reserve is a 20-30 minute walk from Horsham town centre.
Map Reference: WS33
Information:
* Variety of wildlife, plants, birds in beautful setting.
* Visitor centre and cafe.
* School parties welcome.
* Kingfisher, ancient woodlands, dragonflies, woodpeckers, Warblers.

HOVE LAGOON

*The Lagoons and Swans
are a great attraction*

The Kingsway, Hove, East Sussex, BN3 4LX.
Tel: 01273 292974.
Opening hours: Open park.

Directions: Follow A259 coast road
towards Hove.
Map Reference: BH25
Information:
- Children's playground, paddling pool, cafe and toilets.
- Watersports centre.
- Swans.

DID YOU KNOW
*A beaver gulps
air before it dives.
Underwater it gets
about ¹/₂ a mile to a gulp.*

HOVE PARK

Fun for all the family

Old Shoreham Road, Hove, East Sussex.
Tel: 01273 292974.
Opening hours: Tuesday to Saturday,
10am to 5pm. Sunday, 2pm to 5pm.

Directions: On the A270 entrance
opposite the Goldstone Retail Park.
Map Reference: BH26
Information:
- Tennis courts, bowling green, basketball court, children's playground, cafe, miniature steam railway.
- The Goldstone – a huge rock (above) dug up in 1900 is believed to be a sacred Druid stone.
- Parking in residential area.

ST ANDREW'S CHURCH

Guided walks

Waterloo Street, Hove, East Sussex.
Tel: 01273 326491.
Contact: Michael Robin.
Opening hours: Tuesday to Saturday,
11am to 4pm. Ring to arrange.
Admission: Free, but donation to Church
Conservation Trust would be welcome.

Directions: On seafront, Waterloo Street
is opposite the Peace statue.
Map Reference: BH27
Information:
• Beautiful stained glass and late Georgian
  marble monuments.
• Refreshments nearby.
• Check answerphone for current events.
• Dogs are welcome on the beach walks.
• Custodian Michael Robins always leaves a
  dog bowl in the porch so owners can
  allow their dogs to drink after a walk on
  the beach.

ST ANN'S WELL GARDENS

A really beautiful and quiet park which has something for everyone

Davigdor Road, Hove, East Sussex.
Tel: 01273 292974.
Opening hours: Open park.

Directions: Half a mile from Hove
seafront, northwards.
Map Reference: BH28
Information:
• Chalybeate (iron bearing) spring.
• Also a ley line to the South Downs.
• Scented garden, cafe, toilets, tennis,
  bowls, playground and conservation
  areas.
• Green Flag Award.
• Fish pond with biological filter system.
• Many friendly squirrels.

PLACES TO VISIT

WASHBROOKS FARM

Working farm, open to the public

Brighton Road, Hurstpierpoint,
West Sussex, BN6 9EH.
Tel: 01273 832201.
e-mail: enquire@washbrooks.co.uk
web; www.washbrooks.co.uk
Opening hours: Daily, 9.30am to 5pm.
Admission: Adults £4.25. Children (3-14)
£3.75. Seniors £3.75.

Directions: From Brighton, travel north
up A23, turn off at B2117. Follow signs to
Hurstpierpoint. From London, take the
A23 south and turn off at B2118.
Map Reference: WS34
Information:
• Rides, attractions and lovely walks.
• Tea rooms, picnic area, party rooms,
  playrooms and brook walk.
• Birthday parties available.
• Horses, sheep, ponies, pigs and all types
  of farm animals.

BARONS GRANGE AND MOAT FARM

Beautiful views, bridle path leads to
views of Walland & Romney Marsh

Barons Grange, Nr Iden, East Sussex.
Tel: 020 7238 6907.
web: www.defra.gov.uk

Directions: Access is available off the
B2082 under the River Rother.
Map Reference: ES32
Information:
• Rich in frog wildlife – the 'frog chorus' is
  particularly loud in June.
• Dogs must be on leads.
• Layby at new bridge provides
  excellent parking.

DID YOU KNOW?
*A horned toad
can squirt blood
out of its eyes…a fifth
of all it has in fact.*

COOMBES FARM TOURS

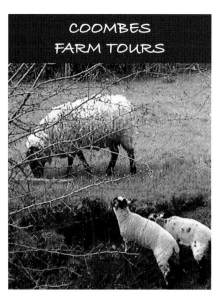

LANCING RING NATURE RESERVE

Working farm with 800 sheep and 90 beef cows set on 1,000 acres

Church Farm, Coombes, Lancing,
West Sussex, BN15 0RS.
Tel: 01273 452028.
e-mail: berty@churchfarm.fsworld.co.uk
web: www.coombes.co.uk
Contact: Jenny Passmore.
Opening hours: Check website for times as they differ throughout the year.
Admission: Adults £5.00. Children £4.00.

Directions: Off A27 at Lancing College, 2 miles on the left.
Map Reference: WS35
Information:
• A 1,000-acre working farm on the South Downs.
• Tours last 1 hour, looking at the farm animals and wildlife.
• Disabled toilets, refreshments. Pre-book for a ploughmans lunch.
• In March and April there is lambing and calving and you might see a lamb or calf being born.
• Sheep shearing days.

Nature reserve with chalky grassland

Lancing, West Sussex.
Tel: 01273 625242.
web: www.adur.gov.uk
Opening hours: Open reserve.

Directions: See website for map.
Map Reference: WS36
Information:
• Local wildlife.

PLACES TO VISIT

PASSIES POND

Great place to see fish

Passies Pond, Coombes Road,
Lancing, West Sussex.
Tel: 01273 465257.
web: www.coombes.co.uk
Opening hours: Open lake.
Admission: Day ticket £8.00.
Concessions £4.00.

Directions: Opposite Old Shoreham
Cement Works.
Map Reference: WS37
Information:
• Coarse fishing, many types of fish and local wildlife.
• Shop, snack bar and toilets.
• Wildlife, bream, carp, tench and many more types of fish.

BLACKBERRY FARM

Working farm open to the public. Lovely place for children and adults. Lots of animals

Whitesmith, Nr Lewes, East Sussex,
BN8 6JD.
Tel: 01825 872912.
Fax: 01825 873082.
e-mail: info@blackberry-farm.co.uk
web: www.blackberry-farm.co.uk
Contact: Rebecca Foxley or Lee Lidbetter.
Opening hours: Daily including Winter,
10am to 5pm.
Admission: Adults £5.00. Children (3-15)
£4.00. Seniors £3.50. Children under 2 Free.

Directions: On A22, 5 miles south
of Uckfield.
Map Reference: ES33
Information:
• Animals, farm and play area for children.
• Tearoom, toilets, play area and tuck shop.
• Daily programmes include pony rides, egg collecting and animal handling and feeding.

THE FARMYARD

Hands on farm with a
large variety of animals

Whitesmith, Lewes, East Sussex, BN8 6JB.
Tel: 01825 872317.
web: www.the-farmyard.co.uk
Contact: Jenny Cottingham.
Opening hours:
Monday to Friday, 2pm to 5pm.
Saturdays and bank holidays, 10am to
5pm. Sunday, closed.
Admission: Adults £3.00. Children £2.30.
Under 3 years, free. Seniors £2.50

Directions: Between Uckfield and
Hailsham on A22 Whitesmith Crossroads.
Map Reference: ES34
Information:
• Hands-on farm with large variety of
  animals and birds to hold or stroke.
• Cold drinks, crisps and sweets.
• Suffolk Punch and a Yak.

LANDPORT BROOKS

Rich in wildlife

Offham Road, Lewes, East Sussex.
Tel: 020 7238 6907.
web: www.defra.gov.uk
Opening hours: Open park.

Directions: Access is via Offham Road
(A2029). Turn at the sign of the "Tally Ho"
pub.
Map Reference: ES35
Information:
• Rich in wildlife, particularly ditch flora
  and fauna.
• Dogs must be on leads.

DID YOU KNOW?
Some hens
lay eggs shaped
like cucumbers.

LEWES BROOKS

Wildlife Walk!

Nr Mountfield Road, Lewes, East Sussex.
Tel: 020 7238 6907.
web: www.defra.gov.uk
Opening hours: Open park.

Directions: Access points situated near Priory School playing fields and near the Southgraham junction off the A26/A27 roundabout.
Map Reference: ES36
Information:
- Restored areas of natural beauty, rich in wildlife.
- Grazing cattle and wildlife.
- Dogs must be on leads.

Catnip does nothing for kittens. Only adult cats.

MIDDLE FARM

Open farm with Cider shop and gift shop. A great day out

Firle, Lewes, East Sussex, BN8 6LJ.
Tel: 01323 811411.
Fax: 01323 811622.
e-mail: info@middlefarm.com
web: www.middlefarm.com
Contact: Helen.
Opening hours: Daily, Summer, 9.30am to 6pm. Winter, 9.30am to 5pm
Admission: Open farm costs £2.50.

Directions: Situated on the main A27 Lewes to Eastbourne Road between villages of Firle and Selmeston.
Map Reference: ES37
Information:
- Plough Monday restaurant, Middle Farm shop, national collection of cider and perry. Gift shop. Lots to see and do.
- Donkeys, chickens, ducks, pigs and Shire Horses.
- Watch Jersey cows being milked!
- Outdoor playground, picnic area and nature trail.

MOUNT CABURN

Nature reserve with beautiful
scenery and wildlife

Nr Lewes, East Sussex.
Tel: 01273 476595.
Opening hours: Open park.

Directions: Southern edge of an isolated
tract of downland 3km from Lewes.
Access is from Glynde village by the
footpath opposite the shop or along the
path opposite Glynde Place.
Map Reference: ES38
Information:
• The Caburn is one of the best
  preserved and most important hill-forts
  in Sussex. Dating from the late Bronze
  Age. The warmth of the south-facing
  slopes allows many plants to thrive.
• From July, chalkhill blue butterflies
  appear in great numbers, feeding on
  marjoram.
• The scarce, day flying Forester Moth
  with its metallic green colours.

RAILWAY LAND LOCAL
NATURE RESERVE

Nature reserve with woodland,
pond and garden

Nr Lewes town centre, Lewes,
East Sussex.
web: www.mmhistory.gov.uk
Contact: Annabelle Kennedy.
Opening hours: Open reserve.

Map Reference: ES39
Information:
• Woodland, pond and Victorian garden.
• Birds, marsh frogs, insects and flora.

PLACES TO VISIT

ARUN DUNES AND SEA NATURE TRAIL

Wildlife walk!

Visitor Centre, 63-65 Surrey Street, Littlehampton, West Sussex.
Tel: 01903 718984.
web: www.naturecoast.org.uk
Opening hours: Open reserve.

Directions: Situated near Littlehampton train station off the B2140.
Map Reference: WS38
Information:
• 1.5-mile wildlife walk from Littlehampton, seeing river, saltmarsh, sand dunes, shingle and marine habitats.
• Facilities available in Littlehampton.
• Sandpipers, eels, spider crabs and dog fish.

BROOKFIELD PARK

Around 8,000 trees

Brookfield Park, Worthing Road, Littlehampton, West Sussex.
Opening hours: Open park.

Map Reference: WS39
Information:
• Woodland, grassland, wild flowers.
• Pond.
• Cycleway, footpath, play area.
• Football area.
• Basketball area.
• Around 8,000 trees.

LOOK AND SEA VISITOR CENTRE

Visitor Centre

63-65 Surrey Street, Littlehampton,
West Sussex, BN17 5AW.
Tel: 01903 718984.
Fax: 01903 718036.
e-mail: info@lookandsea.co.uk
web: www.lookandsea.co.uk
Opening hours: May to October, 10am
to 5pm. November to March, 11am to
4pm Monday to Friday.
Admission: Check for up-to-date prices.

Directions: In Surrey Street near the river.
Map Reference: WS40
Information:
- Meet the Old Boxgrove Man and
  discover how big the Iguanodon
  dinosaur was who roamed nearby
  65 million years ago. Get your hands
  on fossils and check out the views over
  the harbour and Climping Beach.
- Coffee shop and gift shop.
- See website for further details.

MARINA GARDENS

Lovely park to walk your dog
and take the children

St Catherines Road,
Littlehampton, West Sussex.
Opening hours: Open park.

Map Reference: WS41

In an underwater dive, a duck's heartbeat slows to half speed.

PLACES TO VISIT

MEWSBROOK PARK

Lovely park to walk your dog
and take the children

Sea Road, Littlehampton, West Sussex.
Opening hours: Open park.

Map Reference: WS42
Information:
* Boating lake, mini railway, shelters, play areas for children, cafe and the Ruby Gardens conservation area.
* Wildfowl.

WEST BEACH LOCAL NATURE RESERVE

Nature reserve with beautiful
scenery and wildlife

Littlehampton, West Sussex.
Tel: 01903 718984.
e-mail: daphne.fisher@arun.gov.uk
web: www.arun.gov.uk
Opening hours: Call to enquire about tours.

Directions: Call visitor centre on telephone number above.
Map Reference: WS43
Information:
* Aquatic and terestrial oganisms.
* Marine vertebrates and birds.
* Local wildlife habitats, sand dunes and sea.

DID YOU KNOW?

Camels don't spit randomly at the object of their anger. They aim for the eyes.

COWDRAY LEISURE

IPING AND STEDHAM COMMONS

By appointment only. Badger watching. Guided wildlife awareness. School trips catered for

The Estate Office, Easebourne, Midhurst, West Sussex, GU29 0AQ.
Tel: 01730 812423.
Fax: 01730 817962.
e-mail: leisure@cowdray.co.uk
web: www.cowdray.co.uk
Contact: Darron Carver.
Opening hours: By appointment only.
Admission: £70 for an outing. Maximum of 4 in group.

Directions: 1 mile north of Midhurst on the A272.
Map Reference: WS44
Information:
• Guided walks and badger watching.
• Toilets and refreshments in golf club.
• Most indigenous mammals and birds, flora and fauna.

Beautiful scenery with many plant species

Stedham, Nr Midhurst, West Sussex.
Nearest postcode GU29 0PB.
Tel: 01273 492630.
Fax: 01273 494500.
web: www.sussexwt.org.uk
Opening hours: Open park.

Directions: Midhurst is accessible via the A286 or the A272. There is a large car park on the Elsted Road just off the A272.
Map Reference: WS45
Information:
• Birds including warblers and wood lark.
• Many insect varieties.
• Dogs must be on leads.

PLACES TO VISIT

NEWHAVEN FORT

OVINGDEAN CLIFFS

Historic visitor attraction on
stunning 10-acre site.
Dogs welcome on a lead

Newhaven, East Sussex, BN9 9DS.
Tel: 01273 517622.
e-mail: info@newhavenfort.org.uk
web: www.newhavenfort.org.uk
Opening hours: March to October,
10.30am to 6pm. Weekends during
November, 10.30am to 4pm.
Admission: Adults £5.50. Children £3.60.
Seniors £4.60. Family £16.50.

Directions: Situated between Brighton
and Eastbourne on the A259 coast road
and linked to Lewes on the A27.
Map Reference: ES40
Information:
• Cafe and Toilets.
• Many special events throughout the year
  (see website for further details).
• Exhibitions and displays.
• Stunning cliff-top views.

Chalk cliffs with amazing
views over coast and Brighton

Ovingdean, Nr Brighton, East Sussex.
Opening hours: Open park.

Directions: Along the coast road from
Brighton towards Peacehaven.
Map Reference: BH29
Information:
• Lovely walks.
• Site of Special Scientific Interest.
• Cafe.
• Birdwatching area (fulmar, gulls,
  stock dove, peregrine falcon).

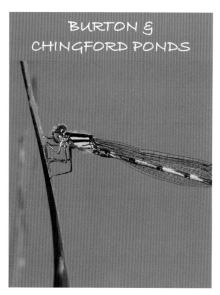

BURTON & CHINGFORD PONDS

Nature reserve with pond wildlife, including wildfowl, plants and insects

Petworth, West Sussex. Nearest postcode GU28 0JR.
Tel: 01273 492630.
Fax: 01273 494500.
web: www.sussexwt.org.uk

Directions: Located between Burton Hill and Crouch Farm.
Map Reference: WS46
Information:
- Pond wildlife including wildfowl, plants and insects.
- Dragonflies, marsh orchids and tussock sedge.
- Dogs must be on leads.
- Parking is limited.
- Surfaced and unsurfaced footpaths.

EBERNOE COMMON AND BUTCHERLAND

National nature reserve with ancient woodland

Ebernoe Common, Nr Petworth, West Sussex. Nearest postcode GU28 9JY.
web: www.sussexwt.org.uk
Opening hours: Open park.

Map Reference: WS47
Information:
- Many dormice and bats.
- Nightingales, fritillary butterflies.
- Dogs must be on leads.

DID YOU KNOW? The knees of an ostrich bend backwards.

PLACES TO VISIT

THE MENS

Nature reserve with woodland!

Crimbourne, Petworth, West Sussex.
Opening hours: Open park.

Directions: Off the A272.
Map Reference: WS48
Information:
- A woodland reverting to natural state with a wild, untamed feel.
- Near cycle network.
- 160 hectares, so compass is advisable.

PETWORTH HOUSE AND PARK

Beautiful park in Victorian setting

Petworth, West Sussex, GU28 0AE.
Tel: 01798 342207.
Fax: 01798 342963.
e-mail: petworth@nationaltrust.org.uk
web: www.nationaltrust.org.uk
Opening hours: Open most of the year. See website
Admission: Adults £7.50. Children £4.00. Family £19.00.

Directions: Located north off the A285.
Map Reference: WS49
Information:
- Wildlife, beautiful landscapes and family attractions.
- House, shop, restaurant, park and pleasure ground.
- Open-air concerts.
- Set in a deer park.
- Introductory talks.

PLACES TO VISIT

PULBOROUGH BROOKS

Superb nature reserve set in the heart of the beautiful Arun Valley. A must-see!

RSPB Pulborough, Wiggonholt, Pulborough, West Sussex, RH20 2EL.
Tel: 01798 875851.
Fax: 01798 873816.
e-mail: pulborough.brooks@rspb.org.uk
web: www.rspb.org.uk
Contact: N Andrews.
Opening hours: Daily, 10am to 5pm.
Admission: Free for RSPB Members. Adults £3.50. Children £1.00. Family £7.00. Concessions £2.50.

Directions: On A283 between Pulborough and Storrington.
Map Reference: WS50
Information:
• Nature trail with viewpoints and hides.
• Tearoom, shop, play area and toilets.
• See events leaflet on arrival.
• Provide electric buggy for the disabled.

WALTHAM BROOKS

Nature reserve

Off Main Road to Pulborough, Pulborough, West Sussex.
Opening hours: Open park.

Directions: Car park at Greatham Bridge.
Map Reference: WS51
Information:
• Wildfowl including teal, redshank, snipe, lapwing and marsh plant.
• Grazing marsh with a large open water area important for birds.
• 43 hectares.

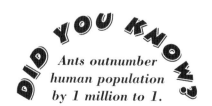

Ants outnumber human population by 1 million to 1.

THE RAYSTEDE CENTRE FOR ANIMAL WELFARE

Over 1,000 animals to see. Dogs, cats, birds, reptiles, equines and small animals

The Raystede Centre, Ringmer, East Sussex, BN8 5AT.
Tel: 01825 840252.
Fax: 01825 840995.
web: www.raystede.org
Contact: Morgan Williams.
Opening hours: Daily, 10am to 4pm.
Admission: Donations welcomed.

Directions: Situated on the B2192 between Ringmer and Halland.
Map Reference: ES41
Information:
• Toilets, refreshments and information centre.
• Annual school outings,
• Spring reports and shows and a quarterly news booklet.
• Dogs, cats, birds and reptiles, horses and small animals.
• Member of the Association of Dogs and Cats Homes.

HAPPY HUNTING GROUNDS

A really lovely spot for your animals' resting place. Beautiful walks and tranquil lake - 22 acres

Little Park Farm, Hooe Road (B2095), Russell's Green, Ninfield, East Sussex, TN33 9EH.
Tel: 01424 892396.
e-mail: tas1@tesco.net
web: www.pet-rest.net
Contact: Tas Cornwell.
Opening hours: 24 hours a day for emergencies. Open daylight hours for walks.
Admission: Donations gratefully accepted for grounds walks.

Directions: Situated on the B2095 between Pevensey Marsh Road and Herstmonceux to Bexhill Road.
Map Reference: ES42
Information:
• Bluebell walks in spring.
• Tranquil lake and woodland walks.
• Blessings conducted – see press or website for details when applicable.
• All pets.
• No bitches in season permitted on the walks.

CAMBER SANDS

Dog walking park with fun for all the family

Camber, Nr Rye, East Sussex.
Tel: 01797 225207.
web: www.eastsussex.gov.uk
Opening hours: Open beach.

Directions: Camber is situated three miles east of Rye. Signposted off the A259.
Map Reference: ES43
Information:
• Dog walking, horse riding and cycling in beautiful setting.
• Car park and toilets.
• Sealife and dune animals and birds.
• Dogs walked in marked zones only.

CASTLE WATER, RYE HARBOUR

Lovely to visit. Bird watching all year with unusual insects

Rye Harbour Nature Reserve, East Sussex, TN36 4LU.
web: www.wildrye.info
Opening hours: Open all times.
Information centre open 10am to 5pm daily (summer only).

Directions: South-east of Rye, signposted off the A259 Winchelsea to Rye Road.
Map Reference: ES44
Information:
• Bird watching, including rare birds.
• Car park, toilets, information centre and bird watching hides.
• Frequent sightings of rare breeds of birds.
• Dogs must be on leads.

DID YOU KNOW?
Bees won't fly when the wind blows at more than 15 mph.

FARM WORLD

Real working farm - something for everyone

Beckley, Nr Rye, East Sussex.
Tel: 01797 260250.
Fax: 01797 260347.
e-mail: enquiries@farmworldrye.co.uk
web: www.farmworldrye.co.uk
Opening hours: Tuesday to Saturday 11am to 5.30pm, term time. Daily during school holidays
Admission: Adults £6.00. Children £5.00. Seniors £5.00.

Directions: A268 between the villages of Newenden and Beckley. Five miles from Rye town centre.
Map Reference: ES45
Information:
• Family day out.
• Toilets and shops.
• Please check website.
• Llamas, rare breed of pigs, ponies, horses and lambs.
• Guide dogs welcome.

FLATROPERS WOOD

Nature reserve with wildlife walks

Rye, East Sussex. Nearest postcode TN31 6TH.
web: www.sussexwt.org.uk
Opening hours: Open park.

Directions: Access from Bixley Lane which joins the A268 2km west of Peasmarsh.
Map Reference: ES46
Information:
• Woodland flowers and plants.
• Variety of trees.
• Woodpeckers, newts and beetles.
• Dogs must be on leads.

SEAFORD HEAD NATURE RESERVE

Beautiful scenery with local wildlife

West of Cuckmere Haven, Seaford, East Sussex.
Tel: 01323 871095.
Opening hours: Open reserve.

Directions: Within the Sussex Downs, between Seaford and Beachy Head.
Map Reference: ES47
Information:
• Vegetable shingle bark, flowers and beautiful cliffs.
• Mammals and reptiles, birds, insects, Chalkhill Blue butterflies and bee-wolf.

DID YOU KNOW?
Every second almost eight portions of fish and chips are sold in the UK.

SEVEN SISTERS COUNTRY PARK

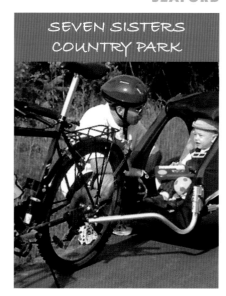

Beautiful wildlife, exhibitions, educational tours, walled garden and restaurant

Sussex Downs Conservation, Exceat, Seaford, East Sussex, BN25 4AD.
Tel: 01323 870280.
Fax: 01323 871070.
e-mail: sevensisters@southdowns-aont.gov.uk
web: www.sevensisters.org.uk
Contact: Katherine.
Opening hours: See website.

Directions: Situated at Exceat just off A259 between Eastbourne and Seaford.
Map Reference: ES48
Information:
• Visitor centre, toilets and restaurant.
• School parties and educational tours.
• Educational centre ideal for dog walkers and cyclists. Interesting history.
• Dogs must be on leads.

WIDEWATER LAGOON

Wonderful lagoon with
Herons and Swans

Shoreham Beach, Shoreham, West Sussex.
web: www.adur.gov.uk
Opening hours: Open lagoon.

Directions: North-west of Shoreham
Beach.
Map Reference: WS52
Information:
• Herons, swans and wildfowl.

HEWENSTREET CIRCUIT

Lovely walk with views
of the South Downs

South Chailey, East Sussex.

Directions: A275 Lewes Road at
Hewenstreet.
Map Reference: ES49
Information:
• 8km walk with lovely views.
• Dogs must be on leads.

DID YOU KNOW?

*Ichthyomancy is
a form of divination
using the heads and
entrails of fish.*

MALLING DOWNS

Country walk and nature reserve

South Malling, East Sussex. Nearest postcode BN8 5AA.
Tel: 01273 494777.
web: www.sussexwt.org.uk
Opening hours: Open nature reserve.

Directions: Head east from Lewes town centre, take small entrance at Wheatsheaf Gardens opposite petrol station.
Map Reference: ES50
Information:
• Winderful views with a variety of fauna and wildlife.
• Many butterfly species including Chalkhill Blue and Adonis. Grazing at times of the year.
• Dogs must be on leads.

SOUTHWATER COUNTRY PARK

Wildlife area and beautiful setting

Cripplegate Lane, Southwater,
West Sussex, RH13 7UN.
Tel: 01403 215263.
e-mail: leisure@horsham.gov.uk
web: www.horsham.gov.uk
Opening hours: Daily, 8am to dusk.

Directions: Located in the southern part of the village of Southwater, off Cripplegate Lane. Cripplegate Lane is off the main Worthing Road.
Map Reference: WS53
Information:
• Recreational activities such as orienteering and canoeing.
• Visitor centre, toilets, cafe are open weekends and school holidays.
• Lizards, kingfishers, nightingales and various dragonflies and butterflies.

HEAVEN FARM

Nature trail with oast house, campsite, ancient woodland, wallabies and deer

Furners Green, Uckfield, East Sussex, TN22 3RG.
Tel: 01825 790226.
Fax: 01825 790881.
e-mail: butler@enterprises@farmline.com
web: www.heavenfarm.co.uk
Contact: John Butler.
Opening hours: March to October, 10am to 5.30pm.
Admission: Camping charges.

Directions: From Brighton, follow A23 north bound to Bolney Junction, follow A272 through Haywards Heath to Chailey, turn left at mini roundabout along A275, then 4 miles on the left.
Map Reference: ES51
Information:
• Nature trail and wildlife. Located on the Greenwich Meridian line.
• Tea rooms, campsite, toilets, museum and gift shop.
• Wallabies and deer.

OUSE BANKS

Pleasant walk through waterside meadows

Leading into Lewes Road, Uckfield, East Sussex.
Tel: 020 7238 5909.
web: www.defra.gov.uk
Opening hours: Open park

Map Reference: ES52
Information:
• Historical interest.

SUSSEX HORSE RESCUE TRUST

Mainly horse and donkey rescue, but also pigs, sheep, cows, llamas, goats, turkeys and chickens

Hempstead Farm, Hempstead Lane, Uckfield, East Sussex, TN22 3DL.
Tel: 01825 762010.
Contact: Jan Roberts.
Opening hours: Sundays only, 11am to 4pm. Easter to September.
Admission: Adults £2.00. Children £1.00.

Directions: London Road north from Uckfield. Turn right into Brown's Lane and 6th turning on left is Hempstead Lane.
Map Reference: ES53
Information:
- Tea bar, barn shop, bric-a-brac, clothes, pony rides and toilets.
- Please phone to find out about special events.
- Education information about animal welfare, primarily equine.

WILDERNESS WOOD

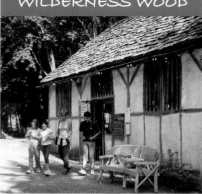

62 acres with lots of paths and trails. Highly recommended but must keep dog under control

Hadlow Down, Nr Uckfield, East Sussex.
Tel: 01825 830509.
Fax: 01825 830977.
e-mail: enquiries@wildernesswood.co.uk
web: www.wildernesswood.co.uk
Contact: Anne Yarrow.
Opening hours: Daily, 10am to 5.30pm
Admission: Adults £3.15. Children £1.90 (3-15). Under-3s free. Family £9.00. Concessions £2.65. Season tickets available and reduced rates from November to February.

Directions: 5 miles north east of Uckfield, in Hadlow Down village on south side of main A272.
Map Reference: ES54
Information:
- Exhibition throughout the year.
- Great place for dog walking.
- Tea room garden with local produce, picnic area and bbq places, play area, gift shop, garden furniture and products including bird boxes, tables and feeders.
- Please see website or phone for details of events this includes Working Horses Day in March.

PLACES TO VISIT

BEWL WATER

CRANE DOWN

Lovely nature reserve and reservoir with beautiful views

Clapham Lane, Nr Wadhurst, East Sussex.
Nearest postcode TN5 7LH.
Tel: 01273 492630.
Fax: 01273 494500.
Visitor centre on reservoirs, northern side
- contact 01892 890661.
web: www.sussexwt.org.uk
Opening hours: Open nature reserve.

Map Reference: ES55
Information:
- Beautiful views, nature, fauna and flora.
- Public footpath around the entire reservoir.
- Birds, tufted duck, goosander, widgeon, gadwell, green sandpiper, greenshank and other birds.
- Dogs must be on leads.
- Refreshments and toilets at visitor centre.

Views of Polegate Windmill and across the Cuckmere

Nr Wannock, East Sussex.
Tel: 020 7238 6907.
web: www.defra.gov.uk
Opening hours: Open park.

Directions: South of Folkington, near Filching Quarry. Path accessible via Mill Way Road next to Cornmill Gardens.
Map Reference: ES56
Information:
- Rich in wildlife.
- Dogs must be on leads.

DID YOU KNOW?

The 'horns' on the great horned owl are really feathers.

Informative features

110   **WORKING ANIMALS:** Who says animals are dumb?

112   **COMPLEMENTARY THERAPIES:**
Heard the phrase, but what does it mean?

117   **ANIMAL CONSERVATION:** Build a 'safari park' in your back garden!

120   **PETS FOR CHILDREN:** Who's the right pet for you?

122   **EQUESTRIAN PURSUITS:** Useful information for horse lovers

127   **INDIGENOUS SPECIES:** Native beasts, or foreign invaders?

130   **ANIMALS IN ART:** Why do we love to look at animals?

132   **RECIPES FOR YOUR PET:**
Homemade pet treats to tickle the taste buds!

136   **TRAINING YOUR HUMAN:** Animal antics, by Flopsy the Rabbit

138   **PHOBIAS:** Who's afraid of the big bad wolf/spider/snake/bat?

142   **GREEN GYMS:** BTCV's Green Gyms - what are they?

144   **ANIMALS IN THE SPIRIT WORLD**

148   **WHERE CAN I SEE ... ?:** Helpful tips for Sussex wildlife hunters

153   **WILDLIFE RESCUE CENTRES:**
What do I do if I find an injured or lost animal?

158   **RECORD-BREAKING ANIMALS:**
Who's the tallest, smallest, oldest, strangest?

160   **PET INSURANCE:** Should I insure my animal?

163   **PERFORMING ANIMALS:** Is it cruel – what can I do to help?

168   **UNUSUAL AND EXOTIC PETS:**
Looking for a small pet with a difference?

172   **PET PASSPORTS:** PETS travel scheme explained

174   **ANIMAL CHARITIES:** Comprehensive listing of charities in Sussex

184   **WHEN A PET DIES:** Coping with the passing of your treasured friend

186   **TRAINING YOUR PET:** Practice makes perfect

188   **PUZZLE PAGES:** Seek your answers from the natural world

190   **OWNING A PET:** A humorous guide to pet-keeping

Who says animals are dumb?

We have harnessed the power, emotion and intelligence of animals to our advantage since the Stone Age, when wild dogs first came close to the campfire in search of warmth and food. It was a logical step for our Homo Sapiens ancestors to form a working bond with these creatures which proved useful for hunting, fetching, carrying and even pulling loads.

Putting animals to work for our personal use may not seem entirely fair, but in fact nurtured working animals are often fitter, healthier and more fulfiled than those who are without 'purpose'. Work brings its own set of stimulation, reward and satisfaction - providing of course that the animal's needs are taken into consideration.

Until the industrial age, most heavy work was assigned to horses, oxen, elephants, asses and camels. Indeed these animals are often still the most effective 'machines' in some environments. If you have ever witnessed the expertise of Indian elephants moving logs or pushing down small trees you cannot have failed to be impressed by the working relationship that makes these enormous beasts willing to work in return for food and care.

Humans use animals for many different purposes, not least for food and clothing. Even unlikely creatures such as spiders have played their part in the development of the modern age. Did you know that spiders' webs were used to fashion the graticule or crossed lines in the eyepieces of bombsights when bombing from the air first threatened the country? It appears that even the thinnest man-made wire was not fine enough for the precision accuracy required.

Today in 21st century Britain, there are still plenty of working creatures. They are used less frequently for ploughing fields, pulling pit carts, grinding corn or powering the hammers of iron forges. But the changing world has opened up new requirements – such as dogs

The camel is described as a 'ship of the desert' as it can carry passengers easily on sand and go without water and food for considerable periods

The power of the elephant is vital in India for clearing woodland and transportation

FEATURES

concerns, but there can be no doubt that we are indeed indebted to creatures that have helped improve human medicine.

Few people relished seeing Ham the space chimp strapped into his capsule when he was launched into space in 1961, and he became an unwitting celebrity when he returned intact after running short of oxygen during the flight and nearly drowning during splashdown. But during the 1880s, Jack the baboon was a joy to watch as he revelled in the task of changing the railway train signals in the Cape, South Africa, for his master who was disabled. He could also pump water from a nearby well, fetch keys in response to whistle signals from approaching trains, do the gardening and push his master to work on a railway trolley!

True, the balance of power lies with the human and it is essential that the advantage is not abused. But because useful working animals are held in high regard, it does mean that their future is assured on a planet where man rules supreme.

trained to sniff for drugs, mountain or earthquake rescue dogs, gun dogs, sheepdogs, guide dogs for the blind, hearing dogs for the deaf, 'bomb' proof horses for mounted police, racing thoroughbreds for the 'sport of kings', birds of prey for entertaining the crowds, rabbiting ferrets and even the humble kitty cat who keeps the number of vermin in the garden shed in check.

Pet therapy is used to soothe the minds of troubled souls and a fluffy rabbit can do wonders for the child who is lost in a private world of sorrow. Who can fail to be cheered by a litter of kittens or a playful pup, or be touched by the sight of a mother sparrow feeding her chick?

Not all useful creatures are so glamorous. A leech or maggots feeding from human blood or flesh is a sight that few wish to see – but they can play an important part in healing wounds where modern medicine has failed to succeed.

The contentious area of drug testing on animals is fraught with its own set of

Border Collies have a natural ability to round up sheep and most are happiest when working

Complementary therapies for animals
Heard the phrase ... but what does it mean?

Complementary or alternative therapy provides 'non-conventional' treatment for a variety of ailments for both humans and animals. As many more people embrace holistic medicine for themselves, they also realise how helpful it can be for their animal companions. Over the years there has been an explosion of interest in natural healing arts for dogs, cats, horses and even rabbits, birds and ferrets.

by Rob Willard

Types of Therapies

Acupuncture

In use for thousands of years, acupuncture was first recorded in China, Japan and other Eastern countries where it began with the discovery that stimulating specific areas of skin affected the functions of various organs and systems of the body. Acupuncture is based upon the concept that the body has energy lines (called meridians) which become blocked or deficient when a person or animal is out of balance, causing various ailments. The use of needles at appropriate acupuncture points redirects this energy and balances the body.

Aromatherapy and essential oils

Aromatic plants and oils have been used for centuries for their medical and culinary benefits. The method developed by aromatherapists and vets working together centres on the fact that creatures know what they need to heal.

Several oils are offered to the animal which will indicate its like or dislike for that particular smell. Distinctive behaviour patterns often occur, such as dogs rolling on their backs, horses shaking their heads, indicating towards the sore point or perhaps stamping one foot. Cats may rub themselves against the practitioner to indicate a positive response. Selected oils (usually diluted) are then given to the animal.

Chiropractic therapy

Literally translated, means 'done by hand'. Chiropractic treatment addresses problems such as imbalances in the skeletal system and joints of the body, muscular ailments and problems with the nervous system. Chiropractic therapy attempts to treat causes rather than symptoms and is based on the principle that many ailments and problems are due to misalignments of the bones of the spine as well as other parts of the body. The most famous form of chiropractic treatment is 'McTimoney', named after John McTimoney who developed and taught his own form of treatment in the early 70s.

Equine craniosacral therapy
This focuses upon the central nervous system of horses, using light touch to optimise body movement. It is a gentle and subtle technique which can be highly effective in addressing a number of conditions including head injuries and traumas, emotional problems, facial nerve paralysis, headshaking, lameness and spinal injuries.

Equine sports massage
Uses a variety of massage techniques which can be helpful for both rehabilitation and prevention of injuries caused by strain or fatigue. It is also beneficial for relieving muscle spasm/tension, increasing circulation and freedom of movement, enhancing muscle tone, improving stamina and overall performance.

Equine Bowen therapy
A gentle, non-intrusive therapy which stimulates the body's inner ability to heal itself. It is based on the principle that reorganisation of the musculature of the body can bring increased energy levels and pain relief. Equine Bowen was developed by the late Thomas Ambrose Bowen.

Herbs and remedies
There are two main areas of herbal remedies: Indian and European. Indian herb remedies are based on the principles of Ayurveda (an ancient healing system). Vets are increasingly utilising the healing properties of these remedies and some European herbs are licensed as veterinary medicines. Herbs have many uses including anti-inflammatory, antiseptic, sedative or stimulant.

Holistic/faith healing
Holistic healing is a form of alternative health care that integrates the whole being in the healing process: body, mind,

emotion, spirit and life force (chi) energy. It is a gentle, non-invasive treatment that utilises natural healing energies via the healer to the patient by the laying of hands. One of the many benefits of holistic healing is that the therapist can often tune into the animal and experience the pain and discomfort that the animal is suffering and thereby direct the healing energies to the exact location of the problem, thus offering immediate benefits to the whole healing process.

Homoeopathy

Homoeopathy works by using remedies that cause the same symptoms as the illness. Homoeopathic medicine uses not only plants but also mineral and animal sources which are diluted homoeopathically and given in minute quantities to stimulate the immune system to fight the disease or illness.

All types of animals from pets to farm animals, exotics to horses can be treated. In many cases it is used to treat chronic diseases, offering a chance to cure where no other options are available. Lifestyle and diet management are also a part of the methodology.

Hydrotherapy

Hydrotherapy is becoming an increasingly popular therapy for horses and dogs. Forms of treatment include cold and hot water hosing, swimming and equine spa. Cold water hosing helps to reduce inflammation, thus reducing the level of pain, and is beneficial for new injuries. Hot water hosing helps increase the blood flow to the site of injury.

Swimming develops the musculoskeletal system, although care must be taken with horses as they are not naturally strong swimmers. Equine spas use the healing properties of sea water to promote healing of leg injuries in horses. During treatment, the handler stands in the middle of a circular pool or walks alongside a long pool to ensure animal safety at all times.

Magnotherapy

It is believed that magnetic energy fields speed up the blood supply which in turn allows more oxygen to enter the bloodstream. This enables a more efficient absorption of nutrients and promotes healing. Types of magnets used for therapy include permanent (or static) magnets, pulsed electromagnetic field magnets and bi-polar magnets, all of which have different effects on the cells of the body. Manufacturers have developed magnetic rugs, beds, collars, boots and strips for dogs, cats, horses and other animals.

FEATURES

Osteopathy

Osteopathy involves examining and treating movement restrictions of the body to help improve mobility and reduce inflammation. Restrictions in the articulations and soft tissues are referred to as osteopathic lesions. The principle of osteopathy is that the body is self-healing and self-regulatory and, if one joint or muscle is blocked or tense, this will affect other parts of the body. The goal of the osteopath is to help restore the animal's natural equilibrium.

Physiotherapy

Chartered physiotherapists are trained to use a variety of techniques such as joint, muscle, ligament and tendon mobilisation and manipulation to restore normal function and help pain relief. This is especially useful for animals requiring specific exercises after surgery or for those with chronic musculo-skeletal problems.

Reiki

This is a Japanese form of healing involving the transfer of energy from practitioner to patient to promote the body's natural ability to heal itself.

Reiki uses specific hand positions that correspond to the major organs and energy centres, such as the heart or adrenal glands. It is helpful for any sort of ailment – physical, mental or emotional – and can reduce stress and anxiety in many animals.

Shiatsu

Mainly used for horses, Shiatsu is based on finger pressure applied to acupressure points to gently stimulate the natural healing ability of the body. In Shiatsu there are 12 paired meridians, the principle being that by working each pair together you can improve the results of each one separately, thus restoring the natural balance. Horses respond well to Shiatsu as it is based on communication and physical contact.

Hydrotherapy is becoming an increasingly popular therapy for horses and dogs

FEATURES

FREQUENTLY ASKED QUESTIONS:

Can any alternative therapist treat my pet?

It is illegal for any lay practitioner to treat animals. This includes aromatherapy, acupuncture and homoeopathy. These therapies can only be applied by a vet who is properly trained and insured.

Is complementary or alternative therapy a good substitute for veterinary treatment?

It is not an alternative. Under the Protection of Animals Act, any sick animal must be taken to a vet. After veterinary diagnosis is established, the vet will recommend a course of treatment that may include complementary therapy.

How do I get alternative therapy for my pet?

Step 1 – visit your vet for a proper diagnosis.
Step 2 – discuss the full range of treatment options with your vet, including complementary therapy.

Where can I train to be an alternative therapist for animals?

There are many organisations that provide training. See the resource list for information. It is essential that you are trained by a recognised institute and that you have full insurance.

London Zoo employs an "Entertainment Director" for the animals.

Summary
Complementary medicine is increasingly becoming accepted as a means of alternative treatment. Vets and pet owners are embracing new techniques and methods, but strict regulation of practitioners and training is likely to become essential in the future as more therapies are developed.

Most people agree that if complementary therapy is likely to produce positive results, it should be tried. The wellbeing of the animal must take priority over other matters, including unfounded prejudice.

USEFUL RESOURCES:

British Holistic Medical Association
www.bhma.org

Foundation for Integrated Medicine
www.fihealth.org.uk

Research Council for Complementary Medicine
www.rccm.org.uk

The National Association of Animal Therapists.
01844 291526

Natural Animal Health
www.natural-animal-health.co.uk

Royal College of Veterinary Surgeons
www.rcvs.org.uk

British Medical Acupuncture Society
www.medical-acupuncture.co.uk

International School of Animal Aromatics
www.ingraham.co.uk

Bowen Association (UK)
www.bowen-technique.co.uk

British Chiropractic Association
www.chiropractic-uk.co.uk

British Herbal Medicine Association
www.bhma.info

Holistic Healers Association
www.ukhealers.info

The Society of Homoeopaths
www.homeopathy-soh.org

The National Federation of Reiki Practitioners
www.nat-fed-of-reiki.freeserve.co.uk

Association of Chartered Physiotherapists in Animal Therapy.
01962 844390

The Shiatsu Society (UK)
www.shiatsu.org

Build a 'safari park' in your back garden!

You don't need to travel to Africa in order to see wildlife in its natural surroundings - it is all around us every minute of the day! Take off those blinkers for a few minutes and absorb the sights and sounds of the English native flora and fauna. You will be truly amazed by the diversity of wildlife that can be found in even the most built-up areas.

Fortunately, there are many designated nature reserves in Britain - almost 3,000 reserves covering over 750,000 acres, and these are vital to wildlife survival. There are around 50 nature conservation trusts which protect most of the sites - but it is up to each and every one of us to create further mini-havens which allow nature to flourish everywhere, not just in formally protected regions.

Everyone who owns and occupies land, however tiny, should regard conservation as part of their responsibility. Neatness is an enemy of many species – so think twice before ripping out hedges, hacking back the shrubbery and uprooting naturally seeded plants. They may not have appeared in your original masterplan of garden design, but nature's designer is always keen to attract wildlife who may appreciate a few additional flowers, seeds, leaves, shade and protection.

Even the tiniest garden will have a corner suitable for a few rotting logs, a heap of leaves, a pile of rocks and pebbles, a few nettles or a semi-wild patch. This is where butterflies will lay their eggs, insects and worms will gather, frogs, toads and newts will seek refuge, birds will rummage and even hedgehogs will feast.

Look at your fences and walls of your dwelling with a fresh eye - there is bound to be room for others to make a home near your house. Position bird and bat boxes in sheltered sites and enjoy watching these creatures investigate and eventually move into their new homes. Allow gaps in your garage for nesting house martins, swallows, bats and even owls, and let your hedges stay shaggy until at least early August to allow birds to raise their young in peace. Install a bird feeder and observe the enormous range of feathered friends who visit.

Plant a tree or two if there's room in your garden and watch how they attract wildlife as they grow. Dig a pond if space allows and you will be surprised just how quickly it is colonised by natural wildlife. Add a few rocky outcrops, plants and groundcover and your pond will become a haven for those who love to live near water. Give it a shallow end where creatures can drink safely without fear of tumbling in and try to resist the temptation to fill it with colourful goldfish – they do look bright and cheerful but tend to eat many of the creatures that you may wish to attract.

Intricate cobwebs with early morning dewdrops

Dragonflies also make the most of an English garden

Allow your lawn to naturalise with species other than grass, particularly avoiding chemicals and fertilisers. Consider leaving an uncut area in which wild flowers will reward you with colourful blooms, delicate leaves and of course a host of bees, butterflies and insects. And if you haven't already begun to reduce your kitchen and garden waste by composting – don't delay! Not only will a small compost heap help reduce the enormous load on landfill sites but your heap will attract a host of creatures such as grass snakes, worms and insects. What's more, your garden will love the result in just a few months' time!

If you are lucky enough to own a field or paddock, leave wide margins around the edge where natural species can colonise and seek refuge from the perils of the 21st century. Woodland can be sensitively managed to allow access by humans whilst leaving native creatures the space and privacy they deserve. If you want to watch badgers, foxes, deer and other wildlife, consider building a small 'hide' so you don't disturb the animals during their daily or nightly forage for food.

Mossy tree stumps are ideal 'living quarters' for many wild animals and insects

DID YOU KNOW?

There are butterflies that smell like chocolate.

There are plenty of opportunities for observing wildlife in its natural surroundings, but you will see nothing until your mind is open. Put aside your worries whilst you stroll purposefully on a wildlife walk and you will reap bountiful rewards. Even in urban sites you will find

treasures in every patch of green.

It is interesting to note that nature's forces are strong enough to invade even the most depressing concrete jungle – there are wild flowers growing from cracks in walls on office blocks, butterflies flitting between window boxes on high-rise flats, mice and voles scurrying along pavements, bats feasting on insects at dusk and frogs paddling by drains and ditches in the busiest towns!

Step into the countryside and the artistic canvas expands. You may be lucky enough to observe a stoat or weasel, the stoat being easily identified by the black tuft on the end of his long-haired tail. In northern areas during winter, the stoat turns white - a clever camouflage which enables him to blend with snow, whilst the summer coloration allows the animal to merge with the woody leaf litter and soil.

You won't have to travel far before seeing rabbits and squirrels, and even shy deer are frequently seen on the edges of woods and fields. Foxes can be spotted in towns, villages and countryside, having adapted to urban life with aplomb. Sit by a pond or lake and feast your eyes on herons, wild ducks, moorhens, coots, swans and a host of water creatures – and you may be lucky enough to spot the elusive kingfisher as he streaks past.

The richness of Britain is all around, and conservation is essential in order to protect not only specific species but the environment in which they live. Conservation cannot be relegated to patches of land here and there, it requires a conscious effort from us all. So every garden, tub and shrub is precious in its own right. Look after the green bits and your life will be filled with colour!

Leaving an area of your garden uncut will attract the likes of butterflies, bees and insects

Who's the right pet for you?

As my family keeps lots of pets, I am an experienced 'pet keeper', you could say. I love all our animals, but there are some drawbacks ...

by Rosie Knight (Age 11)

FEATURES

Dogs

We have two dogs. They are great fun for children to play with, and as they are not actually mine I don't have too much responsibility for them. But I know for a fact that they need a lot of looking after. My dad takes them out for a walk every day, and one of them constantly rounds up the chickens. When we looked after a friend's border collie, it plucked one of the poor chickens until it looked 'oven ready'! Of course they need feeding, grooming and training, not to mention cleaning and stroking. Dogs are lovely but they need lots of attention!

Cats

Cats are so sweet, but there's more to them than meets the eye. I used to have a wonderful cat but he was always 'out and about' – I never knew where he was. Another furry friend I knew was run over. But they can be great pets if you live in a safe area. My friend has had her two cats for years and they are part of the family. But they do catch lots of birds – not so good for that particular household as their mum has a bird phobia and can't bear to clean up the feathers!

Cats can be great pets if you live in a safe area

Rabbits

When we first got Bob my bunny, he would scratch and wriggle when we picked him up but now, after a lot of handling and care, he knows and trusts us. But don't forget, just because a rabbit is shut in a cage, it doesn't mean you can ignore them. Rabbits need to enjoy the freedom of a run every day in a safe place. They love to sniff around in the grass. They also eat more food than you might imagine, and of course they need cleaning out regularly. My friends all love to cuddle Bob – he's practically perfect in every way.

Hamsters

Hamsters look sweet and cuddly. But in my experience they can be vicious! When they bite, I guarantee it hurts!. They need a nice comfy cage with lots of things for them to do. This will keep them interested and make them happy hamsters. They tend to wake up at night – a bit of a problem if you hope to play with them during the daytime.

Fish

We are planning to get some fish for our new garden pond. It's easier than keeping them indoors in a tank because it doesn't need cleaning so often. If the aquarium isn't clean, your pets will become greenfish, not goldfish! These are great, fairly low maintenance pets … but they are not very cuddly!

Horses, ponies and donkeys

I haven't got these, although we do look after two donkeys from time to time. They need stables, paddocks and fields to graze and exercise in, and someone to feed, muck them out and groom them. They are brilliant to ride (once you have paid for all those lessons). I think these are high-maintenance animals and you would have to give them lots of attention every single day. They are also expensive to feed, not forgetting the blacksmith's and vet's bills. They can be dangerous, so be careful that you choose the right one to be your friend.

Dogs are perfect companions, but need lots of attention

Summary

There are lots of other lovely pets such as reptiles (which need to be kept warm), birds (which need a large cage so they can stretch their wings), ducks (which should really have a pond), and even pigs! Whatever pet you consider, make sure you learn about it before it arrives, then you are more likely to know whether or not it is the right pet for you!

Horses and ponies can be 'high-maintenance'

A cat laps milk with the underside of its tongue.

Useful information for horse lovers

Man forged partnerships with horses back in ancient times when the noble animal acted as a beast of burden. Indeed it is still used as such in many countries, where it is valuable for working the land, pulling and carting loads and transporting humans. The long-suffering animal still toils in some regions, having to cope with ill-fitting harness, overwork, sore feet and lack of food and water.

by Pat Crawford

The horse is fortunate in Britain, however, where it is revered by many and used for enjoyment and excellence. In this age of mechanisation and technology, it is heartening to learn that there are more people riding than ever before. Never has there been such a depth of understanding between equine and human, and indeed never before has there been such a wide range of equipment and facilities made available to the equestrian world. Equestrian sports not only gain more followers and participants every year, but expand and develop to include sports that you may not even have heard of!

The world of horses is as complex as it is diverse – read on to whet your appetite and increase your knowledge:

Side or astride?

For centuries it was only considered 'proper' for ladies to ride side saddle. Recent discoveries indicate side saddle riding existed as far back as the first millennium AD, although it was not introduced to Britain until 1382, when Anne of Bohemia, wife of Richard II, created a new fashion. Although very popular in the first part of the 20th century, it was almost totally replaced by astride a very short time later. Today, interest in side saddle riding has seen a resurgence and large and small shows throughout the UK include classes.

Why not book a 'taster' lesson with an instructor registered with The Side Saddle Association? Some instructors are prepared to give lessons on their own horses but, in any case, the vast majority of reasonably schooled horses take to carrying a side saddle without any problems.

The Side Saddle Association can be contacted on: 01509 856025.

Allen Photo Guide 'All About Riding Side Saddle', 24 pages, softback by Patricia and Victoria Spooner, price £4.95, is ideal initial reading for anyone considering taking up this form of riding.

FEATURES

Neddy, steady, go! -
Polocrosse, a fast-growing equestrian sport

Polocrosse

Polocrosse, a fast-growing equestrian sport, is suitable for 'ordinary' horses and riders of all ages. Kent Target Polocrosse caters for enthusiasts in Sussex and Kent and is open to juniors under 18 (£20), senior (£30) and family (£45). Social membership is available at just £10.

Often likened to a cross between polo and lacrosse, the game was imported from Australia. Matches are held against teams from other regions and are frequently followed by barbecues and other social activities. KTPC is a very friendly club and welcomes prospective new members. Why not attend a 'taster' session or to go along and watch?

Contacts: www.kentpolocrosse.co.uk Jason Webb – chairman, coach and selector – 01580 211662 enquiries@australianstockhorses.co.uk Naomi Pearce – club secretary – 07971 780792.

The British Horseball Association

Recently imported from France, horseball is taking off in a big way. Invented by Paul Depons, a former rugby player, it is often compared to a cross between basketball and rugby – and it's certainly fast and furious.

Riders need to be confident and reasonably experienced and horses should be well-schooled and under control because the game involves speed, sudden spurts, half turns and rapid stops.

Most areas of the UK already have access to a group affiliated to the British Horseball Association, the sport's governing body.

Talks, lectures and demonstrations

Ken Lyndon-Dykes, an ex-international level three-day event rider and Society of Master Saddlers' Qualified Saddle Fitter, is available to give talks, lectures and demonstrations for all types of equestrian groups.
Enquiries: 07973 501873.

FEATURES

Why not try a day out with the bloodhounds? (not a fox in sight!)

The Coakham Bloodhounds based near Brightling hunt over beautiful countryside in Sussex and Kent. The hounds follow a scent laid by a human quarry and the hunts vary in length and complexity, some days involving more rugged country and larger jumps than others. When 'caught', the quarry is likely to be covered in very wet licks and kisses!

If you would like to experience a day out with the Coakham Bloodhounds, a welcoming and friendly hunt, you are invited to **telephone for more information on 07729 034546 or 01435 830571.**

Sponsor a bloodhound puppy

Did you know that, for just £100 a year, you're able to sponsor a bloodhound puppy? The Coakham Bloodhounds

welcome new sponsors who are invited to choose a puppy from a selection of photographs. Sponsors name their selected puppy and are presented with a framed photograph signed by the joint 'masters'. They are then kept up-to-date with the puppy's progress and entry into the pack and will be able to foot follow – or spend a day in the saddle – watching their particular hound at work. Sponsorship may be extended for longer periods if desired.

Further information available from Linda Thompson: 01883 723114.

Prior to 1980 anyone could shoe a horse!

Did you know that, until 1980 when the Farrier's Registration Act came fully into force, it was possible for anyone to set up as a farrier? The Act was passed in order to protect the welfare of horses and it is an offence for anyone other that a registered farrier, registered apprentice, veterinary surgeon or veterinary student to carry out farriery except in emergency situations.

If you would like lists of qualified, registered farriers or information about training write to: Farriers' Registration Council, Adam Court, Newark Road, Peterborough, PE1 5PP, www.farriers.reg.gov.uk

Horses and ponies at risk

The endangered species list includes several breeds of horse and pony. The Rare Breeds Survival Trust, an organisation set up more than 25 years ago to save rare breeds of livestock – including horses and ponies – from extinction, lists the following as priority breeds:

Cleveland Bay, Clydesdale, Dales, Dartmoor, Eriskay, Exmoor, Fell, Irish Draught, Suffolk.

The RBST's work is crucial to the survival of these breeds. As with all such bodies, funding and manpower are always problematic.

If you would like to know more about the Trust's work, make a donation or offer your services as a volunteer, contact: **Rare Breeds Survival Trust, Stoneleigh Park, Warwickshire CV8 2BR. Tel: 024 7669 6551 Fax: 024 7669 6706 E-mail: enquiries@rbst.org.uk**

vary in size and are democratically run by elected committees. Programmes reflect members' special interests, with some clubs placing emphasis on schooling and training, others on competition and others on social activities.

Riding clubs are friendly, welcoming places and most are delighted to meet prospective new members. More information available from: **British Riding Clubs, British Horse Society, Stoneleigh Deer Park, Stoneleigh, Kenilworth, Warwickshire, CV8 2XZ.**

FEATURES

British Riding Club movement

Legally and financially, the British Riding Club movement forms a department of the British Horse Society where a staff of six undertakes organisation and administration. Clubs

Hadlow College Equine Department

Hadlow College, numbered among the leading 10% land-based colleges in the UK, has a very successful Equine Department offering a wide range of degree, HND and National Diploma

courses, etc. The college also offers part-time courses leading to the National Award in Horse Management (Equitation), British Horse Society Stages Two and Three and Foundation Degrees (in partnership with the University of Greenwich) in Equine Science and Equine Management.

Hadlow is a friendly, well-equipped college located in an outstanding campus about three miles east of Tonbridge.

Write or call for a prospectus, information or advice: **Hadlow College, Tonbridge, Kent TN11 0AL. Tel: 0500 551434. Fax: 01732 853207. E-mail: enquiries@hadlow.ac.uk www.hadlow.ac.uk**

Foundation courses in saddle fitting

The Society of Master Saddlers welcomes applications for places on a foundation course in saddle fitting from equine vets and physiotherapists, British Horse Society Fellows and Instructors and other professionals working within the equestrian industry. Details of dates, venue, fees, etc. available from:

Society of Master Saddlers, Green Lane Farm, Green Lane, Stonham, Stowmarket, Suffolk IP14 5DS (enclose SAE with enquiries for lists/information). Tel: 01449 711642.

The Society of Master Saddlers

The Society of Master Saddlers is a professional body responsible for promoting craft and skill standards and protecting the welfare and safety interests of horses and riders. Membership is stringently controlled and applicants must fulfil strictly applied criteria. The Society operates the only professional, non-commercially linked saddle fitting qualification available worldwide.

Always look for the badge.

Always use the services of a qualified registered saddle fitter (lists available from chief executive, Society of Master Saddlers, address as above.)

The Worshipful Company of Saddlers

Originating as a guild in the Middle Ages, the Saddlers' Company (0207 726 8661) is among the oldest of the City livery companies and one of the very few to retain enduring links with the trade of its origins. Other livery companies with strong equestrian links include **The Worshipful Company of Loriners (01386 751695) and The Worshipful Company of Farriers (01923 260747).**

Native beasts, or foreign invaders?

A dictionary definition of the word indigenous states: 'originating or occurring naturally (in a country, region etc.); native'. But it is often difficult to know how long an animal has to live in a country to earn that prestigious status.

by Eliza Rhyder

FEATURES

We may expect any animal we see in the British countryside to be indigenous, but in fact many of our most common animals were introduced by invaders and colonisers. Famously, rabbits, the grey squirrel and the collared dove have all been so successful in their host country that they have partially or completely displaced the naturally occurring species.

It is arguable how much the indigenous species was in decline before being supplanted by the more successful interloper. For example, although it is widely assumed that grey squirrels forced out what many would view as the more attractive red, the two species do actually inhabit different environments. There should really be no competition for food – so it is more probable that other factors prompted the decline of the red squirrel and the upsurge of the grey. The balance of coniferous and deciduous woodland has altered, with an increase of the grey squirrels' habitat and decline of the reds'. Popular myth may prefer a more romantic view of the red squirrel valiantly fending off the usurper, but the facts are often more prosaic.

Other species have been introduced for purely practical means: rabbits arrived with the Normans for food, edible snails were brought to us by the Romans, and the marsh frog, whose nocturnal vocalising echoes across Romney Marsh, was more admired for its delicious legs than any desire to increase biodiversity!

Can these species now be classed as 'indigenous'? The fact that they can live in the wild, breeding successfully

A true King among birds – the golden eagle

FEATURES

without any assistance from man, indicates they could fall into the indigenous category. Other more exotic species such as Leonardslee's wallabies in Sussex and flocks of parakeets seen in Cornwall may only have a specious claim to indigenousness. Their foothold in our environment is tenuous, and unfavourable climactic changes could alter their status rapidly and leave them stranded in an alien environment.

In the global village that we now inhabit, there's a potential for many more opportunistic creatures to establish indigenous rights to our island. Let us hope that they will not have the catastrophic effects suffered by islands such as New Zealand and Mauritius, where extinction of native species has been the result of careless intrusion.

Some of our indigenous species have declined to the point of extinction: the wolf for example, which is possibly on the brink of a comeback with a suggestion of a reintroduction policy. However, it is hard to see how this would be practical in such a small and comparatively densely populated country. The possibilities for conflict with man would be endless, with the wolf bound to come off the loser. Parts of Europe have been more successful from the wolf's point of view and small packs remain in the remotest regions.

Otters also succumbed to the march of progress, disappearing along with their habitat. Competition from the non-indigenous mink, a remorseless killer, may also have contributed to their decline. However, the reintroduction of the otter is proving to be successful and thriving colonies in carefully chosen locations are populating the river banks once again. Sussex was once the natural playground of the otter and hopefully it will become so again.

The fat or edible dormouse and common dormouse, although indigenous to southern areas of Britain, are now rarely seen. The edible version was a great delicacy for the Romans and may have even been introduced by them. The common dormouse, although now far from common, is our very own - the same one that was squashed into the teapot by the Mad Hatter at Alice's tea party in Wonderland. It seems, even then, to have had a reputation for being rather dopey and so it may not be so surprising that its survival rate is poor!

The indigenous quality of birds is harder to define due to their migratory habits and ability to hop over the oceans if the wind is in the right direction. For a bird to be classed as indigenous, it would probably have to breed here rather than simply over-winter.

Many people assume that the golden eagle is our largest indigenous bird and this may indeed be true ... but the last surviving English golden eagle now lives a solitary existence in the Lake District

Beavers don't stop growing until they die.

since the demise of its mate just last year. This lone survivor is a male of some seven or eight years old, whereas his partner was over 20. They had not raised any chicks for some years. So unless he can attract a female to his home, the chances are that he will have to search further afield and this may take him away to the Highlands of Scotland, where golden eagles still survive – leaving England with none!

Red kites, another rare bird of prey, have been reintroduced to areas of the country where they were once common, but unfortunately they still have to negotiate the hostility of humans, including some gamekeepers who see them as competition for newly hatched pheasant poults.

With the advent of less intensive agriculture and more land set aside, hopefully these rare indigenous species will be able to make a gradual comeback, to be seen regularly once again in this green and pleasant land. One thing is certain - indigenous species need our continued help if they are to share space on the planet.

Hungry like the wolf ... but is he coming back?

FEATURES

Why do we love to look at animals?

Realistically, symbolically and mythologically, animals have appeared in art from the earliest cave paintings, one of the most famous being at Lascaux in France with its fantastic representation of cattle, deer and ponies galloping across the undulating surface of the cave walls and roof, through to Damien Hurst's preserved cows, pigs and sheep.

by Eliza Rhyder

Animals are often included symbolically in pictures, typically in 15th century Netherlandish art such as the Arnolfini Marriage portrait by Jan van Eyck, where a little dog at the couple's feet represents fidelity. Similarly, Jan Steen's 17th century painting, The Effects of Intemperance, includes a parrot, which symbolised learning by example.

Titian's famous reclining nude, The Venus of Urbino, could be interpreted as a courtesan in her boudoir, but the little dog at her feet would have suggested, certainly to the contemporary viewer, a fidelity that could be at odds with that image. Other similar reclining nudes, such as Giorgione's Dresden Venus and Velasquez's Rokeby Venus, do not include such symbolism and the viewer is allowed to assume that the women in these paintings are what they seem to be.

Aesop's eponymous fables personify, through animals, our human flaws and failings. Perhaps it is easier to face our weaknesses when they are represented by something that is not human, than accept their base and bestial quality in

Cats – a popular subject for painters

human form.

In the 16th century, paintings often included a representation of the senses. Animals associated with these could be a hedgehog or ermine, sharp and soft, for touch; an eagle for sight; a stag for hearing - traditionally associated with an acute sense of sound; monkeys with fruit for taste; a dog for its heightened sense of smell.

Later 17th century genre paintings used a different approach to represent the senses, and Flemish painters of genre scenes used drinkers for taste, fiddlers for hearing and smokers for smell.

The donkey has had a chequered career

in art. It can represent stupidity; the fat drunkard, Silenus, follower of Bacchus, rides an ass, as does Sancho Panza, Don Quixote's faithful squire. In contrast, an ass can also represent humility; it carried the virgin and child as in Jacopo Tintoretto's Flight into Egypt.

In religious art, many saints have animal attributes; St Jerome's is a lion, John the Baptist is always identified with a lamb, as is St Agnes. Even snakes are associated with saints; a serpent in a chalice representing a poisoned cup is the attribute of St John the Evangelist. The viewer of these paintings would know immediately who was portrayed by the animal attributed to them.

Mythological animals play a highly symbolic and important role in art; dragons, unicorns and serpents are represented over and over again. The Latin word draco means dragon or snake and often dragons have serpent-like qualities. The 'lernean hydra' slain by Hercules and Jason's triumph over the hydra protecting the Golden Fleece are portrayed as many-headed snakes.

The similarity between dragons and snakes effectively preys on man's primitive fear. One of the most feared monsters in mythology, the Gorgon, Medusa, was so hideous that she could petrify any living creature from one glance at her face with hair of writhing snakes.

Dragon slaying was a popular pastime from Perseus to St George, and when a dragon appears in chains it symbolises the triumph of good over evil.

The unicorn is another popular mythological creature,

well known to be tamed only by the hand of a virgin.

From the world of the high renaissance and at the other end of the spectrum, we have many examples of animals anthropomorphised through cartoons, especially by Walt Disney. Countless animals, most famously in the case of Mickey Mouse, have fallen prey to Disney's insatiable appetite for the cute and cuddly. Whether this does the animal any favours is debatable – to impose human sensibility and emotion on an animal without self-consciousness can impair our ability to recognise its reality and can compromise the animal's innate dignity and true worth.

There's no doubt that animals in art are immensely popular – both for the artist and the viewer. Indeed, nature itself has always been, and still is, one of the favourite artists' choices. One has only to glance at a painting of a horse by the great George Stubbs to recognise the beauty of the subject. He is one of thousands who have borrowed the emotions associated with grace, splendour and intrigue of beasts large and small in order to recreate just a glimpse of the passion that so many people feel for animals.

Homemade pet treats to tickle the taste buds!

Move aside Jamie Oliver, Alison's Animal Lovers' Guides presents the very best in home cooking … not for school children, not even for adults … but for the tables, kennels, cages and bowls of our beloved PETS!

FEATURES

BIRDIE BREAD

Attract an interesting selection of feathered beasts to your birdtable with this irresistible gastronomic delight:
Mix a cup of wheat flour with a similar amount of cornmeal and oatmeal. Add a cup of plain yoghurt (try making your own), then add about two cups of pureed vegetables or even a couple of jars of vegetable baby food. Add two eggs complete with crushed shells, a packet of frozen mixed vegetables and half a slab of butter. Mix your birdie bread with joy, place in a greased baking dish and bake in a fairly hot oven for about 20 minutes. **The result?**
A delicious loaf that any food-loving beak would love to dip into!

ICE CREAM FOR HIGH FLYERS

Yes, our feathery friends may like to cool off in the hot weather with the help of some birdie ice cream! Here's how to make it:
Beat five eggs until your arm aches, then add some mashed bananas, mashed or cooked apple, any other soft fruit that you may have in the fruit bowl and perhaps some fresh raspberries, strawberries, blackcurrants or blackberries. Tip in one large tub of plain yoghurt, swirl it all around, pour into a dish and put into the freezer. When it is partially frozen, tip into a mixing bowl and mix it with an electric mixer until fluffy. Now pour into several ice cube trays and freeze. Serve on a hot day – no wafer cones required!

CHIRPY COOKIES

The birds will be flocking to sample these delicious biscuits:

Take two cups of flour, add some baking powder, about six tablespoonsful of shortening (any type) and two to three cups of milk. Mix everything together, then add half a cup or so of rolled oats, a teaspoonful of wheat germ and a few cooked mixed vegetables. Shape into individual biscuits and place these on a greased baking tray. Bake in a fairly hot oven until golden brown. Visitors to your bird table will wing their way back, time after time.

GOOFY'S GARLIC BISCUITS

Man's best friend will love these garlic cookies – but you may not want him to breathe over you for the next few hours:

Make approximately one and a half cups of meat stock, either from a cube or from left-over bones. Put into a blender with four cloves of minced garlic and mix on high. Add half a cup or margarine or butter plus one cup of oatmeal and mix well. Stir in $3/4$ cup of powdered milk, the same amount of cornmeal and one beaten egg. Add three cups of wholemeal flour, mixing well. Knead the mixture by hand, adding more flour if necessary. Roll onto a floured surface to $1/2$ inch thick then cut into shapes (bone shapes may appeal to Rover). Place on a greased tray and bake for up to

FEATURES

'Something smells good ...'

60 minutes in a moderate oven. Allow to cool and dry out until hard. Your canine friends will wolf them down with glee!

CRAZY CAT'S CHICKEN CHOMPS

Hide this dish in a safe place so your cat doesn't steal it before you are ready!
Combine one cup of chopped, boiled chicken, steamed carrots and perhaps some broccoli in a mixing bowl, then add some chopped parsley. Pour in a little chicken broth until nice and thick and stir until well mixed. Serve in a bowl and watch her devour every last morsel!

KITTY CAT LOAF

You can cut a piece of this loaf for your cat whenever she feels peckish:
Mix one cup of minced beef with a beaten egg, a piece of ground liver, $1/3$ cup of water and $1/4$ cup rolled oats. Turn into a greased loaf tin and bake in a moderate oven for around 40 minutes. Allow to cool before turning out, then slice and serve with style!

CHEESE CHOMPS

These cheesy treats will set the tongues lolling:
Combine one cup of rolled oats, $1/3$ cup of margarine or butter and one cup of boiling water in a large bowl. Stir in $3/4$ cup cornmeal, one tablespoon sugar, a little meat stock, a little milk, one cup of grated cheddar cheese and one beaten egg. Mix well, then add two cups of either white or wholemeal flour. Mix to a stiff dough consistency and knead until smooth and not too sticky. Roll dough and cut into biscuit shapes. Bake in a moderate oven for up to 45 minutes, until golden brown. Offer to your dog and all his friends and watch them chomp for joy!

LICKY LIVER LUMPS

What dog could possibly resist these carnivorous cookies?
Chop approximately one and a half kilos of liver in a food processor until it resembles chocolate (don't let the children taste as they might get a nasty shock!) Add a few cloves of crushed garlic and blend. Add a cup of wholemeal flour, two cups of white flour, $1/2$ cup of cornmeal and a little grated cheese. Spread the thick mixture evenly on silver foil placed over a baking tray and sprinkle lightly with cornmeal. Bake for about 30 minutes in a moderately hot oven until no pink remains. Cut into pieces and serve to the luckiest dog on earth!

BONZO'S BREAKFAST BARS

Let your pooch start the day in style:
Simply throw all the following ingredients into an enormous bowl, mix and pat onto two greased baking trays:

12 cups of oatmeal; 4 cups of wholemeal flour; 8 eggs; a little oil; a little honey; $1/2$ cup of dark brown sugar; 2 cups milk; up to 4 mashed bananas or mashed vegetables (optional).

Bake in a moderate oven for about an hour and allow to cool slowly whilst still in the oven (this makes them go hard). Break into size according to dog's wishes and feed with glee!

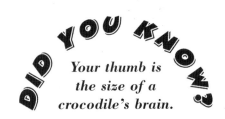

DID YOU KNOW?
Your thumb is the size of a crocodile's brain.

CARROT CRUNCHIES

Help your dog to see in the dark with these crunchy carrot treats!

Grate one large carrot and mix in two tablespoons of honey, one cup of apple sauce (make your own) and $1/2$ teaspoon ginger. Blend them all together, then add $1/2$ cup rolled oats and one and a half cups of flour. Turn the stiff dough out onto a board, press flat and cut out some doggie shapes. Put onto baking tray and brush tops with milk. Bake for 50 minutes in a moderate oven, then leave them in the cooling oven to harden.

Eating carrots has never been so much fun!

TABITHA'S TUNA TASTERS

Your fluffy feline will be purring with delight when she finds out what you have in store for her:

Mix half a cup of tinned tuna fish with half a cup of powdered milk and a similar amount of wholemeal flour. Pour in a beaten egg, one tablespoon of vegetable oil and $1/4$ cup water. Stir well. Turn out onto a board and knead for a minute or so. Make into balls with fingers and flatten each dough ball as you put it onto a greased baking tray. Bake for approximately 10 minutes in a moderate oven. Serve to your cat and she will feel like a purrincess!

FEATURES

Animal antics,
by Flopsy the Rabbit

FEATURES

You might think that we rabbits don't have much power when it comes to training humans. But you would be surprised!

My human is a bit slow to learn, but even she comes running when I rush around thumping my back feet, whacking the side of my hutch with gusto and flinging sawdust onto the ground as I whizz around the corners. She thinks I am probably exercising my male testosterone hormones, but actually I'm just after a bit of attention.

She obeys me when I roll onto my back and wave my legs in the air, at which point she will tickle my tummy and let me out for a run because I'm so sweet. Talking of sweet – I just love those rabbity chocolate drops that I'm only meant to have occasionally. I can make her give me more by drooping my ears and rubbing my nose on the little shelf in my cage where she puts them.

My mate, Tess the dog, has really got the entire family wrapped around her little claw. She's taught them to cuddle and kiss her on command. She just gives the smallest yelp, lifts her paw in the air and hops around on three legs and guess what – all of them come obediently running, patting her lovingly on the head and massaging her paw. She usually gets a generous handful of doggie treats too. Another of her little human-attracting tricks is to bark like mad, pretending there's an intruder lurking behind the hedge. No kidding, you've never seen them move so fast - they shoot out of the house and give her lots of praise for chasing away what they perceive to be a threat! She's also trained them to take her for a walk on the command of fetching her own lead appealingly in her mouth. And she can even bring forward dinner time by manoeuvring her dog bowl into the middle of the kitchen floor and staring at it beseechingly. How's that for pretty slick human training?

Now not all the animals in this household are so smart. Tinkabelle has tried without success to teach the humans to wash themselves in the correct manner. She's demonstrated daily for six years the method of licking all over, paying particular attention to the nether regions. In the haughty way that only a cat can achieve, she's recently declared that human tongues are just too smooth and human bodies just too disabled to reach all the messy bits. She's horrified that they just cover up their sweaty areas with stronger smells instead of licking them clean.

What's more, Tinka has failed to teach them how to eat mice. She's forever bringing home a fat, juicy specimen and laying it carefully on the

kitchen worktop ready for dinner. So great is the temptation for her to nibble at it that she's usually drooling by the time her humans come home. But guess what? They NEVER eat it - not even the tiniest morsel. Not only do they fling it in the dustbin, accompanied by words that I'm embarrassed to recall, but they pour evil-smelling stuff on the worktop and stomp around in a strange mood.
I think their predatory instincts must be severely disordered – or perhaps Tinka's training skills need fine tuning.

Even the goldfish can manage better than that. The whole bunch of them has worked out a routine of 'synchronised swimming' and they've thrown in a bit of leaping like dolphin malarkey too. They time their 'demonstrations' very carefully so as to

create the best impact and eureka!, the humans all crowd around clapping like common sea lions and throwing flakes of food. Needless to say, Tinka's not impressed by their intelligence and more than once I've seen her trying to ensure they reach a sticky end.

I guess some of us animals are just born to teach – they say it's a really worthwhile career. As for me, I consider training humans as purely a hobby – they are full of surprises and are certainly not as dumb as I thought.

Rabbits build nests. Hares don't.

Who's afraid of the big bad wolf/spider/snake/bat?

FEATURES

An anonymous quote, 'Fear is the darkroom where negatives are developed', describes adequately the subject of phobias. Many of the human race struggle with dark feelings that may not be entirely logical – fear of enclosed areas, wide open spaces, flying in aeroplanes, people in white coats, birds, spiders, snakes and bats. Whilst not delving into the reasons why people may be afraid to venture out of doors, into lifts, dental surgeries and aeroplanes, phobias regarding small creatures seem to be more simply explained and understandable.

A phobia, quite simply, is a term for an unrealistic fear. So perhaps if those suffering from a phobia can explain and realise their fear, it ceases to be a phobia. A phobia, however, can be an irrational and excessive fear that may not be banished so easily!

Take spiders, for example. It is very easy to see why people may be afraid. After all, a basic survival instinct may cause us to move away from these eight-legged little beasts, recognising that some spiders have the ability to wound and even kill.

Snakes can invoke a similar instinctive reaction – there are many poisonous species of snake in the world that could possibly harm us, so staying clear of slithery legless creatures may well be the most sensible and cautious approach.

But one would think that we could use our powerful and intelligent brain to rationalise our fear and bring it under control – eliminate the fear completely, in fact.

It is said that 'Applied Kinesiology' can cure many phobias - but perhaps familiarity with some of the creatures most commonly linked to fear may be helpful:

Spiders
If you suffer from arachnophobia, you will scuttle away from eight-legged beasts faster than a rat up a drainpipe. You probably won't ever get close enough to examine their beautiful markings and you certainly won't want to know that the five orders of arachnida that occur in northern Europe also include scorpions, ticks and mites, pseudoscorpions and harvestmen.

Spiders are not only quite beautiful,

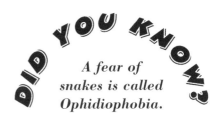

DID YOU KNOW? A fear of snakes is called Ophidiophobia.

but extremely creative and sensitive. Who could possibly pass by a spider's web at dawn, covered in glistening dew, without being amazed at the wondrous process that has taken place during the creation of such a masterpiece?

If you want an example of good parenting skills, look to the various species of spider who nurture their young with tender care. Female wolf spiders carry their babies on their backs for the first week of life, and some species regurgitate food and feed their young mouth-to-mouth. Others catch prey for their spiderlings to feast upon - and often the mother spider cares for her children until they are fully grown.

You may or may not be heartened to learn that, although all spiders bite, most are physically incapable of penetrating human skin and very few will attempt to bite man. Spider bites are not such a menace as mosquitoes, midges, wasps or other biting and stinging insects - but often receive a more negative press.

There are hundreds of different spider types, each with an individual lifestyle. Some of the most common are the Linyphiidae - a large family containing over 400 different species, most with grey or black abdomen, popularly called 'money spiders'. Another large family, Theridiidae, usually spin a web of criss-cross threads in vegetation, whilst Mimetidae invade the webs of other spiders and even eat the occupants! Hahniidae make small ground level webs and Agelenidae spin tubular webs. Some spiders, such as Lycosidae, are hunting creatures that stay mainly on the ground and some, such as the Atypidae, live in a closed tube that is

Photo © Hugh Clark 2005

Brown long-eared bat or vampire? Those suffering from a phobia may not discriminate!

FEATURES

FEATURES

buried below ground level.

So never assume that the poor unfortunate spider that you sucked into the vacuum cleaner or flushed down the sink yesterday, is the same creature that spun the web in the corner of the lounge – not only have you destroyed a living creature that helps keep the home free of flies, but you may have orphaned some babies!

Snakes

It is truly an honour to see a British snake in the wild – these are quite elusive creatures that are shy of humans. If you are lucky enough to see baby snakes, or indeed witness the hatching of snake eggs, you are indeed privileged.

Of the approximately 2,700 different species of snake to be found around the world, just three are indigenous to Britain. These are the grass snake, the smooth snake and the adder.

Grass snakes are probably most frequently seen. They feed on amphibians and fish, swallowed alive, whilst the smooth snake tends to constrict its prey before eating. The adder overpowers prey using venom, and also uses its poison for defence.

The grass snake is probably the largest of Britain's snakes, with a fully grown female specimen averaging around 76cm. Humans have nothing to fear from these sleek creatures, who love to nest in compost heaps and do no harm. If they are caught, they will struggle, before

releasing a foul smelling secretion. This snake may also play dead, lying on its back and sticking out its tongue, or going completely limp! It rarely attempts to bite – and does not harm even if its fangs make contact with human skin.

The smooth snake, as you may expect, is smooth and polished, almost like a slow worm. It is browny-red, or even creamy-yellow in colour, with a lighter shade under the jaw and tail. There's a small dark band on the back of the neck and sometimes some spots, plus a dark line on either side of the head. A fully grown smooth snake may measure around 50cm.

This snake likes heather and it favours ponds, marshy grounds and streams. It feasts upon lizards and lives in Surrey, Hampshire and Dorset. Although calm in nature, it will bite in defence and once locked on, it is reluctant to let go!

The adder begins life as a dullish brown colour and gradually lightens to a yellow, eventually becoming grey. The throat is usually pale and is sometimes marked with black or brown. On the back of the head is a distinctive 'V' or even 'H' marking and there's a zig-zag band along the full length of the back.

Spiders - more scared of us than we are of them?

A fear of animals is called Zoophobia.

The female adder grows to about 55cm and favourite habitats are sandy soils, chalk downs, open woodland and uncultivated fields. It does not like to be near people and usually feeds on lizards and mice.

Of course the adder is famous for its venomous bite, although it is quite rare for a human to be bitten. A snake would always prefer to slither away – but it will attack if cornered. The venom destroys the red blood cells, causing haemorrhage of the blood vessels. It is rarely fatal to an adult person, but does cause swelling, throbbing pain, sometimes vomiting and dizziness, loss of appetite and considerable thirst. Complete recovery is usually achieved within two weeks in a healthy person, but of course, medical assistance should always be sought.

So there we are – even the scariest British snake is probably not as fearsome as you thought!

Bats

If you ever have an opportunity to stroke one of these little mammals, do so. They are soft and furry, warm and incredibly appealing. Some even 'purr' when stroked! Britain is home to around 15 different species, including pipistrelle, long-eared, Daubenton's, Natterer's, serotine and noctule.

Most commonly seen are pipistrelle and long-eared bats – the former being only the length of a matchstick and weighing less than a 2p piece! They love to roost under weatherboarding of houses, preferring modern housing estates to old draughty roofs!

The beautiful long-eared bat is aptly named. In fact, if a human's ears were proportionally as long, they would dangle around our waists! These bats are expert at locating their insect prey and can even detect a moth that is preparing to launch itself, capturing it before it becomes airborne!

Bats do us a great favour – they eat biting insects. They never get tangled up in hair thanks to an excellent navigational system that is second to none.

If you are fortunate enough to have bats roosting in your own property, treasure this rare mammal and delight in its presence.

Boo hisssss – fear of snakes is one of the most common phobias

FEATURES

BTCV's Green Gyms - what are they?

Have you ever puzzled over the logic of so many people expending energy without any 'useful' objective – i.e. the growing number of man-hours that are wasted in a traditional gym? There's no doubt that keeping fit is healthy, fun and good business for the gym providers – but it may not be particularly useful for the community or the environment.

If you don't have a dog to walk, a garden lawn to mow, a hedge to trim, a field to tend, a house to build or a fence to mend, there are probably plenty of people who could use a helping hand. Alternatively, you could join BTCV (formerly the British Trust for Conservation Volunteers) in one of its Green Gyms.

Green Gyms offer an opportunity to take part in nature conservation activities and community gardening. Not only is it free, but you will be helping to enhance your local surroundings whilst improving your own health and perhaps your social life too.

BTCV set up the first Green Gym some seven years ago in Oxford, with the aim of helping people improve their own health. This includes cardiac patients who can benefit through building up their energy levels and increasing stamina. There are now 65 Green Gyms across the country, providing participants with a fresh sense of belonging, a purpose, social interaction,

Weave Ho, Weave H
it's fence building we g

Wading in – pond clearing is an important activity at the Green Gym

improved health and a great sense of achievement. Working outdoors seems to improve mental health and wellbeing as well as providing physical benefits.

Green Gyms are supported by the Office of the Deputy Prime Minister, Primary Trusts, the European Social Fund and other organisations, and they use council land, private land including some organic farms and community land for their important work. Funding pays for office space, equipment and training costs for volunteers. Volunteers work throughout the year, unless really extreme weather conditions prevail.

Sessions run for three hours, although participants can do just five minutes work if they prefer! Activities range from gentle to strenuous, everyone works at his or her own pace and experienced leaders demonstrate what's required. No experience is necessary, but enthusiasm is essential.

There are several Green Gyms up and running in Sussex, including the Greenspace Project in the Hastings region –

an area that is fortunate to have a wealth of important wildlife sites. Meanwhile, the Rother Green Gym around Battle, Bexhill and Rye, also has many opportunities for volunteers to get involved.

BTVC and Plumpton College in Sussex are working together to provide NVQ Level 1 in 'Land-based operations'. This part-time course consists of two days per week for 31 weeks and students of all ages learn about woodland management, coppicing, hedgelaying, tree planting, fencing and chainsaw use. Courses are offered in Lewes and Hastings and both transport and protective clothing are provided. They are free under LSC (Learning Skills Council) and do not affect anyone claiming benefits.

Also operating in the Hastings region is the Wednesday Conservation volunteers who meet every week at 9.30am by Hastings Railway Station. They carry out practical work in some beautiful conservation areas in the region.

Typical projects include rhododendron control, waymarking, invasive species control, footpath maintenance, ride clearance and scrub clearance.

BTCV is a registered charity no 261009. Volunteers should usually be 18 years and over, although children are welcome on many projects, with the oldest being over 80. All members should have current tetanus immunity. Whilst working with BTCV, volunteers are insured for Public Liability and Personal Accident.

Tempted to offer your services? Contact Tim Hills on 01424 446395, visit the website: www.btcv.org or e-mail information@btcv.org.uk for further information.

FEATURES

Animals in the Spirit World

It was believed by the Native American Indians that each animal has its own meaning and holds its own message. If you were to see an abundance of a certain animal or an animal stood out to you, it was believed that the Great Spirit (God) was trying to get a message through to you. Clairvoyant mediums still use these symbols today. Here are some examples:

by Rosie Finey

FEATURES

 Alligator
aggression, survival

 Ant
group minded, teamwork

 Antelope
action

 Armadillo
defended

 Badger
aggressive

 Bat
guardian, macabre

 Bear
power, gentle strength

 Bear Paw
power, direction

 Beaver
builder, gatherer,
accomplishment

 Beetle
hidden knowing

 Bighorn Sheep
conqueror

 Bluebird
happiness

 Blue Jay
pushy

 Buffalo
sacredness, strength

 Bull
sexual energy

 Butterfly
friendly

 Camel
ornery

 Canary
joy

 Cardinal/Red Bird
beauty

 Cat
independent

Chameleon
adaptable

Chickadee
optimism

Chicken
foolish

Cockroach
lowest

Cougar
leadership, swiftness

Cow
docile

Coyote
prankster

Crane
solitude, independence

Cricket
disharmony

Deer
love, kindness,
gracefulness, loveliness

Dog
loyal

Dolphin
kindness, teaching

Domestic Goose
quarrelsome

Domestic Sheep
follower

Donkey
helpful

Dragonfly
flighty, carefree

Eagle
success, prosperity,
highest power

Elephant
old memory

Elk
nobility, strength, brave

Flamingo
grace

Fly
parasite

Fox
cunning, intelligent

Frog
connection to water
element, sorcery

Goat
friendly

Grizzly Bear
Mother Nature's
pharmacist

Hawk
messenger of the sky,
opportunity

Heron
spiritual

Horse (race)
high strung

Horse (working)
plodding

FEATURES

Horse (wild)
freedom

Hummingbird
optimism, sweetness, joy

Lark
weather

Lizard
conservation, agility,
old wisdom

Llama
practical

Lynx
psychic

Magpie
knowledge

Meadowlark
protective

Mockingbird
imitative

Mole
lack foresight

Moose
longevity,
headstrong, pride

Mouse
busy

Mule
stubborn

Ostrich
stubborn

Otter
grace, empathy, playful

Owl
wisdom, patience,
truth, diviner

Parrot
playful

Peacock
ostentatious

Pelican
saver

Pig
intelligence

Pigeon
inertia

Pigeon (in air)
mission

Porcupine
protected

Possum
playful

Quail
family

Rabbit
alertness, nurturing,
gentle

Raccoon
enterprising

Rat
survivalist

Raven
trickster, teacher, hoarders, portent

Red-Headed Woodpecker
resourceful

Roadrunner
traveller

Robin
balance

Salmon
instinct, persistence, determination

Seagull
freedom

Seahorse
confidence, grace

Shark
survival, hunter, killer

Skunk
defended

Snake
shrewdness, transformation, challenger

Snow Goose
fidelity

Sparrows
ordinary

Spider
creative, connection of past to future, deceit

Squirrel
resourceful

Sturgeon
dominant

Swan
grace, balance, innocence

Turkey
forgetful

Turtle
self-contained, creative, old wisdom

Whale
universal mind

Wild Duck
adventure

Wild Pheasant
quick

Wolf
loyalty, perseverance, success, organiser

FEATURES

DID YOU KNOW
The best talker among chatty birds is the Mynah.

Helpful tips for Sussex wildlife hunters

You've got the book, bought the tee shirt, now all you need is a glimpse of a particular animal in order to make your wildlife hunt complete. But where can you see our wonderful British wildlife in its natural state? Here are a few tips to help you on your journey:

Water vole

Ratty in Wind of the Willows is really our beloved water vole, a shy creature who has declined in numbers by over 90% in the last 20 years. If you are a casual wildlife watcher it's doubtful that you will have ever seen one – you need to know where to look and then you need lots of patience! Water voles need good clean water, they won't tolerate pollution and can't survive in dry areas, as their name suggests. The East Sussex Coastal Plain has a couple of strongholds for the endangered water vole in this county – including Pett Levels nature reserve in Rye. The good news is that this animal responds quickly when water management improves, so it is possible that you will find Ratty in areas that are well managed, with good levels of water and little pollution.

Otters

We all love this cheeky little chappie, with his playful nature and semi-amphibious lifestyle. But where can we see one in Sussex? Back in the 1950s, otters were numerous, particularly around the Arun, Adur and Western Rother areas. But hunting, combined with the poisoning of fish and eels by chemicals that were once widely used on crops and farm stock, saw the rapid decline of this beautiful animal. No evidence of them was found from the mid 1970s onwards. Recently, however, otters are reappearing in both East and West Sussex, some due to re-introductions. An otter road-kill victim on the Sussex/Hampshire borders in 2001 confirmed that the animals were crossing through the Western Rother region into Sussex from Hampshire, where there are already established breeding otters. Further evidence has also suggested that otters are present at Wallers Haven in Pevensey, Rye Harbour and Rustington. Sightings have also recently been recorded around the Pulborough Brooks area on the river Arun.

Wading birds

Mud, glorious mud, is what is loved most by many waders such as oystercatchers, godwits, turnstones, dunlins and avocets. There are about 200 species of wading birds that love to feed in soft mud and sand at the water's edge. Those with short beaks such as ringed plover, knot, sanderling, turnstone and dunlin pick food from the

FEATURES

Photo: courtesy Drusillas Zoo Park

FEATURES

Otters can now be seen in both East and West Sussex

surface, whilst longer-beaked birds such as redshank oystercatcher, snipe, avocet and curlew dig down deeper for worms and shellfish. Pagham Harbour in West Sussex together with Chichester and Langstone Harbours form the largest area of mud in the south. Birdwatchers should be armed with a good pair of binoculars and be prepared to sit and watch for at least a couple of hours – just a few minutes is not enough to see the wealth of wading birds that will appear.

Birds of prey

The sparrowhawk is now one of the most commonly seen birds of prey. It loves set-aside land and even visits garden bird tables … not to feed in a picturesque manner from nuts and seeds, but to snatch other birds such as blue tits whilst they feast! The female sparrowhawk is larger than the male, preying on bigger birds including

pigeons, doves and thrushes. Kestrels are also quite common in Sussex – usually seen hovering above roadways, in open countryside and even along motorway verges. The hobby is an uncommon visitor from Africa, whilst the buzzard is gradually making its way up from the west country and there have been recent sightings in Sussex. The latter can often be identified by the mewing 'kiew' sound as it soars effortlessly on thermal winds. It prefers open hillsides and wooded valleys and likes to nest in trees and on cliff ledges. Other Sussex visitors include Montagu's harrier, hen harrier and marsh harrier.

Nightingale

Beachy Head in Sussex may not be the first place you would associate with nightingales, but in fact they breed here very successfully. They love the dense clipped scrub that is hidden away in valleys and around field edges, and seem to appreciate the sea air! This bird is usually noted by its song – not always delivered at night, but noticeable for its rich tone, variety of notes and sheer volume. The splendid song lasts only for around three spring months during the breeding season. Nightingales are found all over Sussex, particularly in deciduous woodland and thickets of blackthorn.

DID YOU KNOW? All birds have three lids over each eye.

Kingfishers and herons

Most people lucky enough to see a kingfisher glimpse only a flash of azure blue as this beautiful bird flashes past. It is a shy creature that lives near rivers and lakes, or even coastal creeks and pools. A kingfisher's nesting place is excavated in the bank of a slow-running stream – so there's no point in looking

upwards into trees and shrubs in order to find a nest! Kingfishers feed on fish, tadpoles, insects and molluscs and the nest is soon littered with regurgitated fish bones. The bird can be found in wetland habitats all over Sussex including Warnham Nature Reserve in Horsham, Woods Mill at Henfield, several sites around Hastings and at both Darwell and Weirwood Reservoirs in East Sussex.

These locations are also favoured by the watchful heron, which waits patiently in the shallows, hoping to feast upon fish and other small creatures. Herons nest in heronries in large trees or shrubs, also in reed-beds and even on cliff edges. They use the same nest year after year. You gain the best chance of seeing either bird by choosing footpaths near rivers, streams and lakes, walking slowly and quietly and listening for clues such as the shrill 'cheee' call of the kingfisher.

Badgers

This black, white and grey mammal is a wonderful Sussex resident and can be seen all over the county, particularly loving woods with sandy soils that are easy to dig. A badger sett is usually a big mound of sandy soil, with many entrances and exits. It may be hidden under tree roots, with just the entrance holes visible. Setts are used over several generations and large spoil heaps

Who's a pretty bird then? – the very colourful kingfisher

'Hareing' about – you will have to be quick to see this one

FEATURES

accumulate outside each entrance. Trees such as elder are often used as scratching posts, enabling badgers to clear soil from under their nails. Badgers usually emerge at dusk and after dark. They are shy beasts, so badger watchers need to keep quiet and use that precious commodity - patience!

Hares

You may never have seen a brown hare … but they are here in Sussex! They love lowland pasture – open fields and even ploughed fields. March is the easiest time to spot them – the mad March hare does indeed exhibit seemingly mad behaviour – not usually male hares doing battle but probably females trying to put off an over-amorous male! Hares are certainly not as common as they used to be, due to changes in farming practices over the years. However, they do love set-aside land and like to hide in long grass that has been left to seed naturally.

Moles

Proud gardeners who like neat lawns may not want a mole to take up residence! They make numerous molehills that may spoil the appearance of a manicured lawn – but surely the price is worth paying? This is a

wonderful creature who is not quite blind - but he doesn't need to use his eyes very often as he is usually underground. Moles prefer nice soft soil, so the Sussex sandy and mixed terrain is just right. If you see a molehill that is slightly larger than the others, this may well be the sight of the football-sized nest. Moles eat worms and insects and the resulting molehills are simply the excess soil that comes out of the tunnels. A bonus for gardeners is the fact that the soil in molehills is beautifully mined, soft and crumbly – just right for pots and hanging baskets!

Snakes

Grass snakes and adders are species that can be found in Sussex. The adder is the most feared and is, in fact, quite common. It loves rough grassland such as heaths – but is shy and will prefer to slither away when disturbed. Grass snakes like damper locations such as the edges of ponds and the compost heap, where they will lay a clutch of up to 40 eggs. Early morning is the best time to catch a glimpse of either – when they are warming up in the sun.

Herons can be seen on many a river bank

FEATURES

Dolphins, whales and seals

You may be lucky enough to spot bottle-nosed dolphins off the coast of Sussex, although these welcome visitors usually prefer to swim slightly further west. They are often seen at Durlston Head, south of Swanage, where a visitor centre at this country park has a hydrophone set up, allowing visitors to actually hear dolphins about 80% of the time! Dolphins are most frequently spotted swimming up to 200 metres from the shoreline and there may be anything from one solitary animal to 12 in a group. Other species are occasionally reported off the Sussex coast, including long-finned pilot whales, common porpoises, common dolphins and both grey and common seals.

Of course there are hundreds more species of animals that can be seen in and around Sussex, including stoats, weasels, foxes, deer, squirrels, mice, lizards, fish, birds and insects. Some Sussex free-roaming residents are particularly surprising, such as the famous wallabies from Leonardslee! They all share the richness that makes this beautiful county unique and we should never cease to celebrate the wonder of nature that is all around.

DID YOU KNOW?
A group of whales is called a pod.

What do I do if I find an injured or lost animal?

You can imagine the scenario – you are driving home on a cold winter's evening and see a poor dejected bundle at the side of the road. Upon inspection, it reveals itself to be an injured deer. What do you do? Then there's the hedgehog who has a nasty injury from your garden strimmer, the clutch of baby sparrows who have been orphaned by your neighbour's cat, the badger who has been caught in an illegal snare so it is trapped by its paw, and the family of foxes who are suffering from mange. Not to mention that domestic rabbit that you found down the street, the family of kittens looking for a good home and the old dog that needs a new owner.

Firstly, if there's a potential hazard to humans or if you suspect something illegal, phone the police. For example, an injured deer on a road could cause an accident, so the police should be alerted. Secondly, there are numerous animal charities and rescue centres that you can contact for advice and guidance. Some may suggest you bring an injured animal to them, providing it is easily transportable. Others will offer advice over the telephone that will allow you to treat the animal yourself before releasing it into the wild. Others specialise in finding homes for unwanted pets.

Sometimes the experts may advise you to leave a wild animal where you found it – for instance, baby birds are often 'rescued' during their first few days out of the nest, even though they are following nature's course and not in need of any assistance. On other occasions, a charity representative may be willing to come to the animal - but of course this may not

DID YOU KNOW

Anteaters don't have any teeth.

always be immediate.

Meanwhile, you will want to do the very best for the animal concerned. If it's obviously a lost pet, the RSPCA, police or local vet may be able to help. Many animals carry a microchip under their skin, giving details of the owner - in which case a vet can usually scan the animal in order to read the details. The local council Dog Warden is also a good contact.

Some animal helplines are operational 24 hours a day, others work during office hours only. Here's a list of just some of the animal rescue centres and charities in Sussex dealing with wildlife and domestic animals. The information is believed to be correct at the time of going to press:

FEATURES

Animaline, Broadhurst Manor Road, Horsted Keynes, Haywards Heath, West Sussex: 01342 810596. Animal rights and welfare charity, also a woodland sanctuary for rescued animals and birds. www.carlalane.com

Badger Rescue, London Road, Forest Row, East Sussex: 01444 417822. Deals with all types of badger problems. www.badgerland.co.uk

Barnjet Shelter, Cuttinglye Road, Crawley Down, Crawley, West Sussex: 01342 712387. A shelter for Cats Protection League. www.cats.org.uk

Blue Cross Adoption Centre for equine and small animals. St Francis Fields, Northiam, East Sussex: 01797 252243. Finds homes for rescued dogs, cats, horses and ponies. www.bluecross.org.uk

Brent Lodge Bird & Wildlife Trust, Cow Lane, Sidlesham, Chichester, West Sussex: 01243 641672. A bird and wildlife hospital that offers treatment, rehabilitation and release of injured wild birds and small mammals. www.brentlodge.org

Brownbread Horse Rescue Centre, Ashburnham, Battle: 01424 892381. Equestrian rescue centre that is concerned with the welfare and rehabilitation of horses and ponies. www.horsedata.co.uk

Cat Rescue, Overhill Drive, Brighton, East Sussex: 01273 500474. Rescues and rehomes cats.

Cat and Rabbit Rescue Centre, Chalder Lane, Sidlesham, Chichester, West Sussex: 01243 641409. Offers advice and help on cat and rabbit care plus humane feral control. www.crrc.co.uk

Cats Protection, Brighton & Hove: 01273 279138. Rescue and rehoming of cats. www.brightoncatsprotection.org.uk

Cats Protection, Hailsham: 01323 440101. Rescue and rehoming of cats. www.cats.org.uk

Cats Protection, Kings Road, Horsham, West Sussex: 01403 221900, helpline: 01403 221919. Offers rescue and rehoming of stray and unwanted cats plus advice on cat care. www.cats.org.uk

Celia Hammond Animal Trust, High Street, Wadhurst, East Sussex: 01892 783367. Rescues and rehomes cats, includes care and advice regarding feral cat colonies. www.celiahammond.org

Court Lodge Farm Sanctuary for Farm Animals, Etchingham Road, Burwash, Etchingham, East Sussex: 01435 882340. A sanctuary for farm animals including calves, lambs, ponies, donkeys and horses including shire horses.

Dogs Trust Rescue Centre, Brighton Road, Shoreham-by-Sea, West Sussex: 01273 452576. Offers rescue and protection for dogs.

Most predators attack at head level.

East Sussex Wildlife Rescue and Ambulance Service, Stone Cross, Eastbourne, East Sussex: A 24-hour rescue and ambulance service for wildlife in East Sussex, Brighton and Hove: 07815 078234.
www.wildlifeambulance.co.uk

Feline Foster Cat Welfare Association, Battle Road, St Leonards-on-Sea, East Sussex: 01424 432687. A sanctuary and rescue centre for stray, unwanted and abandoned cats and kittens. www.lostcatsbrighton. mysite.wanadoo-members.co.uk

The Fox Project, operating in East Sussex, parts of Kent, Surrey and South East London. Care, treatment and rehabilitation of sick and injured foxes and abandoned fox cubs. Advice lines: Urban Fox Deterrence: 0906 272 4411; Mange treatment: 0906 272 4422; Head office: 01892 545468.
www.foxproject.org.uk

Foxhollow Animal Sanctuary, Priors Leaze Lane, Hambrook, Chichester, West Sussex: 01243 574871. Rescues abandoned, abused and unwanted pets and farm animals.

Guinea Pig Rescue Centre, Northdown Road, Newhaven, East Sussex: 07957 630096. Dedicated to the caring and rehoming of unwanted guinea pigs. www.diddly-di.fsnet.co.uk

Hastings Animal Concern, covering East Sussex: 01424 812055. Offers health advice, information, news and events concerned with animal cruelty. www.geocities.com

FEATURES

FEATURES

Hastings Badger Protection Society, Park Wood Road, Hastings, East Sussex: 01424 751482. Advice and protection for badgers. www.hbps.cwc.net

Hen Heaven, Stonepit Lane, Henfield, West Sussex: 07754 550193. A sanctuary for turkeys and chickens.

International Animal Rescue, Uckfield, East Sussex. A rescue and rehabilitation organisation that has centres in Goa, Tamil Nadu and Agra in India as well as in Malta. Comes to the aid of wild and domestic animals including rehabilitation of dogs, cats, monkeys, reptiles, sacred cows plus a bear sanctuary that provides a caring home for ex. 'dancing bears' in India. Also carries out bird rescue in Malta. www.iar.org.uk

Kit Wilson Trust for Animal Welfare, Animal Rescue Centre, Stonehurst Lane, Hadlow Down, Uckfield, East Sussex: 01825 830444. Promotes welfare of animals. Cares for ill treated, neglected and abandoned animals and birds. www.charitiesdirect.com

Labrador Rescue, Normandy Drive, East Preston, Littlehampton, West Sussex: 01903 782059. A rescue and rehoming service for Labrador dogs. www.cats-dogs.co.uk

Lord Whisky Animal Sanctuary, Roundstone Lane, Angmering, Littlehampton, West Sussex: 01303 862622.

Mallydams Wood Wildlife Sanctuary & Study Centre, Fairlight, Hastings, East Sussex: 01424 812055.

Rescues and rehabilitates wildlife and seabirds. RSPCA unit plus training and study centre.

Mid Sussex Badger Protection Group, Station Road, Hailsham, East Sussex: 01323 442198. Mobile: 07778 152576. Protects and advises on badgers.

Mount Noddy, RSPCA Animal Rescue Centre, Black Mill Lane, Eartham, Chichester, West Sussex: 01243 773359. www.rspca.org.uk

Paws & Claws Animal Rescue Service, Penland Road, Haywards Heath, West Sussex: 01444 413846. www.cats-dogs.co.uk

People's Dispensary for Sick Animals, Preston Park, Brighton, East Sussex: 01273 566595. Offers veterinary services for sick animals. www.pdsa.org.uk

Portslade Retreat Horse and Animal Rescue, Cross Road, Southwick, Brighton, East Sussex: 01273 389700. A shelter and retreat for rescued horses and ponies, plus sheep, chicken and lambs. www.retreathorserescue.co.uk

Raystede Centre for Animal Welfare Ltd, The Broyle, Ringmer, Lewes, East Sussex: 01825 840252. A treatment centre for domestic animals. Also has limited rescue and rehabilitation facilities for wildlife. www.raystede.org

RSPCA Head Office, Southwater, Horsham, West Sussex: 0870 010 1181. The headquarters of the RSPCA. www.rspca.org.uk

Southdowns Badger Protection Society, Court Farm Road, Newhaven, East Sussex: 01273 514942. Includes a 24 hour phone service offering badger protection and advice.

Squirrel Rescue, Carden Cresent, Patcham, Brighton, East Sussex. Rescue service for squirrels.

Sussex Bat Hospital, Forest Row, East Sussex: 01342 823189. Rescuing injured bats. www.sussexbatgroup.org.uk

Sussex Horse Rescue Trust, Hempstead Lane, Uckfield, East Sussex: 01825 762010. A care centre for horses, ponies and donkeys. Includes a loan scheme.

Sussex Wildlife Trust, Shoreham Road, Henfield, West Sussex: 01273 492630. www.sussexwt.org.uk

Warnham Animal Sanctuary, Mayes Lane, Warnham, Horsham, West Sussex: 01403 268095. Helping dogs, cats and donkeys. Also a German shepherd dog and dachshund rescue centre. www.warnhamanimalsanctuary.org.uk

Wildlife Rescue - Arundel, Church Street, Amberley, Arundel, West Sussex: 01798 831715. Rescuing birds and small mammals, not aquatic mammals. www.britishwildlifehelpline.com

Wildlife Rescue - Brighton, Wickhurst Road, Brighton, East Sussex: 01273 422705. A rescue service for large birds, raptors, also badgers and foxes.

Wildlife Rescue - Pulborough, Nutbourne, Pulborough, West Sussex: 01798 32628. Rescuing squirrels, birds and hedgehogs. www.britishwildlifehelpline.com

Worthing and District Animal Rescue Service, Park Lane, Ashington, Pulborough, West Sussex: 01903 217788.

Worthing Cat Welfare Trust, Orchard Avenue, Worthing, West Sussex: 01903 202251. Rescues and rehomes stray and unwanted cats and kittens.

FEATURES

DID YOU KNOW
A group of Kangaroos is called a mob.

FEATURES

Who's the tallest, smallest, oldest, strangest?

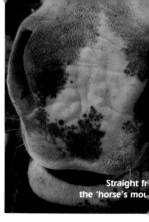

Straight fr
the 'horse's mou

We know that creatures are both great and small, but did you know that the very tiniest dog was thought to be a Yorkshire terrier who measured under three inches tall and under four inches long? Put this little chap beside the tallest horse, measuring 19 hands and 1inch (195.58cm), and he wouldn't even reach the top of his hoof line!

The smallest mammal of all is the tiny Kitti's hog-nosed bat from Thailand, who has a compact little body the size of a wasp, at around 3cm. And if anyone ever calls you a 'little twit', you can astonish them with the fact that the smallest owl is the aptly named elf owl from USA and Mexico, with a length of around 13cm. If you are rudely referred to as a lumbering hippo, you can quote the details of the

Cougar, mountain lion, puma ... ?

smallest hippopotamus, the pygmy from West Africa, measuring in at a length of around 1.6m – and just about knee height.

No prizes for guessing that the tallest land mammal is a giraffe from Africa, who can reach a maximum of about 5.8m, whilst the largest land mammal is the African elephant, who weighs up to 8 tonnes. What is the very largest mammal of all? The blue whale of course, who may grow to around 35m and weigh about 130 tonnes.

Can you guess what the maximum age for a pony might be? Try 54 years - clocked up by a Welsh/Arab cross! There has been a 15 year old rabbit, a 34 year old cat, a 22 year old goat, a 35 year old parrot and a goldfish who reached the grand old age of 43!

The slowest mammal is not any human you may know getting out of bed in the mornings, but the three-toed sloth of South America, who speeds along at around 2 metres per minute on the ground but more than twice that amount in the trees. And if you really want to amaze your friends, you can tell them about a fish that climbs trees – the climbing perch from south Asia!

The slowest fish is actually the seahorse, who floats calmly through the ocean at around 0.001mph, and the most poisonous mollusc is the blue-ringed octopus from Australia and southeast Asia, who can kill a human without any effort whatsoever.

Much nicer to meet on a warm sunny day is the smallest bird – a bee hummingbird from Cuba, who measures only 57mm. But don't be lured by the largest butterfly – Queen Alexandra's birdwing, a poisonous species that has a wingspan of about 28cm.

Those people fascinated by creepy-crawlies may already know that the most venomous spider is none other than the Brazilian wandering spider – let's hope he doesn't wander too far from home then! The most poisonous fish is the puffer fish from the Red Sea – who can actually be eaten by humans, providing he is cooked correctly. And if you have been troubled by wasp nests during the summer, take heart that it wasn't the biggest on record that was found in Japan, with a circumference of 2.44m (8ft).

You may think that name-calling is a rather unkind human thing. But have a guess what mammal has the most English names of all? It's the cougar, well perhaps I mean puma, no, mountain lion, also known as the red tiger, the Florida panther and no less than 35 other names. But why? Best ask the creature with the largest animal brain – the sperm whale, whose vital organ tips the scales at around 9kg - compared to the average human brain, which weighs about 1.4kg.

Giraffes can grow
as tall as 5.8 metres.

FEATURES

Should I insure my animal?

FEATURES

Living in a nation of animal lovers, UK pets are often very much loved members of our households. So as for any other treasured living being, we should ensure that they are properly cared for both in sickness and in health. A healthy pet is a happy pet, giving in return many happy moments and great satisfaction.

by Yvonne Neilson

A pet's owner is responsible for its well-being - a pet is for life, and the expenses, worry and responsibility are all an integral part of owning an animal. Therefore, it stands to reason that insuring your pet could bring great peace of mind. After all, vets bills have been known to make very large holes in the pocket!

Nowadays one can insure just about anything, from footballers' legs to priceless items of jewellery. Both house and car owners want their investments to be safe and secure, and the same applies to pets.

Current pet insurances not only cover expensive vet bills, but most of them will also include loss and theft policies, and most importantly, third party liability. Any pet, however docile, may inadvertently cause damage to others or property - whether by intention or misfortune. A dog can run out into a road and cause a car to swerve into a garden fence, damaging two people's property in addition to possibly injuring the driving and passengers.

In our modern world, where there seems to be an increasing trend to apportion 'blame', people are becoming

very much more aware of difficult, long and costly compensation legal fees. A court case can often set the participants back by thousands of pounds - unless of course they have a current insurance policy that covers them for such a misfortune.

If you have an expensive breed of pet, or an animal that is prone to illness or injury, health insurance is certainly worth considering. Most major insurance companies offer pet insurances. However, if you own an exotic animal, certain companies may not provide cover. Your vet may be able to offer advice as to which insurance companies will best suit your particular needs.

Some insurance companies specialise in horses and these should also be able to insure riders, competitors, trailers and horse boxes. Horse insurance covers can also include loss, theft or damage to saddlery and tack.

Before taking out any insurance, make sure you read carefully the full policy terms and conditions, as there are many exceptions that might apply to you or your pet. Having a pet insurance does not

necessarily mean your pet will always be covered. Also, if you wish to travel abroad with your pet, make sure your insurance specifically covers this – and check whether certain conditions apply.

Age is also a conditioning factor; some companies will not insure pets under a few months old or over a certain age. Other companies decline to insure dogs under the Dangerous Dogs Act. Insurance companies may have registered vets with whom they work – so check first which ones you can use.

The following pages contain a summary of what most insurance policies in Great Britain may cover:

- Illness or injury for 12 months. The policy will cover your pet's injury or illness commencing 10-14 days from the date you signed the contract. No previous incidents to that specific date may apply.
- Causing accidents or injury to a third party. This includes to a property or person. But it will not cover yourself, a member of your family or any person working with you.
- Dental care is NOT covered unless necessary after illness or accident.
- Inoculations are not included.
- Preventative treatments are not included.
- Vet bills up to a certain amount. This is usually pre-arranged.
- Pregnancy or birth is not included. If the pet has to be hospitalised for birth, kennels fees will not usually be paid.

- Kennel bills if the animal has to be hospitalised. Again there is a restriction on the amount of days.
- Euthanasia is not included, unless it is due to illness.
- In the case of loss/theft, insurance companies will sometimes pay a certain fee towards the reward and advertising fees. If the pet is not found after a specified amount of days, the cost of the pet will be refunded.
- Death due to illness or accident; insurance companies will pay the cost of the pet.
- Holiday cancellation fees if a pet falls ill and you cannot travel due to this.
- Third part liability if a pet causes damage to a third party or property, eg. dogs worrying sheep. Not included here are working animals, i.e. security dogs, pets used for racing.

So, how much does it cost? Pet insurance can cost from as little as £5 per month up to a few hundred pounds, depending on your type of pet or the policy cover you choose. This, of course, is subject to your needs and requirements. Do get a few quotes from different companies as prices vary notably. Please be advised that prices may vary from region to region (vet fees are different, loss/theft more likely in certain areas, etc.)

Most major insurance companies will be able to insure your pet, but always remember to seek advice from your vet, since not all policies will suit you or your pets needs. Shop around and get different quotes from various companies – prices may vary. Should you wish to contract a certain insurance policy, make sure you read all the clauses and are fully aware of the exceptions.

www.animalloversguides.co.uk

Performing animals: is it cruel – what can I do to help?

In some settings, animals are used to entertain the mammals with the most developed brain – humans. There are different schools of thought as to whether this is acceptable and over the last few decades many activities involving animals have been reduced or banned in the UK. Over the years, people have become more aware of the suffering and cruelty that some animals have to endure, not just focusing on physical abuse but also considering their physiological and psychological needs and a perceived quality of life.

by Rob Willard

Circuses, zoos and animal sports are three of the obvious fields for concern – but there are also other areas in which animals are encouraged to perform, including dancing bears and trained monkeys for tourist photographs outside the UK. Creatures are frequently used in film-making, television advertisements and live shows – and because filming is not witnessed by most members of the public, few worry about the conditions under which the animals live or work.

A person who exhibits or trains a performing animal in the UK must be registered. The Performing Animals (Regulation) Act 1925, which applies to Great Britain (but not Northern Ireland), requires any person who exhibits or trains performing animals to register with his/her local authority. The local authority must maintain a register of such individuals, which is available for public inspection. There have been many reported cases of animal cruelty and neglect in the film and advertising industry, but the situation is generally improving. Campaigns and animal rights groups are constantly striving for tougher legislation and regulations for people who exhibit and train animals for entertainment.

Circuses

The image many people have of the circus is of a spectacular and wonderful world full of colour, music, fun and excitement, where acrobats, clowns, trapeze artists and lion tamers perform amazing feats to delight the audience.

Many people who see a circus with performing animals are unaware of the implications that lie behind this illusion of harmless fun. Exotic circus animals are sometimes forced to perform confusing, physically uncomfortable and unnatural tricks. Trainers have been found to use a variety of painful tools including whips, muzzles, electric prods, tight collars and bull hooks.

Equally importantly, living conditions for some circus animals are simply appalling. Some may be chained in darkness and many are unable to move sufficiently, or allowed to enjoy natural behaviour. Circuses can be on the road for many months each year, with animals confined in small 'beast wagons'.

UK circus facts

Great progress has been achieved over the last few years. There are officially only seven circuses remaining in the UK that use animals. However, it is possible that a circus may change its name, or it

A free bear is a happy bear

may use its performances to promote circuses that are operating abroad, without outside supervision covering animal acts. The Association of Circus Proprietors is largely self-governing and therefore could possibly be accused of making its own rules and recommendations.

Currently there seems to be no specific law governing animals in circuses. They are exempt from zoo laws as well as laws covering 'dangerous wild animals' kept as pets. However, if a circus is parked on council land, the council can inspect or ask the circus to move. In the UK, over 200 local authorities have banned animal circuses from council land.

Zoos

During the 1980s, around 250 zoos existed in the United Kingdom, but numbers rapidly declined as the public became more aware and deeply concerned about animals kept in captivity in small enclosures. Today, most zoos claim that they perform several vital functions: conservation of species, study and understanding of animals and education – all of which hold the long-term interests of the animals at heart.

Many believe that species kept in zoos are facing extinction and captivity offers one of the few hopes for ultimate survival. It is, of course, important to remember to think in terms of centuries instead of years, and if mass extinction is to be avoided, captive breeding in zoos may well be an answer, albeit not ideal. Only a few species in the UK have actually been returned to the wild with any degree of success so far, but the knowledge and understanding that is gained by studying these animals in

Too much monkey business?

FEATURES

captivity has to give them a better chance of sharing the planet with the dominant species. Many animals in zoos, including elephants, African lions and giraffes, are not immediately under threat in the wild, and some people are concerned that they are simply used as exhibits – with performances and tricks being used to increase visitor numbers.

Of course, confinement in zoos is rarely ideal for any animal, although increased knowledge of an animal's

needs means that enclosures are now usually designed as imaginatively as possible, attempting to recreate the terrain that would form natural surroundings for a species. Some zoos are better equipped than others, but unfortunately abnormal behaviour in zoo animals is still quite common. Visitors may notice some animals swaying repetitively, pacing and even self mutilating.

Zoos in the UK are governed by the Zoo Licensing Act 1981, which sets minimum standards for zoo management. There's no doubt that zoos have improved immensely over the past few decades. One only has to compare zoos in the UK with those in countries with fewer regulations, or

DID YOU KNOW?

Chimps play many games - peekaboo is one of their favourites.

indeed to study photographs of zoos in this country just 50 years ago, to fully appreciate the comparatively recent progress that has been achieved for animal welfare in the UK.

Sports and competition

There are many controversial sports and competitive activities that involve animals, including racing, carriage driving, showing, hunting and trialling. Some promote the excellence of certain breeds, such as thoroughbred horses, Arab horses, working sheepdogs and others. But others take the finer points of breeding to extremes and produce unnatural features in animals that may be desirable in the show ring, but are not so positive for the animal itself. The lovable dachshund suffers with slipped discs due to its long back and short legs, whilst bulldogs may have painful sores in their facial skin folds.

Some animals are 'entertaining' just doing their own thing in their own way

Whilst some people express an interest in the abilities of animals to perform, others are concerned with success, status and profit. Where money is concerned, there are huge temptations for illegal activity. Many prize-winning dogs and horses are kept in excellent conditions, but for some animals used in sport or competition, living conditions can be poor.

Factors for concern are methods which ensure the best performances (or even to fixing a race by ensuring a loss): these include drugs, electrical stimuli, whips and so on. For horses, the track itself poses dangers; falls and fractures are common in both jump and flat races.

Greyhounds can also be prone to injury and mistreatment and sometimes die prematurely due to over-exertion and stress.

Blood sports

The brutal blood sports of cockfighting and dog fighting, which peaked during the late 80s were a popular and profitable pastime for the UK underground community. Fortunately, changes in the law made during the last decade now mean that even being a spectator at a cockfight or possessing equipment that could be used in one are criminal offences. Blood sports continue to exist on a smaller scale, with public awareness, campaigns, heavier sentences and fines being used as effective deterrents. Other types of blood sports include hunting, fishing, hare coursing and badger baiting. Hunting with hounds and hare coursing in England and Wales became illegal on 18th February 2005.

How you can help

If you decide to visit a venue with performing animals, you may want to ask yourself what stresses the animals are under. Are they exhibiting their normal behaviour? Do they look contented? Is it entertaining? Is it fun? Ask their keepers or qualified staff for information if you are not sure - they may be able to reassure you. If not, express your concerns in writing to the establishment concerned. You can take it further if you are not satisfied with the response. If you are concerned about the legality of the operation, contact the police. The local council may also be a point of reference.

The following recommendations may also help:

• Support only animal-free circuses.
• If you know of an animal circus that is heading for a town near you, contact your local council to promote a ban.
• If you see an act of animal cruelty or if you hear of any illegal blood sports taking place in your area, call the police or a local animal welfare organisation.
• Become a fundraiser or a volunteer for a recognised charity.
• Raise awareness in local councils, schools and animal welfare groups.
• Support organisations that protect wildlife in the wild.
• Write a letter of protest to your MP or to your Member of the European Parliament.
• Write a letter to a local newspaper.
• Collect signatures for petitions.
• Educate yourself and others.
• Offer information to schools in order that students may be educated to recognise animal cruelty.

Resources / References

The Captive Animals' Protection Society
PO Box 573, Preston, PR1 9WW
Phone/fax 0845 330 3911
email info@captiveanimals.org
www.captiveanimals.org

Animal Cruelty Investigation Group and the Animal Welfare Information Service
P.O. Box 8, Halesworth
Suffolk. IP19 0JL
www.acigawis.freeserve.co.uk

Animal Defenders
261 Goldhawk Road
London, W12 9PE
www.animaldefenders.org.uk

Born Free Foundation
3 Grove House, Foundry Lane,
Horsham, West Sussex, RH13 5PL
www.bornfree.org.uk

Respect for Animals,
PO Box 500 Nottingham, NG1 3AS
www.respectforanimals.org

Animal Defenders International
www.ad-international.org

Animal Concerns
www.animalconcerns.org

FEATURES

DID YOU KNOW

Identical twins smell the same to bloodhounds.

Looking for a small pet with a difference?

Here are some suggestions ...

FEATURES

We've all heard of hamsters, guinea pigs, rabbits and gerbils, and it's well known that they can make charming small pets. But perhaps you want a pet with a difference? There's something rather more exciting about the thought of owning a chinchilla, a degu, a tree frog or a gecko ... but what exactly are these animals, and could they be suitable for you?

Firstly, think about the housing arrangement you can afford in both space and expense. A **chinchilla**, for example, needs a large cage - wide rather than tall. Although this rodent is related to the hamster, it is much larger and has characteristic luxurious fur that is usually grey but can be white, brown, black and even 'violet'. These charming creatures hail from high up in the Andes mountains of South America and they are nocturnal animals that sleep most of the day. Your bedroom is therefore not the place for the cage, as they can make a considerable amount of noise as they rush about during the night. They are fairly easy to keep as pets, but do need to chew because their strong incisor teeth continue to grow throughout their long lives of up to 20 years. A chinchilla is surprisingly fast and he appreciates coming out for exercise on a regular basis. A chinchilla owner may also need to be speedy in order to catch up with him – and should be vigilant in order to

ensure that this little animal doesn't chew the antique furniture, the TV cable or the library books!

Consider a **degu** if you prefer something a little smaller. He comes from Chile, looks rather like a gerbil and likes to climb. A tall cage would be preferable to a sawdust-filled aquarium, although the latter can make a good base for a home, with a top cage securely fastened on. This sociable little creature likes the company of another degus. Keep two or more of the same sex together, or consider breeding them if you have a market for the countless babies that will soon appear. They are largely nocturnal but also wake for short periods during the daytime. They rarely bite humans and are said to make good pets.

To the casual passer-by, a **jird** is just another gerbil, or could even be mistaken for a degu. It has a sharper, more pointed nose, however, and likes to burrow. Like gerbils, jirds come from South and West Africa through to Far

Photo: courtesy Drusillas Zoo Park

FEATURES

**Incy, wincy spider?
I don't think so!**

East Asia. In captivity they eat a good quality rodent mix and are said to be rather slower and easier to handle than gerbils.

A **duprasi** looks similar again, but this creature that hails from the north Sahara desert lives largely in underground tunnels. He is most active at dusk and has been known to nip the odd finger that strays too close. They are said to be sociable animals, but tend to bite each other - they therefore require plenty of space that enables them to keep their distance.

Perhaps a reptile might be more to your liking? There are many reptiles that could make suitable pets, providing you provide the correct environment and ensure that their diet is suitable. The

leopard gecko is a lizard with skin like velvet. They are marked with leopard-like spots and come from arid regions of India and Pakistan. These live on the ground, unlike some of their climbing cousins. They dig in sand and clamber on rocks and logs. Leopard geckos can live up to 20 years in captivity, so this is a long-term pet who likes a humid micro-climate so that he does not dehydrate. He needs a vivarium with a hot spot and various cooler areas, provided by a heater pad at one end of the habitat and shelters in which to hide away. Leopard geckos are nocturnal so won't need overhead light bulbs or ultra-violet lamps. They eat live food such as crickets, so these are not for the squeamish!

Chameleons are well known for their ability to change colour. One of the most adaptable species, the veiled chameleon, is considered ideal for a pet keeper who is willing to devote time and effort to this animal's care. The

DID YOU KNOW? *A flea can jump 120 times its own length.*

Anyone for crickets?
A leopard-gecko's staple diet

Photo: courtesy Drusillas Zoo Park

weather, with a heat lamp to keep chills at bay. Mediterranean tortoises are herbivores, loving fruit and vegetables, flowers and weeds. They occasionally eat meat and also enjoy specially prepared tortoise pellet concentrate that contains vitamins and minerals. Tortoises need to hibernate in winter, ideally in a secure crate filled with shredded paper or straw, stored in a cool but frost-free environment.

chameleon needs a large vivarium with living plants and branches included within the design. It needs a basking area in which to warm up, probably provided by a couple of spotlights plus a shaded area and perhaps a fluorescent light tube too. This animal enjoys heavy dew or condensation, provided by a mist spray, a pool of water and ideally good ventilation provided by a fan (placed safely out of the way of the creature). Angry chameleons will turn black. They have pigment-filled cells just beneath the surface of the skin and can change colour according to their environment. They like to eat live food such as flying or climbing insects and also eat leaves, fruit and vegetables.

Just a few decades ago, practically every garden had a poor unfortunate **tortoise**, often attached to a piece of string by means of a hole drilled through its shell. Fortunately, pet keepers have been alerted to the error of their ways and tortoises are now only available to serious collectors and pet keepers who care about the animal's needs. Adult tortoises can be kept outside during the British summer, in a well-fenced garden. They are surprisingly agile and will escape where possible! Ideally they need shelter from the cooler and wetter

DID YOU KNOW?

Tortoises can live up to 200 years.

Who can resist a **tree frog**, the acrobat of the amphibian world? These comical creatures are found in warmer climates around the world and many of them spend most of their lives, as you might expect, in trees. They can climb almost any vertical surface, even glass! Tree frogs require a tall vivarium filled with branches and climbing surfaces.

They may be s
but tortoises can
up to 200 y

hat's green and sticky?
y a stick insect, of course!

Photo: courtesy Drusillas Zoo Park

Moss, stones, pebbles and bark chippings make an ideal ground base. They need a large bowl of water, daily misting with a spray and a good even warm temperature during daytime. Tree frogs in captivity will eat small dead creatures such as other frogs, lizards and even baby pink mice. They also eat large crickets, earthworms and small locusts. They usually tolerate handling quite well, but take care not to damage their delicate skin.

Some people find the entire notion of **snakes** revolting, whilst others love them! There are many different varieties than can be kept as pets, including **kingsnakes**, **corn snakes** and even the small **royal python**. Kingsnakes feed on other snakes in the wild, but will eat almost any prey in captivity including birds, frogs, rodents and lizards. They grow to about 120cm in length and can live for up to 15 years. Snakes need dry vivariums with hiding areas and a shallow water dish. They take time to get used to being handled, but usually tame very well and rarely bite. Corn snakes are one of the most commonly kept snakes – they are easy to look after, eat well and are usually of good temperament. They can exist in captivity almost entirely on mice, although they may also enjoy frogs and lizards. The

royal python grows to an average length of about 100cm. He appreciates the occasional spray mist using warm water and is often difficult to feed. Royal pythons have a tendency to fast in captivity, refusing food for several weeks at a time. A captive royal python has been known to fast for 26 months! In the wild they eat live food, but may accept warm dead mice, birds, rats and even raw chicken. A python kills its prey by squeezing and a reticulated python, the world's longest snake, is said to be capable of eating a small bear!

There are plenty more unusual and exotic small pets - for instance invertebrates such as stick insects, leaf insects, giant millipedes and praying mantis. In fact, 97% of all living animals are invertebrates – creatures without a backbone – so there are quite a few pet possibilities amongst them!

Some people love to keep spiders such as tarantulas as pets, and this is perhaps not as dangerous as you may think. Did you know that despite its reputation, there appear to have been no human deaths caused by this spider? Its venom is similar in strength to a bee sting, however, and some people are allergic to venoms. Handling spiders, incidentally, may not be advisable to anyone of a nervous nature!

It is said that even scorpions can make interesting pets. The largest is the imperial scorpion that comes from Africa. It is actually not considered dangerous to humans – but these creatures are definitely not for the faint-hearted!

If it's something soft and cuddly you are after, the invertebrates are probably not for you. There's a lot to be said for rabbits and guinea pigs, after all!

PETS travel scheme
Does my pet need a passport?

Many people love to take their pet with them on holiday, but for many years only those taking holidays in the UK could do so. As appealing as the image of trekking across foreign lands in the company of a four-legged friend could be, who could ever imagine a line of animals queuing for passport control at the airport?

by Bernie Fiddimore

Until recently, animals taken abroad always had to endure quarantine when they returned home. The quarantine period used to be six months, a long time in the life of a dog or cat. This meant that animals would only ever travel abroad in extreme or exceptional circumstances – perhaps the owners were emigrating or a homeless animal may have been adopted by (fairly wealthy) holidaymakers who just could not bear to leave it behind.

In recent years, the quarantine period was reduced to three months and then in 2000, the Pet Travel Scheme (PETS) was launched. Under the scheme, some animals could be brought into the UK without having to go through quarantine.

The Scheme, managed by the Department for the Environment, Food and Rural Affairs (DEFRA), decreed that the majority of EU countries and certain countries outside the EU that are considered rabies-free, should be included in PETS.

PETS covers cats, dogs, ferrets, rabbits and rodents. There are very strict requirements for anyone travelling with an animal and it is essential that the correct

information is researched according to the country you intend to visit.

All animals must be microchipped and vaccinated against rabies. A blood test is then taken a month later to check for rabies antibodies and many countries insist upon flea, tick and tapeworm treatments. These treatments also have to be carried out before an animal re-enters the UK.

Animals travelling to countries outside those listed in the scheme will not be allowed to re-enter the UK within six months, or will automatically be subject to the quarantine period being imposed. Dogs, cats and ferrets entering the UK from non-qualifying countries will also still have to go through quarantine.

In July 2004 the scheme was simplified by the introduction of European Union (EU) Pet Passports. A passport is a form of certification that allows cats and dogs to travel within the EU. It replaces the old PETS certificate. However, cats and dogs with valid PETS certificates issued before 2004 can use them until they expire.

The new legislation also allows pet rodents (guinea pigs, rats, chinchillas)

and rabbits to travel freely within the EU, with no certification usually being required. They are also usually free to travel without a travel ticket and are not required to be checked at the Pets Control Booth.

There are, however, many methods of travel and it is important to check with the travel provider what facilities are available. Many airlines still do not transport even small pets, and neither does Eurostar, although Eurotunnel accepts pet travellers for an additional fee. Most airlines that do transport animals insist on a particular specification of travel box according to the type of animal to be contained. These generally have to be purchased rather than hired, thereby adding to the cost of travel.

As the world becomes more and more like a global village, it seems that almost anything is possible. Travel facilities now make even the most remote corners of the globe accessible for those who have the

time and money. But the legal process is still a lengthy and time-consuming task – and in the same way that people need to make sure their documentation is up to date and in order before booking a ticket, the same applies to travelling pets.

In some cases, arranging for a pet to travel overseas can take at least six months of planning, and has been known to take nearly a year. So your pooch may enjoy a summer holiday abroad with the family, but not unless you have planned it well in advance!

INFORMATION

For lists of routes, advice about documentation plus general information: www.defra.gov.uk/animals/quarantine/pets

Pet Travel Scheme (PETS) helpline 0870 241 1710 Monday to Friday 8.30am to 5.00pm.

Eurostar Travel visit www.eurotunnel.com/ukcMain/ukcPetTravel

---

Animal charities

These kind organisations, which are dedicated to the welfare of animals, are all charities that rely on donations or legacies in order to continue their good work. You may wish to consider such a donation or legacy in the future. We have listed as many animal charities that we could find, local and national, for your information.

by Rosie Finey

Sussex Branch	Description	National
Action for Animals Charity No local branch	Charity No. 1068487 Our aim is to prevent animal cruelty and promote kindness to animals worldwide.	Action for Animals Charity PO Box 986, Southampton SO19 5TR Tel: Not available www.actionforanimals.org
Animal Aid No local branch	Charity No. Not available We campaign peacefully against all forms of animal abuse and promote a cruelty-free lifestyle.	Animal Aid The Old Chapel, Bradford Street Tonbridge, Kent, TN9 1AW Tel: 01732 364546 www.animalaid.org.uk
Animals in Distress Sanctuary No local branch	Charity No. 515886 Care of abandoned, neglected animals.	Animals in Distress Sanctuary 55 Silver Street, Irlam, Manchester, M44 6HT Tel: 0906 680 1215 www.animals-in-distress.net
Animals in Mind (AIM) No local branch	Charity No. 1063919 To help people that have problem pets and dogs that were being rehomed or destroyed due to behaviour problems	Animals in Mind (AIM) 31 Magdalen Way, Worle, North Somerset, BS22 7PG Tel: 01934 516714 www.members.aol.com
Birdlife International No local branch	Charity No. 207076 Focusing on birds and the sites and habitats on which they depend. Working to improve the quality of life for birds and wildlife	Birdlife International Global Office Wellbrook Court, Girton Road, Cambridge, CB3 0NA Tel: 01223 277318 www.birdlife.org
Blue Cross Equine Rescue St Francis Fields, Northiam, Sussex, TN31 6LP Tel: 01797 252243	Charity No. 224392 The Blue Cross is an animal welfare charity	Headquarters, Blue Cross, Shilton Road Burford, Oxon, OX18 4PF Tel: 01993 822651 www.bluecross.org.uk
Border Collie Trust GB No local branch	Charity No. 1053585 Our purpose built kennels are our base and rescue centre for the work the Trust undertakes in the care, rescue and rehoming of Border Collies and Collie X's.	Border Collie Trust GB Heathway, Colton, Rugeley, Staffs, WS15 3LY Tel: 0871 560 2282 www.bordercollietrustgb.org.uk

Sussex Branch	Description	National
Border Collie Rescue No local branch	Charity No. 3037504 We take in, care for, rehabilitate, retrain and rehome unwanted Border Collies and working Sheepdogs.	Border Collie Rescue 57 Market Place, Richmond, North Yorkshire, DL10 4JQ Tel: 0870 444838 www.bordercollierescue.org
Brent Lodge Headquarters, Cow Lane, Sidlesham, Chichester, West Sussex, PO20 7LN Tel: 01243 641672 www.brentlodge.org	Charity No. 276179 A bird and wildlife hospital	Brent Lodge As local branch
British Chelonia Group No local branch	Charity No. 801818 Care and Conservation of Tortoises, Terrapins and Turtles worldwide.	British Chelonia Group PO Box 1176, Chippenham, Wiltshire, SN15 1XB Tel: No number available www.britishcheloniagroup.org.uk
British Hedgehog Preservation Society No local branch	Charity No. 326885 Helping and protecting hedgehogs.	British Hedgehog Preservation Soc. Hedgehog House, Dhustone Ludlow, Shropshire, SY8 3PL Tel: 01584 890801 www.software-technics.com/bhps
British Horse Society No local branch	Charity No. 210504 Focusing on horse welfare, horse and rider safety, access and rights of way, training and education and providing a voluntary system of approving livery yards and riding schools, making sure high standards are met.	British Horse Society Stoneleigh, Deer Park, Kenilworth Warwickshire, CV8 2XZ Tel: 08701 202244 www.bhs.org.uk
British Ornithologists' Union No local branch	Charity No. Not available To understand bird's biology and aid their conservation.	British Ornithologists' Union Department of Zoology, University of Oxford, South Parks Road Oxford, OX1 3PS Tel: 01865 281842 www.bou.org.uk
Brook Hospital for Animals No local branch	Charity No. 1085760 Relieving the suffering of horses, donkeys and mules working for poor people in the developing world.	Brook Hospitals for Animals 21 Panton Street London, SW1Y 4DR Tel: 020 7930 0210 www.thebrook.org
Brownbread Horse Rescue Ashburnham, Battle East Sussex, TN33 9NX Tel: 01424 892381 www.brownbread_rescue.250free.com/Page/info.html	Charity No. 1029341 The Centre takes in any horse, any time, for any reason.	No national branch
Canine Concern Ravopi, Elsted Road Bexhill, East Sussex, TN39 3BG Tel: 01424 843661	Charity No. 328237 Registered charity for pet owners to take their dogs (cats and rabbits)into hospitals and homes etc. for residents to stroke and enjoy.	Head Office Smocks, Wellington Somerset, TA21 9PW Tel: 01823 664300
Canine Lifeline UK No local branch	Charity Lifeline	Canine Lifeline UK C/O 26 Queen Street, Boston, Lincolnshire, PE21 8XB Tel: 08707 581401 www.caninelifeline.fsnet.co.uk

FEATURES

Sussex Branch	Description	National
Canine Partners for Independence Mill Lane, Heyshott, Midhurst, West Sussex, GU29 0ED Tel: 08456 580480 www.c-p-i.org.uk	Charity No. 803680 We aim to transform the lives of people with disabilities ("Partners") by partnering them with highly trained assistance dogs, enabling them to live more independently and enjoy an enhanced lifestyle.	No national office
Cat and Kitten Rescue of Chandlers Ford No local branch	Charity No. Not available A small independent rescue service. Based in Hampshire. Cats and kittens in environs of Chandlers.	Cat and Kitten Rescue of Chandlers Ford, Based in Hampshire Ford, Hampshire Tel: 023 80253563 www.catandkitten.co.uk
Care for the Wild International The Granary, Tickfold Farm Kingsfold, West Sussex, RH12 3SE Tel: 01306 627900 www.careforthewild.com	Charity No. 288802 Provide immediate aid to wildlife in distress anywhere in the world. We work with the local people and Government bodies in an attempt to alleviate suffering.	Care for the Wild International Head Office Kingsfold, West Sussex
Cat Action Trust No local branch	Charity No. 1063947 The Original Cat Action Trust, the pioneer society for ferals, was founded in 1977 to help the feral cat.	The Original Cat Action Trust 11 Lower Barn Road, Purley Surrey, CR8 1HY www.catactiontrust.org.uk
Cats Protection League 63 London Road St Leonards on Sea, East Sussex, TN37 6AY Tel: 01243 602777 www.cats.org.uk	Charity No. 203644 Cats Protection has grown to become the UK's leading feline welfare charity.	Cats Protection League Chelwood Gate, Hayward's Heath West Sussex, RH17 7TT Tel: 08702 099099
Celia Hammond Animal Trust (CHAT), Greenacres, Stubb Lane, Brede, Near Hastings, East Sussex Tel: 01424 882198 www.celiahammond.org	Charity No. 293787 Celia became involved in rescuing, neutering and rehoming stray and unwanted animals.	Celia Hammond Animal Trust High Street, Wadhurst East Sussex, TN5 6AG Tel: 01892 783367
Dogs for homing PO Box 126, Burgess Hill West Sussex, RH15 0SL Tel: 01273 843897 www.happybreed.co.uk/dogs_for_homing.htm	Charity No. 267284 Rehoming of dogs.	No national office
Dogs for the Disabled No local branch	Charity No. 1092960 Dogs for the Disabled trains dogs to help disabled people live life more independently.	Dogs for the Disabled The Francis Day Centre Blacklocks Hill, Banbury, Oxon, OX17 2BS Tel: 08700 776600 www.dogsforthedisabled.org
Dogs Trust (formerly NCDL) Brighton Road, Shoreham by Sea, West Sussex, BN43 5LT Tel: 01273 452576	Charity No. 227523 Founded in 1891, Dogs Trust has always campaigned on dog welfare related issues to ensure a safe and happy future for our four-legged friends.	Headquarters, Dogs Trust 17 Wakley Street London, EC1V 7RQ Tel: 020 7837 0006 www.dogstrust.org.uk
Edinburgh Dog and Cat Home No local branch	Charity No. SCO 06914 We are one of the few independent homes in Scotland, taking in many hundreds of stray and unwanted dogs and cats every year.	Edinburgh Dog and Cat Home 26 Seafield Road East Edinburgh, EH15 1EH Tel: 0131 669 5331 www.edch.org.uk

Sussex Branch	Description	National
English Springer Spaniel Rescue No local branch	Charity No. 1076924 This allows us to raise funds to continue to find homes and give help to hundreds of Springer waifs and strays.	English Springer Spaniel Rescue 26 Whitewater Drive, Salford, Manchester M7 3AP Tel: 01282 697692 www.englishspringerrescue.org.uk
Fauna and Flora International No local branch	Charity No. Not available Renowned for its science-based approach, FFI has pioneered sustainable conservation work that tackles problems holistically, providing solutions that simultaneously help wildlife, humans and the environment	Fauna and Flora International **Headquarters in the USA** Great Eastern House, Tenison Road Cambridge, CB1 2TT Tel: 01223 571000 www.fauna-flora.org
Feline Advisory Bureau (FAB) No local branch	Charity No. 254641 The charity is dedicated to promoting the health and welfare of cats through improved feline knowledge to help us all care better for our cats.	Feline Advisory Bureau (FAB) Taeselbury, High Street Tisbury, Wiltshire, SP3 6LD Tel: 0870 742 2278 www.fabcats.org
Folly Wildlife Rescue No local branch	Charity No. 1091857 Working for the wildlife, relying solely on fundraising and donations.	Folly Wildlife Rescue Folly Cottage, Danegate Eridge Green, Tunbridge Wells Kent, TN39 9JB Tel: 01892 750865 www.follywildliferescue.org.uk

German Shepherd Dog Helpline
See website for more details. Phone numbers available for your area
www.gsdhelpline.com/

Great Dane Rescue No address available Contact via the website Tel: 01460 52676 www.daneline.co.uk	Charity No. Not available We are in desperate need of short-term foster homes for many of our Great Danes who are in need of tender loving care.	No address available Contact via the website www.daneline.co.uk
Greatwood Sanctuary No local branch	Charity No. 1077080 Caring for retired horses.	Greatwood Sanctuary Rainscombe Hill Farm, Clench Common, Marlborough, Wiltshire, SN8 4DT Tel: 01672 514535 www.racehorsesgreatwood.org
Green Fields Rescue No local branch	Charity No. Not available Rescue centre for rabbits and guinea pigs.	Green Fields Rescue 29 Beedon Drive Easthampstead Grange, Bracknell Berkshire, RG12 8GJ Tel: 01344 488208 www.greenfieldsrescue.co.uk
Greyhound Rescue West of England No local branch	Charity No. 1056676 Rehoming of greyhounds	Greyhound Rescue W of England PO Box 3695 Bath, BA2 8XJ Tel: 07000 785092 www.grwe.co.uk
Guide Dogs for the Blind Association Mallard, Bishops Lane Robertsbridge, TN32 5ED Tel: 01580 882204 www.guidedogs.org.uk	Charity No. 209617 We have been providing blind and partially sighted people with the freedom and independence a guide dog gives for nearly 75 years.	Guide Dogs for the Blind Association Burghfield Common Reading, RG7 3YG Tel: 0118 983 5555

FEATURES

FEATURES

Sussex Branch	Description	National
Hastings Animal Concern No national office www.geocities.com/animalconcern	HAC aims to provide accurate events locally and regionally on animal cruelty and this contains information, advice, news and this site contains many links to animal care and protection related organisations in the UK and throughout the world.	
Hastings Badger Protection Society 304 Bexhill Road, St Leonards on Sea East Sussex, TN38 8AL Tel: 01424 439168 www.hbps.cwc.net	Charity No. 1014678 Help for badgers.	Hastings Badger Protection Society No national branch.
Hearing Dogs for Deaf People No local branch	Charity No. Not available This charity continues to train dogs to alert deaf people to specific sounds, whether at home, workplace or public buildings.	Hearing Dogs for Deaf People The Grange, Wycombe Road Saunderton, Princes Risborough Bucks, HP27 9NS Tel: 01844 348 100 www.hearing-dogs.co.uk
Hereford & Worcester Animal Rescue No local branch	Charity No. 1104481 Rehoming of stray, abandoned and unwanted dogs.	Hereford and Worcester Animal Rescue All contact via the website or phone - Tel: 01553 828845 www.hwanimalrescue.org
Home of Rest for Horses No local branch	Charity No. 231748 The home promotes the health and welfare of welfare of horses through support for needy cases, education and research to reduce disease and suffering.	Home of Rest for Horses Westcroft Stables, Slad Lane Princes Risborough, Bucks, HP27 0PP Tel: 01494 488464 www.homeofrestforhorses.co.uk
IFAW 87-90 Albert Embankment London, SE1 7UD Tel: 020 7587 6700 www.ifaw.org/ifaw	Charity No. Not available Protection of animals and their habitats	IFAW Headquarters in America
International League for the Protection of Horses No local branch	Charity No. 206658 Equine welfare and stopping cruelty to horses.	International League for the Protection of Horses Anne Colvin House, Snetterton Norfolk, NR16 2LR Tel: 0870 871 1927 www.ilph.org
International Otter Survival Fund No local branch	Charity No. SC003875 Care for the otter	International Otter Survival Fund 7 Black Park, Broadford Isle of Skye IV49 9DE Tel: 01471 822 487 www.otter.org
Labrador Rescue Swallow Barn Netherfield, Battle	Charity No. 1105955 We aim to unite pure bred and first cross Labrador Retrievers with loving new homes.	Labrador Rescue See local branch as headquarters East Sussex www.Labrador-rescue.org.uk
Lincolnshire Greyhound Trust No local branch www.lincolnshire.gov.uk	Charity No. Not available The Retired Greyhound Trust (RGT) is a charity set up to relieve the stress and suffering of Racing Greyhounds and to help find them good homes as pets.	Lincolnshire Greyhound Trust Address not published Tel: 01522 569825

Sussex Branch	Description	National
London Wildlife Trust	Charity No. 283895 Protecting London's and the country's wildlife. The Wildlife Trusts care for almost 2,500 nature reserves.	London Wildlife Trust Skyline House, 200 Union Street London SE1 0LW Tel: 020 7261 0447 www.wildlondon.org.uk
National Animal Welfare Trust No local branch	Charity No. 1090499 The Trust operates rescue centres for unwanted, ill-treated and abandoned animals and birds.	National Animal Welfare Trust Tyler's Way, Watford By Pass, Watford, Herts, WD25 8WT Tel: 020 8950 0177 www.nawt.org.uk
Paws for Kids No local branch	Charity No. 1084861 A unique charity in the UK which fosters the pet animals of women and children escaping domestic violence.	Paws for Kids PO Box 329 Bolton, BL6 5FT Tel: 01204 698999 www.pawsforkids.org.uk
PDSA Local Shop Hastings & St Leonards PetAid Practice East Sussex Tel: 0800 731 2502	Charity No. 208217 PDSA cares for the pets of needy people by providing free veterinary services to their sick and injured pets and by promoting responsible pet ownership.	PDSA Freepost Telford, TF2 9YQ Tel: 0800 0199166 www.pdsa.org.uk
People and Dogs Society (PADS) No local branch	Charity No. 1005973 We relieve suffering and distress in dogs by promoting responsible dog ownership and by solving dog-related problems.	People and Dogs Society (PADS) 45B Ashgap Lane, Normanton, West Yorkshire, WF6 2DT Tel: 01924-897732 www.padsonline.org
PETA UK No local branch	Charity No. Not available People for the Ethical Treatment of Animals believes that animals deserve the most basic rights - consideration of their own best interests, regardless of whether they are useful to humans.	PETA UK Other offices around the world PO Box 36668 London, SE1 1WA Tel: 020 7357 9229 www.peta.org.uk
Redwings Horse Sanctuary No local branch	Charity No. 1068911 To provide and promote the welfare, care and protection of horses, ponies, donkeys and mules.	Redwings Horse Sanctuary Hapton, Norwich, NR15 1SP Tel: 01508 481000 www.redwings.co.uk
Royal Society for the Protection of Birds 2nd Floor, 42 Frederick Place Brighton, East Sussex BN1 4EA	Charity No. 207076 To secure a healthy environment for birds and wildlife.	Royal Society for the Protection of Birds Headquarters, The Lodge, Sandy, Bedfordshire, SG19 2DL Tel: 01767 680551 www.rspb.org
RSPCA Animal Centre Mount Noddy Black Mill Lane, Eartham, Nr Chichester, West Sussex PO18 0LL Tel: 01243 773359 www.rspca.org.uk	Charity No. 219099 Helping sick animals	RSPCA Headquarters Tel: 0870 333 5999
Save the Rhino International No local branch	Charity No. 1035072 Committed to ensuring the survival of the rhinoceros species in the wild	Save the Rhino International 16 Winchester Walk London SE1 9AQ Tel: 020 7357 7474 www.savetherhino.org

ANIMAL CHARITIES

Sussex Branch	Description	National
Sebakwe Black Rhino Trust No local branch	Charity No. 328461 To conserve part of the remaining population of black rhino.	Sebakwe Black Rhino Trust **Headquarters in Zimbabwe** Manor Farm, Ascott under Wychwood Oxon, OX7 6AL Tel: 01993 830278 www.blackrhino.org
Support Dogs No local branch	Charity No. 1088281 This charity trains Seizure Alert Dogs for people with epilepsy and disability. Assistance Dogs for people with physical disabilities.	Support Dogs 21 Jessops Riverside Brightside Lane, Sheffield, S9 2RX Tel: 0870 609 3476 www.support-dogs.org.uk
The British Butterfly Conservation Society Ltd No local branch	Charity No. 254937 The aim of protecting native butterflies from destruction of habitat and other threats.	The British Butterfly Conservation Society Ltd Manor Yard, East Lulworth Wareham, Dorset, BH20 5QP Tel: 0870 7744309 www.butterfly-conservation.org
The British Deer Society No local branch	Charity No. Not available To conserve the six species of deer wild within the UK.	The British Deer Society Fordingbridge, Hampshire, SP6 1EF Tel: 01425 655434 www.bds.org.uk
The British Herpetological Society No local branch	Charity No. Not available Care of reptiles and amphibians.	The British Herpetological Society c/o The Zoological Society of London Regents Park, London, NW1 4RY Email: president@thebhs.org www.thebhs.org
The Fox Project No local branch	Charity No. Not available A charity dedicated to the red fox.	The Fox Project The Southborough Centre, Draper Street, Southborough, Tunbridge Wells, Kent, TN4 0PG Tel: 01892 545468 www.foxproject.org.uk
The Great Dane Adoption Society No local branch	Charity No. 1091717 We relieve the suffering and distress of dogs, in particular the breed known as Great Danes, who are in need of attention by reason of homelessness, by the provision of temporary shelter, veterinary treatment and by finding permanent homes for such dogs.	The Great Dane Adoption Society Tudor Cottage, Bury Road, Brockley Green, Suffolk, IP29 4AG Tel: 0870 7874691 www.danes.org.uk
The Dogs Home Battersea No local branch	Charity No. 206394 Battersea Dogs Home has three centres, all dedicated to caring for lost and abandoned dogs and cats.	The Dogs Home Battersea HQ 4 Battersea Park Road London, SW8 4AA Tel: 020 7622 3626 www.dogshome.org
The Bat Conservation Trust No local branch	Charity No. 1012361 To legally protect bats and their roosts as their numbers are declining.	The Bat Conservation Trust 15 Cloisters Hse, 8 Battersea Park Rd London, SW8 4BG Tel: 0845 1300 228 www.bats.org.uk

FEATURES

www.animalloversguides.co.uk

Sussex Branch	Description	National
The David Shepherd Conservation Foundation No local branch	Charity No. 289646 An adaptable, non-bureaucratic organisation, the Foundation is flexible, responding promptly to conservation threats, supporting trusted, reputable individuals and organisations operating in the field.	The David Shepherd Conservation Foundation 61 Smithbrook Kilns Cranleigh, Surrey, GU6 8JJ Tel: 01483 272323 www.davidshepherd.org
The Diana Brimblecombe Animal Rescue Centre No local branch	Charity No. 288473 Animal Rescue Centre.	The Diana Brimblecombe Animal Rescue Centre Nelsons Lane Hurst, RG10 0RR Tel: 0118 9341122 www.dbarc.org.uk
The Donkey Sanctuary No local branch Worldwide branches - see website for details	Charity No. 264818 To prevent suffering of donkeys worldwide and to offer advice, training and support.	The Donkey Sanctuary The Donkey Sanctuary, Sidmouth, Devon, EX10 0NU Tel: 01395 578222 www.thedonkeysanctuary.org.uk
The Hillside Animal Sanctuary No local branch	Charity No. 3027738 Hillside was founded in 1995 to help and campaign for animals in need and most importantly, to bring public awareness to the millions of animals suffering every day in the intensive factory farming industry.	The Hillside Animal Sanctuary Hill Top Farm, Hall Lane, Frettenham, Norwich, NR12 7LT Tel: 01603 736 200 www.hillside.org.uk
The Humane Slaughter Association No local branch	Charity No. 209563 The Humane Slaughter Association (HSA) is the only registered charity committed to the welfare of animals in markets, during transport and to the point of slaughter.	The Humane Slaughter Association The Old School, Brewhouse Hill Wheathampstead, Herts, AL4 8AN Tel: 01582 831919 www.hsa.org.uk
The Mammal Society No local branch	Charity No. Not available To protect British mammals, halt the decline of threatened species, and advise on all issues affecting British mammals.	The Mammal Society 2b Inworth Street London SW11 3EP Tel: 020 7350 2200 www.abdn.ac.uk/mammal
The Mayhew Animal Home No local branch	Charity No. 1077588 Animal home and humane education and training centre.	The Mayhew Animal Home Trenmar Gardens London NW10 6BJ Tel: 020 8969 0178 www.mayhewanimalhome.org
The Moggery No local branch	Charity No. 1070330 Cat rehoming Centre	The Moggery Address not published Tel: 0117 9243128 www.themoggery.co.uk
The Otter Trust No local branch	Charity No. Not available The Otter Trust is a registered charity, founded by Philip and Jeanne Wayre in 1971. The main aims of the Trust are to encourage the conservation of otters throughout the world, with particular emphasis on the British otter.	The Otter Trust Earsham, Bungay Suffolk, NR35 2AF Tel: 01986 893480 www.ottertrust.org.uk

FEATURES

Sussex Branch	Description	National
The Parrot Line UK www.parrotline.org	Charity No. To be advised	Site under construction - coming soon
The Rabbit Welfare Fund PO Box 603, Horsham West Sussex RH13 5WL Tel: 0870 046 5249 www.houserabbit.co.uk	Charity No. 1085689 Welfare of rabbits.	The Rabbit Welfare Fund No National Branch
The Raystede Centre for Animal Welfare Ltd Raystede, Ringmer East Sussex, BN8 5AJ Tel: 01825 840252 www.raystede.org	Charity No. 237696 To prevent and relieve cruelty to animals and protect them from unnecessary suffering.	The Raystede Centre for Animal Welfare Ltd No national branch
The Seahorse Trust No local branch	Charity No. 1086027 Conservation of the natural world. We care about the welfare of seahorses.	Headquarters 36 Greatwood Terrace Topsham, Devon, EX3 0EB Tel: 01392 875930 www.theseahorsetrust.co.uk
The Siamese Cat Club Welfare Trust No local branch	Charity No. 1072366 We look after the welfare of Siamese cats. We operate a rescue and rehoming service and we foster unwanted cats.	The Siamese Cat Club Welfare Trust Lots of contacts around country Email: sccwt@siameserescue.org.uk www.siameserescue.org.uk
The Suffolk Horse Society No local branch	Charity No. 220756 To keep the Suffolk Horse breeding.	The Suffolk Horse Society The Market Hill, Woodbridge Suffolk, IP12 4LU Tel: 01394 380643 www.suffolkhorsesociety.org.uk
The Whale and Dolphin Conservation Society No local branch	Charity No. 1014705 The global voice for the protection of whales, dolphins and their environment.	The Whale and Dolphin Conservation Society Brookfield House, 38 St Paul Street Chippenham, Wiltshire, SN15 1LJ Tel: 0870 870 0027 www.wdcs.org.uk
The World Parrot Trust No local branch Worldwide branches - see website for details	Charity No. Not available Parrot conservation and welfare.	The World Parrot Trust Glanmor House, Hayle, Cornwall, TR27 4HB Tel: 01736 751026 www.worldparrottrust.org
Tortoise Trust No local branch	Charity No. Not available Campaign against illegal collecting and trade and pet store abuse.	BM Tortoise London, WC1N 3XX Tel: 01267 211578 www.tortoisetrust.org
Traffic No local branch	Charity No. 1076722. A donation to TRAFFIC supports research and action to ensure that trade in wild plants and animals is not a threat to the conservation of nature.	Traffic Worldwide branches. See website for details 219 Huntingdon Road, Cambridge, CB3 0DL Tel: 01223 277427 www.traffic.org
Vale Wildlife Rescue No local branch	Charity No. 702888 We at the Vale Rescue offer help to thousands of casualties every year by treating them and where possible, releasing them back into the wild.	Vale Wildlife Rescue Station Road, Beckford, Tewkesbury Gloucestershire, GL20 7AN Tel: 01386 882288 www.vwr.org.uk

FEATURES

Sussex Branch	Description	National
Veteran Horse Society No local branch	Charity No. 1104072 Rehabilitation centre for horses.	Veteran Horse Society Hendre Fawr Farm St Dogmaels, Cardigan North Pembrokeshire, SA43 3LZ Tel: 0870 242 6653 www.veteran-horse-society.co.uk
Wetnose Animal Campaign No local branch	Charity No. Not available Raising money and awareness for the sick and needy animals in the smaller Animal Rescue Centres.	Wetnose Animal Campaign Newgate Lodge, Newgate Kirby Cane, Norfolk, NR35 2PP Tel: 01508 518 650 www.wetnoseanimalaid.com
Wildfowl and Wetlands Trust Mill Road, Arundel Sussex, BN18 9PB Tel: 01903 883355	Charity No. 1030884 Our mission is to conserve wetlands and their biodiversity.	Wildfowl and Wetlands Trust WWT Slimbridge, Gloucester, GL2 7BT Tel: 0870 334 4000 www.wwt.org.uk
Wildlife Rescue Ambulance Service Stone Cross, Eastbourne, East Sussex, BN24 5QU www.wildlifeambulance.co.uk	Charity No. Not available 24-hour rescue service	Wildlife Rescue Ambulance Service No national branch
Woodgreen Animal Shelters No local branch	Charity No. Not available We take in unwanted and lost animals.	Wood Green Animal Shelters HQ Godmanchester Shelter Kings Bush Farm, London Road Godmanchester, Cambs, PE29 2NH Tel: 08701 904090 www.woodgreen.org.uk
World Society for the Protection of Animals No local branch	Charity No. 1081849 WSPA works with more than 500 member organisations to raise the standards of animal welfare throughout the world.	World Society for the Protection of Animals Worldwide branches. See website for details. 89 Albert Embankment London, SE1 7TP Tel: 020 7587 5000 www.wspa.org.uk
Worthing and District Cats Protection Branch 16 Dankton Lane Sompting, Lancing, West Sussex, BN15 0EA Tel: 01903 200332 www.worthingcatsprotection.org.uk	Charity No. 203644 Cats Protection was founded in 1927 and is the oldest national charity with over 250 branches nationally devoted solely to the welfare of cats.	Worthing and District Cats Protection Branch No national branch
Worthing Animal Clinic 30/32 Newland Road Worthing, West Sussex BN11 1JR Tel: 01903 202248 www.worthinganimal.co.uk	Charity No. 211467 Vet care to pets with limited means.	Worthing Animal Clinic No national branch
Worthing Cat Welfare Trust 36 Orchard Avenue Worthing, West Sussex BN14 7PY Tel: 01903 202251 www.worthingcatwelfare.co.uk	Charity No. 1049596 The charity consists of cat lovers who care for sick and distressed animals.	Worthing Cat Welfare Trust No national branch

FEATURES

When a pet dies
Coping with the passing of your treasured friend

If you have shared many years together, the death of your pet will not be unexpected. However, this does not mean to say that it will be easy. Likewise, if your pet dies prematurely, the shock of the event can be extremely traumatic. Psychologists generally agree that the feelings experienced by a bereaved pet owner are similar to those felt after losing a human friend or relative. The gap left by a faithful dog or cat can feel like a gaping chasm – and other people may not provide much sympathy or understanding, simply because the loss was not a human one.

Firstly, you may have to make the decision as to when to let your pet go. Less than one quarter of dogs die peacefully due to old age – which means that it may be you who decides when the time is right for euthanasia. If your animal is no longer able to eat and drink sufficiently in order to maintain normal bodily functions, or if it breathes with difficulty and cannot walk and move without pain, perhaps the time is right.

Of course, the vet may be able to offer medication to improve the general health of your pet, and his or her advice should always be sought.

The word euthanasia means 'gentle or easy death', and it takes the form of an intravenous injection of barbiturate. The animal should feel only the prick of the needle and it is unconscious within just a few seconds. If your animal is nervous about visiting the vet, a sedative given at home may make that final journey a little easier. Owners can usually choose whether to stay with their animal while the euthanasia takes place, or they can leave the surgery while the vet performs the procedure. It is always a good idea to see the body afterwards in order to say a final farewell.

It is important to think about the disposal of the body before you visit with the animal - you may find it difficult to make a decision immediately after such an upsetting event. There are basically two options: cremation and burial.

Domestic pet remains can usually be buried in your own garden or in a pet cemetery. If choosing the former, contact your local authority to check there are no objections. Deceased pets are classed as clinical waste and they should be buried at least 1.25 metres down, away from water courses, underground pipes and cables. Use biodegradable wrappings such as a blanket or towel rather than plastic. A grave can be a source of great comfort and the long-

In loving memory of Widgit. Disobedient to the last.
ROB WILLARD. SUMMER 2005

FEATURES

term benefits of remembering your old friend by the grave should not be underestimated.

If you cannot or do not want to bury your animal in the garden but like the idea of being able to visit a burial grave, consider a pet cemetery. This is a more expensive option, however, and may cost up to £350. The service usually includes collecting the pet's body, preparing the grave and performing the burial. The pet cemetery may also sell coffins, memorial stones and sometimes offer a memorial service too. There is sometimes an annual maintenance charge to pay.

Cremation is becoming increasingly popular. It is considered to be both practical and hygienic. If you decide to leave the body at the veterinary surgery, it will usually be routinely disposed of by means of a communal cremation. The ashes are generally buried at the crematorium.

You may be able to keep your pet's own ashes by arranging an individual cremation, either through the vet or directly with a crematorium. This can cost up to £150 and a full range of services may be offered. They may include a certificate stating that the ashes returned in a receptacle to you are those solely of your pet. There may be a memorial garden where they can be scattered or you may choose to keep the ashes.

Ask your vet for details of your local contact. Alternatively, The Association of Private Pet Cemeteries and Crematoria can provide details of your nearest establishment. Visit the website at **www.appcc.org.uk**.

You will probably experience many emotions after your loss, including shock, denial, anger, guilt and possibly depression. Give yourself plenty of time to accept and recover from the event and don't be ashamed to get help if you don't think you are coping. Talk about your loss and consider attending a local support group for bereaved pet owners if there is one available. Meanwhile, look after your physical needs and indulge in small pleasures. Treat your inner feelings as you would a small child and you will gradually come to terms with your loss.

Finally, when your spirits lift when you see a puppy's wagging tail, or when your eyes light up on hearing the purr of a kitten, you will know it's time to start the entire process again! After all, we animal lovers all know that the pain of loss is a small price to pay for the potential years of unconditional comfort and love that come from having a pet.

Practice makes perfect
How to help an animal fit in with your life

Acquiring a pet is probably the easiest stage of owning an animal. Responsible pet owners then set about the task of training it. This applies to almost every type of animal - from the simplest goldfish through to the largest horse. You may think that fish don't need training, and to a certain extent this may be true. But they soon learn when to expect meals and will benefit from learning how to endure being moved from their aquarium or pond with the least possible upset.

In many cases such as the above, repetition is the key to success. Your goldfish will soon know that you feed him first thing in the morning and he will become visibly excited when he sees you approaching. Your pet rabbit may wriggle and squirm when you first pick him up, but he will learn that you mean him no harm and that the experience can be enjoyable. Your pet snake will need to be taught how to behave while being handled and your cat will be a more acceptable member of the family if he doesn't sharpen his claws on the antique furniture.

Of course, dogs respond exceptionally well to training. They can easily understand human speech and as a pack animal, their social needs can be adequately met within a human family. Training should encourage the basic natural instincts of a dog. Those dogs that are developed for working should do what comes naturally and learn the human words for their various manoeuvres. If their instincts are undesirable, however, their energy can be directed into more socially acceptable activities.

Informal training should take place almost immediately an animal joins a household. You must show your pet that you are the leader – therefore you decide when to feed and exercise him. Badly behaved dogs can be a menace to everyone, and a dog that bites people or other animals represents a danger that should be permanently removed.

Get into the habit of training your dog to allow you to take away his feed bowl at any time you wish. Use an appropriate word to stop the animal eating mid-way through his meal, take away the bowl for a few seconds and providing he did not grumble, praise your dog and allow him to continue his food. Training your dog around food is one of the most important lessons he can learn, for the natural instinct of a hunting dog is to guard his food possessively.

Coming when called is another highly valuable lesson. You can do this right from day one by calling your dog to come for dinner. He will want the food and will therefore naturally be willing to oblige. Coming to you should be an enjoyable exercise – no dog is going to want to come running to an owner who then shouts angry abuse at him. Don't allow your dog to jump up as this can be socially unacceptable. Encourage him to sit when he meets new people and his reward can be a tasty treat or a loving stroke.

be. An ill-mannered horse, for example, can be a real danger to humans, especially children. A horse, pony or donkey will need to be taught good manners such as not biting or kicking, standing still while it is being groomed or tacked up, and of course behaving predictably while being ridden.

The training of any animal cannot not be rushed. Schooling a horse can take several years and training a dog may last

Dogs and their owners both benefit from good training

Formal training with a dog can involve walking to heel, fetching, waiting, staying and all sorts of associated changes of position. This can be done as a group in training classes, or at home. As with any training, the emphasis should be on fun – a bored dog will soon lose interest and stop wanting to please the leader of the pack.

In general terms, the larger the animal, the more important training can

its entire lifetime! As with children, having a pet is both an honour and a responsibility that should not be taken lightly. The result, however, is well worth the effort. Not only will your pet blend in with your family life in the easiest and most enjoyable way, but your relationship with the animal will be enriched because of the understanding and communication that you have developed.

Puzzle pages
Seek your answers from the natural world

QUICK CROSSWORD

ACROSS:
2 A system of chronology tells us we are backward (3)
5 Lions do it without cooking (4)
7 A spider likes to do what is not religious (4)
8 Horsing around with Greek mythology (7)
10 Dark tunes in the wind (11)
13 This female features in a well known song (3)
15 A variegated horse (6)
17 The early one doesn't catch the fastest (4)
18 Soft feathers are on their way down (5)

DOWN:
1 Eight reasons to have a phobia (8)
2 Unbleached linen (4)
3 Monkeying around without a tail (3)
4 This spotted cat could be good at tennis (6)
6 This rodent is good at giving thanks back (3)
9 An industrious small, social insect (3)
11 American burrowing rodent is good at fetching (6)
12 From a chrysalis doth a butterfly ......(6)
14 JK Rowling uses them as postmen (4)
16 You palindrome (3)

YOU'RE HAVING A LAUGH!

Why did the cow cross the road?
Because the chicken was on holiday

What's the fastest animal?
A railway lion

Why are owls the funniest creatures?
Because they think everything is a hoot

What did the Scotsman say when he was locked in the toilet?
A kangaroot, a kangaroot

Why do sheep always itch and scratch on fences?
Because they all have fleece

Why did the bald man have pictures of rabbits tattooed on his head?
He thought they might look like hares

WORDSEARCH

Find 30 hidden words that fall within the subjects of habitats, exotic animals and British animals:
Rainforest; gardens; desert; woodland; sea; wetland; mountains; lowland; river; lake; meercat; lioness; tortoise; dolphin; whale; giraffe; elephant; cheetah; wombat; gorilla; alsatian; donkey; peacock; woodpecker; sparrow; crab; kingfisher; squirrel; newt; vole.

```
M A L A S B T E H I K C O C A E P R O X S L L T
E E Y B E L I D S O E B E L Z I Q U I N N O T D
N W E V A C A B D H E I J L K M F P N Q W W R P
U P L R H Y L F E D C X N B V I W E T L A N D S
A S E Z C Y S B N I K E L O V T R E A N T D G N
I E D L R A A Y T R Q A S H B V C N T F N I M I
S E O J A V T X R T Y U A S M N D V I U U R K A
H K N D B I I K P M U Y R Q P E A C O C K A P T
K A K H O H A T E E H C R U Y G F D J K I O L N
E L E P H A N T G E W L A I E D U H G S N Q U U
F G Y Y U J H O K I J I U R Y F T D Y H G J T O
G T F F Y U K R Y F D R I V E R Y H U I F J O M
H I U Y N E W T O P R K N E W C R T L I I K J T
Y G T F T F Y O U H E R D L E H N I I E S L M S
B B G V F C M I G N K Y N U O P A T O J H G F E
L N M L G O I S T L C B I C E S A L N O E T I R
E G I R A F F E A Y E I H H G B N M E L R A H O
R C X D R R T Y B E P K P J H G F D S E L A E F
R O P I D F D C M A D M L N B Z Q A S L R T Y N
I J H S E A R T O K O O O K J A I E I N B V C I
U R Y U N O K J W W O O D L A N D R L N B V D A
Q K A L S P A R R O W E S T G V O X Y U I O L R
S I F T H R I T W W E L D O P G A E L O P R I T
```

FEATURES

Owning a pet
A humourous guide to pet-keeping

The first rule to observe on the road to owning an animal is that of unselfishness. Never again will you be able to put yourself first.

Much like children, your pet will ensure that your own needs and desires come at the bottom of the pecking order. This applies particularly if you have a dog or cat, who tend to rule the timetable completely. It is also relevant for hoofed animals such as horses, ponies and donkeys, who ensure that you bear their needs in mind at all times and whatever the weather. Come to think of it, the same rule applies to caged animals such as birds, rabbits, mice, hamsters and guinea pigs, chickens, reptiles, insects, arachnids and fish. Just about everything, then.

Not only do these creatures need feeding at regular intervals, exercising, cleaning, stimulating, training, stroking and soothing, but they also need love, care and compassion. Sometimes you won't feel that you are capable of either loving or feeling compassion for the hamster that just drew blood from your thumb, for the dog that brought muddy footprints into the lounge or for the pony that just crushed all the bones in your toes.

So the second step to becoming a pet owner is to practise your acting skills. You must pretend to adore your animal every minute of the day, whatever it gets up to. And even if you scold your pet severely, it should always be able to trust your behaviour. Your dog will quickly understand that you are seething about the muddy carpet, your hamster

will definitely feel the vibes of rage that emit just when he was hoping to tuck into a juicy treat and your pony will be quite offended by your swear words as you soothe your crumpled toes – but the punishment should not be unjust. You may feel like altering the appearance of your pet forever, but if you lash out in anger you will destroy all the valuable trust that you had been carefully building for weeks and even months.

The third rule to observe before you become a pet keeper is to research your animal. A red setter or a border collie is not suitable for a high rise flat. A dalmatian is probably not the best companion for a little old lady with arthritis and a horse may not be ideal for someone who works 24/7. A tarantula will not guarantee restful sleep in a household containing a member with an arachnid phobia and a cat may not be perfect for those suffering from certain allergies.

Finally, remind yourself constantly that your animal is enriching your life. This is in spite of the fact that your purse is always empty. Animals are expensive and they will endeavour to help you empty your pockets of cash on a regular basis. Not only is there food to consider, but housing, bedding, vet bills, insurance, holiday care and many other unforeseen costs. Of course the rewards are well worth it … if only I could remember what they are.

Directory of services

192-193   Alternative Therapies

194   Animal Artists

195-197   Animal Sanctuaries

198-206   Animal Supplies
- Pet Foods
- Pet Shops

207-209   Aquatics

210-213   Attractions

214-219   Boarding

220   Charity Organisations

221-223   Club & Societies

224-235   Conservation

236-246   Country Parks & Gardens

247-250   Dog Training
- Animal Behaviourists

251-257   Equine
- Livery Stables
- Riding Schools
- Saddle & Harness Makers
- Stable Manufacturers
- Stud Farms

258-261   Grooming Services

262-263   Hotels & B&Bs

264   Pet Heaven
- Crematorium & Cemeteries

265-268   Pet Minding

269   Pet Services & Information

270-277   Veterinary Surgeries

278-280   Working Animal Centres

BEXHILL-ON-SEA

Equine Shiatsu Practitioner
Practitioner for horses and ponies
Sessions for riders available also
3a Collington Mansions, Collington Avenue,
Bexhill on Sea, East Sussex, TN39 3PU.
Tel: 07913 058762.
e-mail: shiatsukaren@tesco.net
Contact: Karen Pennell.
Opening hours: By appointment.

A wealth of experience in equine management
and consultancy, offering Shiatsu and physical
therapy with comprehensive service for equines
and owners. Professional, reliable, fully
qualified, registered and insured. Friendly and
down to earth. Holistic approach. Shiatsu has
been developed for horses using ancient
wisdom and modern theories and physical
techniques. Pressure points, meridian work,
stretches, rotations, percussion and massage.
A relaxing experience aiming to rebalance the
body and mind. Vets must be aware of this
treatment taking place.

BRIGHTON

Rose Holistic Health
Complementary Therapist
67 Ewhurst Road, Brighton,
East Sussex, BN2 4AL.
Tel: 01273 299611.
e-mail: joroseholistic@yahoo.co.uk
web: www.roseholistichealth.com
Contact: Jo Rose.
Opening hours: Tuesday to Friday, some
Sundays (courses).
Course costs: £60 per person for initial day
and £25 for follow up half-day workshop.

Over 7 years' experience, can come to you.
Combining Reiki and kinesiology. Runs Reiki
Practitioner and Intuitive Healing courses for
animal lovers Course venues all have facilities.
Refreshments offered. 1st Degree Reiki
Practitioner Courses:- For Horse Lovers' - 4th
June, nr Hassocks, For Dog Lovers' - 6th
August (venue tba), For Horse Lovers' - 1st
October, Upper Beeding. Specialises in horses
and dogs. Also a British Horse Society
Intermediate Riding teacher. From September
will be offering Touch for Health Kinesiology
Training. Please call for more details.

EAST HOATHLY, Nr Lewes

East Hoathly Pet Centre
Homeopathy, Herbal Medicine,
Acupuncture and Chiropractic treatment
The Holistic Veterinary Centre,
The Village Works, London Road,
East Hoathly, Lewes, East Sussex, BN8 6QA.
Tel: 01825 840966.
Opening hours: By appointment only.
Cover all of Sussex, Kent and Surrey. Any animal
tended to. Home and stable visits.

DIRECTORY

FELPHAM, Nr Bognor Regis

Colour Therapy Healing
Private complementary therapy practice
High Banks, 108 Limmer Lane, Felpham,
Nr Bognor Regis, West Sussex, PO22 7LP.
Tel: 01243 585609. **Fax:** 01243 585609.
e-mail: valerie@colourtherapyhealing.com
web: www.colourtherapyhealing.com
Contact: Valerie Logan-Clarke.

Opening hours: 9.30am to 5.30pm.
Regular monthly one-day workshops on colour
therapy for humans and other animals.

PUNNETT'S TOWN

Equilibrium Therapy
All types of horses treated
St Vito, Flitterbrook Lane, Punnetts Town,
Nr Heathfield, East Sussex, TN21 9PQ.
Tel: 01435 830701.
e-mail: saminuk@hotmail.com
web: www.equilibriumtherapy.co.uk
Contact: S. Richardson.
Opening hours: Monday to Saturday.
Fees: £30 per treatment, plus travel costs.

SIDLESHAM

Therapaws
Swimming pool and canine agility
Street End Lane, Sidlesham, Chichester,
West Sussex, PO20 7RG.
Tel: 01243 641114.
Contact: Julie Grantham.
Opening hours: Tuesday to Friday, 9am to
5pm. Saturday, 8.30am to 3pm.
Admission: Prices available.

Directions: B2145 to Selsey. Second village is
Sidlesham. At pub on sharp bend, turn left and
it is signposted.

ST LEONARDS ON SEA

Internal Arts
Specialises in horses, dogs and cats.
Member of the Holistic Healing Association
61 Westfield Lane, St Leonards on Sea
East Sussex TN37 7NF.
Tel: 07950 264204.
e-mail: info@internalarts.co.uk
web: www.internalarts.co.uk/healing
Contact: Rob Willard.
Service available all week, not set times.
Will travel to clients.

Directions: Junction off A21 towards Ashford
and Westfield.

TWINEHAM

Canine Hydro Healing
Specialises in dogs
Hillmans Farm and Business Centre
Bolney Chapel Road, Twineham
West Sussex, RH17 5NN.
Tel: 01444 882938. **Fax:** 01444 882938.
web: www.k9hh.co.uk
Contact: Helen McDonald.
Opening hours: Monday to Friday,
9am to 5pm. Saturday, 9am to 1pm.

Directions: Off A23/M23 motorway, next to
Hickstead Show Jumping Ground.

WEST CHILTINGTON

The White Orchid
Large heated indoor hydrotherapy pool
for dogs. Treat animals with Reiki
Harbolets Road, West Chiltington,
West Sussex, RH20 2LG.
Tel: 01798 815191.
Contact: Mandy Govier.
Opening hours: Tuesday to Saturday,
10am to 6.30pm.
Admission: A price list is available.

Directions: On B2133. Directions available.

DIRECTORY

BEXHILL-ON-SEA

The Studio
Capture those special memories
live in our studio
31 Sackville Road, Bexhill on Sea,
East Sussex, TN39 3JD.
Tel: 01424 212301.
e-mail: sue@thestudiobexhilll.co.uk
Contact: Sue Jackson.
Opening hours: By appointment.

Directions: From Bexhill town centre, turn into
Western Road and Sackville Road is at the end.
Friendly, relaxed, air-conditioned studio or on
location. Capturing special memories of your
cherished pet. Refreshments available.
Photograph any pet you have.

BOGNOR REGIS

Hells Bells Art & Illustration
Unique Animal Portrait Service
47 Essex Road, Bognor Regis,
West Sussex, PO21 2BU.
Tel: 01243 870815.
e-mail: hellsbells@keepontrucking.co.uk
Contact: Helen Yeo.
Traditional, fine art, portraits and humorous
cariacatures of your pet can be commissioned.
Experienced animal artist – official illustrator for
Animal Lovers' Guides. Will create your personal
portrait to your exacting specifications, creating
a unique work of art. Horses and household
pets a speciality. Signed limited edition prints
are also available.

*Only female
ants can sting.*

SALEHURST, ROBERTSBRIDGE

Hayley Tipler
Beautifully detailed portraits and
illustrations from photographs
13 Andrews Close, Salehurst, Robertsbridge,
East Sussex, TN32 5PB.
Tel: 01580 880633.
e-mail: hayleyandthierry@aol.com
Contact: Hayley Tipler.
Opening hours: By appointment.
Wonderful portraits and illustrations of your
pet. All animals undertaken.

WILMINGTON

Josie Tipler Animal Portraits
Quiet country studio of animal
loving artist with cats, dogs, chickens
and a donkey!
Magpie Cottage, Hayreed Lane
(Off Thornwell Road), Wilmington, Polegate,
East Sussex, BN26 6RR.
Tel: 01323 485153.
web: www.josietipler.co.uk
Contact: Josie Tipler.
Directions: From A27 Polegate to Lewes. Turn
right at Wilmington into Thornwell Road. Hayreed
Lane is on your left after about one mile.

Opening hours: By appointment.
Quiet country studio. Refreshments available
during exhibitions. Art classes for adults and
children (details on application). Open studios and
exhibitions in June and September. Dogs, cats,
horses and any animal painted in watercolour or
acrylics, pencil or chalk pastel. I have occasional
stalls at craft and animal events.

CHICHESTER

Noah's Ark

Get close to many small animals and
reptiles that have been rescued

133 Almodington Lane, Chichester,
West Sussex, PO20 7JR (based at Earnley
Butterflies and Gardens)
Tel: 07961 516731.
web: www.noahs-ark.freeuk.com
Opening hours: Open all year around except
Christmas Eve, Christmas Day and Boxing Day.
Call to enquire.

Directions: Off the A27 Chichester bypass.
Learn about the reptiles' needs at the
education centre. Help the animals by
sponsorships or donations. Boarding facilities
available. Picnic area, refreshments, crazy golf
and gift shop. Call to enquire about events.
Farmyard animals, chinchillas, chipmunks and
rabbits. Lizards, snakes and tortoises.

EASTBOURNE

East Sussex Wildlife Rescue

Rescue and rehabilitation of animals

c/o 8 Stour Close, Stone Cross, Eastbourne,
East Sussex, BN24 5QU.
Tel: 07815 078234.
e-mail: info@wildlifeambulance.co.uk
web: www.wildlifeambulance.co.uk
Rescue service for all types of animals. 24-hour
emergency line. Provides education and training.
Run by volunteers. Receive about 2,000-3,000
calls per year. Facilities for rehabilitation provide
advice and supporters' group.

FINDON VILLAGE

Paws Animal Sanctuary

Sanctuary for donkeys, horses, dogs,
cats, rabbits, ferrets, chinchillas, chickens
and mice

Squirrels Cottage, 15 The Oval, Findon Village,
West Sussex, BN14 0TN.
Tel: 01903 872734.
Contact: Stacey McSpirit.
Opening hours: 24-hour advice line.

Open to the public on open days. Saturdays for
rehoming, delivering and adopting. Also specialise
in gerbils, parrots, lovebirds and canaries.

HADLOW DOWN

Kit Wilson Trust for Animal Welfare

Rehoming of cats, dogs and other
domestic animals

Kit Wilson Trust, Stonehurst Lane
Hadlow Down, Nr Uckfield.
East Sussex, TN22 4ED.
Tel: 01825 830444. **Fax:** 01825 830887.
e-mail: colette.kwt@tiscali.co.uk
web: www.kitwilsontrust.org.uk
Opening hours: By appointment only.

See website for details of events. Wildlife
rehabiliation, cats, dogs, horses, donkeys, goats,
birds and small rodents. Reception and toilets.
Limited disabled access. Please call before visiting.

HORSTED KEYNES

Animaline

Wildlife Rescue Centre

Broadhurst Manor, Broadhurst Manor Road,
Horsted Keynes, Nr Haywards Heath,
West Sussex, RH17 7BS.
Tel: 01342 810596. **Fax:** 01342 811377.
web: www.animaline@carlalane.com
Contact: Carla Lane.
Opening hours: Not open to public.

DIRECTORY

MIDHURST

Bulldog Rescue and Rehoming Service
Rehoming Bulldogs across the country
PO Box 18, Midhurst, West Sussex, GU29 9YU.
Tel: 01730 810531. **Fax:** 01730 815422.
e-mail: bulldogrescue@btinternet.com
web: www.bulldogrescue.co.uk
Contact: David and Tania Holmes.
Opening hours: Monday, Tuesday, Thursday
and Friday, 11am to 5pm.
Directions: See website for details.
Bulldog rescue and rehoming centre. We will
do our very best to find the right home for
each dog that passes through the rescue
system from our extensive list of people right
across the country willing to offer a second
chance to this most loveable of breeds. See
website for details.

NATIONAL

Bichon Frise Rescue
Bichon Frise Rescue Group
Part of a national organisation.
No public premises.
Tel: 01323 521522.
e-mail: derek@thebriggs.plus.com
web: www.bichonfriserescue.co.uk
Contact: Derek A Briggs.
Opening hours: Not open to public.
By arrangement only.

NEWHAVEN

The Guinea Pig Rescue Centre
Animal rescue centre
6 Northdown Road, Newhaven,
East Sussex, BN9 9JB.
Tel: 01273 512248. **Fax:** 01273 512248.
e-mail: illingworthlouis@aol.com
Contact: Louise Jenkins.
Opening hours: Daily, 9am to 7pm.

Directions: Off the A259 South Coast Road.
We attend the Animal Lovers' Day at Brighton
Greyhound Stadium. Rehoming of guinea pigs.

PEACEHAVEN

Cat Rescue
Rehoming of cats and rabbits
19 Fairlight Avenue, Telscombe Cliffs,
Peacehaven, East Sussex, BN10 7BN.
Tel: 01273 580464.
Contact: Debbie Campain.
Opening hours: 10am to 4pm.

Rescue cats, rabbits and guinea pigs.

RINGMER

The Raystede Centre for Animal Welfare
Over 1,000 animals to see. No admission
though donations are welcome
The Raystede Centre, Raystede, Ringmer,
East Sussex, BN8 5AT.
Tel: 01825 840252. **Fax:** 01825 840995.
Web: www.raystede.org
Contact: Morgan Williams.
Opening hours: Daily, 10am and 4pm.
Admission: No charge.

Directions: Situated on the B2192 between
Ringmer and Halland.

SIDLEY, NR BEXHILL

Barby Keel Animal Sanctuary
A sanctuary for all unwanted animals
Freezeland Lane, Sidley, Bexhill,
East Sussex, TN39 5JD.
Tel: 01424 222032.
Contact: Barby Keel.
Opening hours: Sundays, 2-5pm. Every other
day by appointment.
Admission: Charge on open days.

Early August open days.

SIDLESHAM, NR CHICHESTER

The Cat & Rabbit Rescue Centre
Rescues cats, rabbits and guinea pigs
Holborow Lodge, Chalder Lane, Sidlesham,
Chichester, West Sussex, PO20 7RJ.
Tel: 01243 641409.
e-mail: info@crrc.co.uk
web: www.crrc.co.uk
Contact: Monique Turk.
Opening hours: Visits by appointment only.
Admission: Only event days.

Further details available by phone.

TUNBRIDGE WELLS

The Folly Wildlife Rescue Trust
Dedicated to the rescue of injured,
orphaned or distressed wildlife
Folly Cottage, Danegate, Eridge Green,
Tunbridge Wells, Kent, TN3 9JB.
Tel: 01892 750865. **Fax:** 01892 750337.
e-mail: info@follywildliferescue.org.uk
web: www.follywildliferescue.org.uk
Contact: Mr D Risley.
Opening hours: By appointment.

Directions: See website for details.
Thousands of animals are treated at the centre
and the vast majority of these are successfully
returned to the wild. It is our aim and ambition
to open a purpose-designated wildlife hospital
where the optimum facilities to treat and
rehabilitate casualties can be provided, together
with an Education Centre where the important
work of raising public awareness of wildlife can
be built upon.

UCKFIELD

Sussex Horse Rescue Trust
Mainly horse and donkey rescue, but also
pigs, sheep, cows, llamas, goats and chickens
Hempstead Farm, Hempstead Lane,
Uckfield, East Sussex, TN22 3DL.
Tel: 01825 762010.
Contact: Pauline Grant.
Opening hours: Sundays only, 11am to 4pm
Easter to September.
Admission: Adults £2.00 Children £1.00

Directions: London Road north from Uckfield.
Turn right into Browns Lane and sixth turning
on left is Hempstead Lane.
Tea bar, barn shop, bric-a-brac, clothes, pony
rides and toilets. Please phone to find out
about special events. Education information
about animal welfare, primarily equine.

WOODINGDEAN

Roger's Wildlife Rescue
Wildlife Rescue Centre
37 Downs Valley Road, Woodingdean,
Brighton, East Sussex, BN2 6RG.
Tel: 01273 308268.
e-mail: fleurmusselle@tiscali.co.uk
Contact: Roger Musselle.
Opening hours: By appointment – please call.

DIRECTORY

BRIGHTON

Dog Dogs Bakery
Healthy handmade dog treats
4 Briarcroft Road, Brighton,
East Sussex, BN2 6LL.
Tel: 01273 275128. **Fax:** 01273 273850.
e-mail: people@dogdogs.co.uk
web: www.dogdogs.co.uk
Contact: Samantha King-Grant.
Opening hours: Online ordering.

Dog treats handmade with love, biscuits and
cakes for dogs. Personalised, healthy and
yummy. Order online as we do not yet have a
store front.

CROWBOROUGH

The Pet Food Shop
Wide range of animal feeds and supplies.
No animals sold here
Croft Road, Crowborough,
East Sussex, TN6 1DL.
Tel: 01892 662961.
Opening hours: Monday to Friday, 9am
to 5.30pm. Saturday, 9am to 5pm.

Bird seed to hamster food sold here.

EASTBOURNE

Enterprise Centre
All animal food and accessories sold
Enterprise Centre, Station Parade, Eastbourne,
East Sussex, BN21 1BD.
Tel: 01323 725593.
Contact: A Reynolds.
Opening hours: Monday to Saturday, 9am to
5pm.

Directions: By Eastbourne Railway Station.
Free local home delivery.

EASTERGATE

SPR Centre
Animal feeds. Horses and poultry specialists
Greenfields Farm, Fontwell Avenue, Eastergate,
Chichester, West Sussex, PO20 3RU.
Tel: 01243 542815. **Fax:** 01243 544662.
e-mail: info@sprcentre.co.uk
web: www.sprcentre.co.uk
Contact: David Bland.
Opening hours: Monday to Friday, 8.30am
to 6pm. Saturday and Sunday, 9am to 6pm.

Directions: A29 south of Fontwell Avenue.

EAST GRINSTEAD

Hayden Feeds
Everything your pet could wish for, feed
and accessories
Orchard Farm, Holty Road, East Grinstead,
West Sussex, RH19 3PP.
Tel: 01342 323113.
Contact: Joan Hayden.
Opening hours:
6 days a week, 9.15am to 5.30pm.

Directions: On A264 about 1 mile from centre
of town.
Some Saturday smallholder open events with
10% discount. Horses, farm animals, dogs,
cats, chickens plus hutches.

GORING-BY-SEA

Shoreline Pet Supplies
Pet food specialist
278 Goring Road, Goring-by-Sea, Worthing,
West Sussex, BN12 4PE.
Tel: 01903 243100.
e-mail: shoreline-pets@btconnect.com
Contact: Davina Angell.
Opening hours: Monday to Saturday, 9am
to 5.30pm. Sunday, 10am to 1pm. Closed on
bank holidays.

Directions: In the Mulberry Parade.

LEWES

Oscar Pet Foods
Free home delivery pet shop for cats
and dogs
18 Hawkenbury Way, Lewes,
East Sussex, BN7 1LT.
Tel: 01273 479064.
e-mail: tracy.amarsh@btinternet.com
web: www.oscars.co.uk
Contacts: Cliff and Tracy Marsh.
Home delivery throughout Sussex.
We attend various open days including Plumpton
College and RSPCA Patcham. Food for dogs, cats,
small furry animals and specialise in dogs with poor
appetites, skin and coat conditions.

LONDON

Husse
Pet food delivery with a full range for dogs
and cats. Free to your door with local
distributors
H Office, Unit 8, Windsor Pk Estate,
50 Windsor Avenue, London, SW19 2TJ.
Tel: 020 8544 0111. **Fax:** 020 8544 0304.
e-mail: uk@husse.com
web: www.husse.com
Contact: Dominque Smith.
Opening hours: Please ring. Various distributors.

NR UCKFIELD

Hurstwood Feeds Ltd
All animal and pet foods
Vulcan House Farm, Coopers Green,
Nr Uckfield, East Sussex, TN22 4AT.
Tel: 01825 733073.
Contact: Elaine Maybury.
Opening hours: Monday to Saturday,
8.30am to 5.30pm.

Directions: On A272 between Coopers Green
and Buxted.

PEACEHAVEN

Bonnie's News & Pet Supplies
Bulk pet supplies, horsefeed and wild
bird products
140-144 South Coast Road, Peacehaven,
East Sussex, BN10 8ER.
Tel: 01273 580777.
e-mail: mandymoss2000@yahoo.com
Contact: Amanda.
Opening hours: Monday to Friday, 6.30am
to 5pm. Wednesday and Saturday, 6.30am
to 1pm.

DIRECTORY

DIRECTORY

SHOREHAM-BY-SEA

Living World

Specialises in pigeon sundries and
horse feeds

28 Kingston Broadway,
Shoreham-by-Sea, West Sussex.
Tel: 01273 595779.
Contact: Ian Hollis.
Opening hours: Monday to Friday, 9am to
5.30pm. Saturday, 9am to 5pm.

Directions: Kingston Broadway runs parallel with
Old Shoreham Road. Adjacent to Holmbush
Shopping Centre. Stockists of GEM, Verselle Laga
and Buctons Corn.

ST LEONARDS ON SEA

The Dawg's Biscuits

Bakery selling dawganic healthy
homemade dog treats

65 Norman Road, St Leonards on Sea,
East Sussex, TN38 0EG.
Tel: 01424 424682.
e-mail: talkbix@dog-treat.co.uk
web: www.dog-treat.co.uk
Contact: Valerie May.
Opening hours: Monday to Friday, 10am
to 1pm and 3pm to 5.30pm.

Treats for dogs and cats.

Oscar Pet Foods

Free home delivery of pet food and
accessories. Free nutritional advice to help
you choose the right food for your dogs
and cats. Free try before you buy and
money backguarantee. Home
microchipping service

St Leonards on Sea, East Sussex.
Tel: 01424 753367.
e-mail: djarvis@oscars.co.uk
Web: www.oscars.co.uk
Contact: David and Dawn Jarvis
Home delivery only.

NATIONWIDE

Oscar Pet Foods

Free home delivery of pet food and
accessories. Free nutritional advice to help
you choose the right food for your dogs
and cats. Free try before you buy and
money backguarantee. Home
microchipping service

Horsham, West Sussex.
Tel: 01403 791756.
Email: tim.ives@oscars.co.uk
Web: www.oscars.co.uk
Contact: Tim Ives.
Home delivery only.

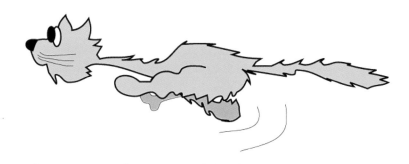

BARNHAM

Elite Pets

Bird specialist at the Barnham Windmill.
Everything for the serious bird keeper, plus
guinea pigs, rabbits, hamsters
Units 13-18, Parsonage Farm, Yapton Road,
Barnham, West Sussex, PO22 0BD.
Tel: 01243 554311.
Contact: Clive Porter.
Opening hours: Tuesday to Saturday, 9am to
5pm. Sunday, 10am to 4pm. Monday, closed.

Directions: At Barnham Windmill on B2233
between Barnham and Yapton.
Tea room on site. Specialise in birds. Dogs must
be kept under control in livestock rooms.

BOGNOR REGIS

Aldwick Pets

Specialise in small animals. Do
microchipping and free claw clipping.
Board small animals
87 Aldwick Road, Bognor Regis,
West Sussex, PO21 2NW.
Tel: 01243 869444.
e-mail: aldwickpets@aol.com
web: www.freewebs.com/aldwickpets
Contact: Sam Bolton.
Opening hours: Monday to Saturday, 9.30am
to 6pm. Sunday, 10.30am to 4.30pm.
Wednesday, closed.

Directions: Opposite Tesco Express, near the
junction with Nywood Lane.

It is illegal to get a fish drunk in the state of Ohio.

BRIGHTON

K9 by Igloo Designs

Designers and producers of
upmarket pet accessories
Unit 4, Level 6, New England House,
New England Street, Brighton,
East Sussex, BN1 4GH.
Tel: 01273 686263.
Fax: 01273 677287.
e-mail: info@igloodesigns.co.uk
web: www.igloodesigns.co.uk
Contact: Samantha Ruffell-Smith.
Opening hours: Monday to Friday,
Mail order 9am to 5.30pm.

Pampermepet

Speciality clothes for Chihauhaus
16 Imperial Arcade, Brighton,
East Sussex, BN1 3EA.
Tel: 01273 746273.
e-mail: pampermepet@hotmail.com
web: www.pampermepet.co.uk
Contact: Roisin Murphy.
Opening hours: Monday to Saturday, 10am
to 6pm. Sunday, 11am to 4pm.

Directions: From London off M23.
We also do speciality shows in the area.

Repco Herpetological Supply

Specialist supplier of captive bred reptiles
132 Preston Drove, Brighton,
East Sussex, BN1 6FJ.
Tel: 01273 553303.
e-mail: simcrun@aol.com
web: www.repcoreptiles.co.uk
Contact: Rob Crunden.
Opening hours: Monday to Saturday, 9am
to 5.30pm.

Directions: Near to Preston Park, just off A23.
Reptiles and amphibians with some tarantulas.

BURGESS HILL

Feathers and Firs
Parrot specialist
289a London Road, Burgess Hill,
West Sussex, RH15 9RU,
Tel: 01444 239545,
Contact: Richard Callant.
Opening hours: Tuesday to Saturday, 9am to 6pm. Sunday, 10am to 4pm. Monday, closed.

CROWBOROUGH

Ultimate Animals
An Aladin's cave of pet supplies for all kinds of pets
1 Beech View Parade, Walshes Road,
Crowborough, East Sussex, TN6 3RA.
Tel: 01892 667733. **Fax:** 01892 660151.
e-mail: info@ultimateanimals.co.uk
web: www.ultimateanimals.co.uk
Contact: Dianne Augustine.
Opening hours: Monday to Friday, 9am to 5.30pm. Saturday, 9am to 5pm. Sundays and bank holidays, closed.

Everyday and extra special pet products are supplied by friendly staff. Visit our shop or shop online.

DITCHLING

Garden Pride Garden Centre
Fish and pet centre as well as garden centre
Common Lane, Ditchling, Hassocks,
East Sussex, BN6 8TP.
Tel: 01273 846844. **Fax:** 01273 845540.
e-mail: info@garden-pride.com
web: www.garden-pride.com
Contact: David Jermyn.
Opening hours: Monday to Saturday, 9am to 6pm. Sunday, 10.30am to 4.30pm.

Directions: 3/4 of a mile north of Ditchling village on the B2112.
Disabled toilet also available. Dogs must be on a lead.

EAST GRINSTEAD

Goughs
Specialise in small animals
34 Railway Approach, East Grinstead,
West Sussex, RH19 1BP.
Tel: 01342 322255.
Contact: Beki Maycock.
Opening hours: Monday, Tuesday, Thursday, Friday and Saturday, 9am to 5.30pm. Wednesday, closed.

Directions: 700 yards from railway station, near town centre.
Specialise in small animals such as rabbits, guinea pigs, hamsters. Lots of knowledge about other animals.

HASTINGS

Pet Pride
Pet shop and grooming parlour
370 Old London Road, Hastings,
East Sussex, TN35 5BB.
Tel: 01424 425238.
Contact: Mrs Anne Webb.
Opening hours: Monday to Saturday, 9am
to 5pm. Wednesday, 9am to 1pm only.
Directions: On the A259.

HAYWARDS HEATH

The Pet and Garden Warehouse
One-stop shop for entire pet needs
Unit 1, 30 Bridge Road, Haywards Heath,
West Sussex, RH16 1TX.
Tel: 01444 474019. **Fax:** 01444 474074.
Contact: Stuart Goacher.
Opening hours: Monday to Saturday, 8am
to 6pm. Sunday, 10am to 2pm.

HOLLINGTON

Tammy's Pet Store
Specialise in tropical and cold water fish.
Guinea pigs and rabbits (some bred on
premises)
118 Battle Road, Hollington,
East Sussex, TN37 7AN.
Tel: 01424 424988.
Contact: Angela Glyn-Gareth.
Opening hours: Monday, Tuesday, Thursday,
Friday and Saturday, 9am to 1pm and 2pm to
5.30pm.

Directions: On the corner of Battle and
Ashbrooke Road.

HOVE

Pet Pet Pet
Specialise in fluffy or scaly animals
5 West Way, Hove, East Sussex, BN3 8LD.
Tel: 01273 884949.
Contact: Nick Pannett.
Opening hours: Monday to Friday, 9am
to 6pm. Sunday, 12noon to 4pm.

Directions: Opposite Grenadier Pub off
Hangleton Road.

HURSTPIERPOINT

Pierpoint Pet Supplies
Offer advice on nutrition and specialise in
holistic treatments
97 High Street, Hurstpierpoint,
West Sussex, BN6 9RE.
Tel: 01273 832368.
e-mail: pierpointpets@hotmail.com
web: www.pierpointpetsupplies.co.uk
Contact: Liane Ward-Cleaveley.
Opening hours: Monday to Friday, 9.15am
to 5pm. Saturday, 9.15am to 4pm.

Directions: Turning off A23 – southbound
through Sayers Common and Albourne. Left at
traffic lights through to High Street. Opposite
New Inn Pub. All animals welcome.

DIRECTORY

DID YOU KNOW?
No two cows
have identical
nose prints.

IFIELD, CRAWLEY

Ifield Park Animal & Country Centre
Pet and clothing store, cattery and kennels, equestrian
Bonnetts Lane, Ifield, Crawley,
West Sussex, RH11 0NY.
Tel: 01293 511832.
e-mail: sales@ifield-park.co.uk
web: www.ifield-park.co.uk
Contact: Dan Griffith.
Opening hours: 8am to 5.30pm.

Directions: See website for map.

LANGLEY GREEN, CRAWLEY

The Pet Shop
Hand-reared birds, reptiles and kittens
10 Langley Parade, Langley Green, Crawley,
West Sussex, RH11 7RS.
Tel: 01293 520883.
e-mail: petshoplangley@aol.com
Contact: Peter Shiers.
Opening hours: Monday to Saturday,
9am to 6pm.

Directions: 2 miles from the town centre.

LEWES

Fur Feathers 'n' Fins
Wide selection of pet supplies and friendly atmosphere
41 Cliffe High Street, Lewes,
East Sussex, BN7 2AN.
Tel: 01273 473970.
Opening hours: Monday to Saturday, 8.45am
to 5.30pm.

Directions: Situated east of A26 close to
River Ouse.

NORTHIAM

Northiam DIY & Garden
Pet accessories and many other items
Main Street, Northiam, East Sussex, TN31 6NB.
Tel: 01797 252162. **Fax:** 01797 252162.
Contact: Adrian Mowle.
Opening hours: Monday to Saturday,
8am to 5pm.

PEACEHAVEN

Animal Fare
Pet supplies – wide range of sundries and supplies
44 South East Road, Peacehaven,
East Sussex, BN10 8ST.
Tel: 01273 583301.
Opening hours: 9am to 5pm

Directions: Accessible off main High Street
through Peacehaven.

DIRECTORY

PULBOROUGH

Stopham Pets
Pet shop
81 Lower Street, Pulborough,
West Sussex, RH20 2BP.
Tel: 01798 873674.

RYE

Alfie Greys
Sell English-bred parrots
Units 20-23, Ropewalk Shopping Centre,
Ropewalk, Rye, East Sussex, TN31 7NA.
Tel: 01797 227495.
Contact: Nigel Bixley.
Opening hours:
Monday to Saturday, 9am to 5pm.

Cafe on site. Specialise in parrots.

The Pette Shoppe
111a High Street, Rye, East Sussex, TN36 4LA.
Tel: 01797 222401.
Contact: Jill Wilson.
Opening hours:
Monday to Saturday, 9am to 5.30pm.

Directions: At the beginning of Rye high street
on the left-hand side.

SEAFORD

Pet Love
Specialised products not available in
supermarkets
9 Talland Parade, Saxon Lane,
Seaford, East Sussex.
Tel: 01323 897929.
Contact: Linda Dobson.
Opening hours:
Monday to Saturday, 8.30am to 5pm.

Directions: Take road opposite library. Next left
and we are near jewellers.
Toilets available for customers.

SHOREHAM-BY-SEA

Paradise Pets
Specialise in parrots and parakeets
24 Brunswick Road, Shoreham-by-Sea,
West Sussex, BN43 5WB.
Tel: 01273 452580. **Fax:** 01273 441234.
e-mail: paradisepets@aol.com
web: www.paradise-pets.co.uk
Contact: Ben Capelin.
Opening hours:
Monday to Saturday, 9am to 5.30pm.

Directions: Opposite main post office from
Shoreham railway station.

DIRECTORY

Most bears are left-pawed.

TTL Shop
Online pet shop – specialise in dog items
16 Mill Hill Close, Shoreham-by-Sea,
West Sussex, BN43 5TP.
Tel: 01273 440949.
e-mail: john@ttlshop.co.uk
web: www.ttlshop.co.uk
Contact: John White.
Not open to public. Only internet access.

Discount days announced.

SIDLESHAM, CHICHESTER

The Animal Park
Over 200 birds. Also peacocks, terrapins
and chipmunks
Inside Old Liberty Gardens, Selsey Road,
Sidlesham, Chichester, West Sussex, PO20 7NE.
Tel: 01243 649001. **Fax:** 01243 649003.
web: www.animalark.co.me.uk
Contact: Mr N Gregory.
Opening hours: Monday to Saturday, 9am
to 5.30pm. Sunday, 10am to 4pm.

Directions: From A27 at Chichester, take B145
to Selsey, 4 miles on the left.
Coffee and snack bar.

STEYNING

Steyning Pet Shop
Dog nutritionist and microchipper trained
46 High Street, Steyning, West Sussex,
BN43 3RD.
Tel: 01903 814455. **Fax:** 01903 814455.
e-mail: petfood2go@aol.com
Contact: Neil Bennison.
Opening hours: 9am to 5pm.

Directions: Located in Steyning High Street
next to post office.

Pets Corner
Various pet shops around South England -
see website. All over South
Tel: 0800 169 6098.
e-mail: info@petscorner.co.uk
web: www.petscorner.co.uk
Contact: Dean Richmond.
See website for store times and different shops
in your area.

UCKFIELD

Bell Walk Pet Supplies
Pet supplies - wide range of products
Market Hall, Bell Walk, Uckfield,
East Sussex, TN22 5DQ.
Tel: 01825 768797.
Opening hours: Monday to Saturday, 8.30am
to 5pm.

Health foods and quality products. Any product
can be ordered.

Southern Aviaries
Aviary supplies with delivery available
Tinkers Lane, Hadlow Down, Nr Uckfield,
East Sussex, TN22 4EV.
Tel: 01825 830283.
Fax: 01825 830241.
e-mail: southernaviaries@totalise.co.uk
web: www.1066.net/southernaviaries
Opening hours: 9am to 1pm and 2pm to 5pm.
Closed on Sundays and Mondays.

Directions: Situated between Cross in Hand and
Blackboys off the B2102.
Aviary equipment from cages to ceramic heaters.
Many types of custom-designed aviaries.

CHICHESTER

Reef Aquatics
Aquatic Shop
26 The Hornet, Chichester,
West Sussex, PO19 7SG.
Tel: 01243 773361.
Contact: Dan Weston.
Opening hours:
Monday to Saturday, 9am to 5.30pm
Sunday, 10am to 4pm.

Directions: A27 into Chichester.
Car parking is pay and display around the corner.

BRIGHTON

Sealife Centre Brighton
Wonderful place to visit with new tropical
reef complete with underwater tunnel
Marine Parade, Brighton, East Sussex, BN2 1TB.
Tel: 01273 604234. **Fax:** 01273 681840.
web: www.sealifeeurope.com
Contact: Danielle Crane.
Opening hours: Daily, 10am to 5pm.
Admission: Adults £9.95. Children (3-14)
£7.50. Seniors £8.50. Students £8.50.
Family £32.90. Disabled children £6.50.

Directions: On the Marine Parade, near
Brighton Pier. See website for more details.
Concentrates on conservation, education and
entertainment. Over 150 species and 50
displays. Toilets, Victorian tea rooms and gift
shop. Giant turtles, sharks, rays, tropical reef
and seahorses. Guide dogs welcome.

CROWBOROUGH

Pondakoi Aquatics
Koi and tropical fish available
Sussex County Gardens, Mark Cross,
Crowborough, East Sussex, TN6 3PJ.
Tel: 01892 853388. **Fax:** 01892 853388.
Opening hours:
Monday to Saturday, 9am to 5.30pm.

Small animals, fish and bird seeds.

HAILSHAM

Dicker Aquatics
Aquatic ponds and tropical fish
Wyevale Garden Centre, Lower Dicker,
Hailsham, East Sussex, BN27 4BJ.
Tel: 01323 844655.
Opening hours: 9am to 5pm.

Also supply dog foods.

Horseshoe
crabs chew food
with their legs.

HASTINGS

Underwater World
Variety of marine life for all
the family to enjoy
Underwater World, Rock-a-nore Road,
Hastings, East Sussex, TN34 3DW.
Tel: 01424 718776. **Fax:** 01424 718757.
e-mail: tracey@discoverhastings.co.uk
web: www.discoverhastings.co.uk
Opening hours: Easter to October, 10am
to 5.30pm. October to Easter, 11am to 4pm.
Admission: Adults £6.20. Children £4.20.
Seniors £5.20.

Directions: A259 links Hastings to Channel
Ports and the Channel Tunnel to the East and
Brighton to the West. The A21 links Hastings to
the M25. In Hastings, head towards fishing
huts by cliff railway and follow signposts.
Mammals to sea creatures. Fish of all types.
Very educational. Gift shop, coffee shop and
toilets. See website for details of events. Sharks,
seahorses, crabs, coral reefs, 70 species to view
and enjoy. Guide dogs allowed.

HORSHAM

Pond Restoration and Maintenance Ltd
Pond maintenance – high quality of service
Silverlea, Southwater Street, Southwater,
Horsham, West Sussex, RH13 9BN.
Tel: 01403 730103. **Fax:** 01403 730103.
web: www.pond-maintenance.co.uk
Contact: Ross Charman.
Opening hours: 8am to 6pm. Visits arranged
by appointment.
Travel to client. High quality and reliable service.
General pond, fish and aquaria maintenance.

LANCING

Passies Pond
Great place for coarse fishing
Passies Pond, Coombes Road,
Lancing, West Sussex.
Tel: 01273 465257.
web: www.coombes.co.uk
Opening hours: Open lake.
Admission: Day ticket £8.00. Concessions £4.00.

Directions: Opposite Old Shoreham
Cement Works.
Coarse fishing, many types of fish and local
wildlife. Shop, snack bar and toilets. Wildlife,
bream, carp, tench and many more types of fish.

NEWICK

Newick Aquatics
Specialise in building ponds
9 Newlands Park Way, Newick,
East Sussex, BN8 4PG.
Tel: 01825 723719.
Opening hours: By appointment only

POLEGATE

Devotedly Discus Ltd
Specialise in Discus Fish
32-34 High Street, Polegate,
East Sussex, BN26 6AJ.
Tel: 01323 483689. **Fax:** 01323 483689.
e-mail: enquiries@devotedly-discus.co.uk
web: www.devotedly-discuss.co.uk
Contact: M J Evenden.
Opening hours: Summer, 8am to 6pm
Winter, 9am to 5pm.

Directions: In the High Street, opposite
Barclays Bank.

SEAFORD

Seaford Aquatics
Specialise in cold water and tropical fish
14 Sutton Road, Seaford,
East Sussex, BN25 1RU.
Tel: 01323 897623.
web: www.seafordaquatics.co.uk
Opening hours:
Monday to Saturday, 9am to 5pm.

Directions: In the town centre.
Also stocks ponds.

DIRECTORY

DIRECTORY

ALFRISTON

Drusillas Park
Zoo and leisure attractions with playground and shops
Alfriston, East Sussex, BN26 5QS.
Tel: 01323 874100. **Fax:** 01323 874101.
e-mail: info@drusillas.co.uk
web: www.drusillas.co.uk
Opening hours: Winter, 10am to 4pm.
Summer, 10am to 5pm. Closed Christmas
and Boxing Day.
Admission: Phone first as prices change.

Directions: Between Eastbourne and Brighton,
just off A27. About seven miles from Eastbourne
and 15 miles from Brighton. Zoo, leisure
attractions, train, and playground. Two
restaurants, five shops and five toilet blocks.
See website or www.animalloversguides.co.uk for
events throughout the year. Lar gibbons are new
at the Zoo. Guide dogs are welcome.

ARUNDEL

Arundel Boatyard and
Riverside Tea Gardens
Boatyard with boats for hire.
Cruises along the River Arun
Arundel Boatyard, Mill Road, Arundel,
West Sussex, BN18 9PA.
Tel: 01903 882609.
e-mail: arundelboats@hotmail.com
web: http://.carol-buller.tripod.com
Contact: Carol Buller.
Opening hours: Seasonal, March to October
Boats: 10am to 4pm. Tea garden: 9am to 5pm

Directions: On A27, between Chichester and
Brighton. Mill Road is by old bridge next to Post
Office. Boatyard is via Mill Road.
Boat hire, cruises, riverside tea gardens. Tea
gardens, water for dogs and gift shop. Arundel
Festival at the end of August.

BILLINGSHURST

Fishers Farm Park
A unique place to visit –
a wonderful day out for the family
Newpound Lane, Wisborough Green,
Billingshurst, West Sussex, RH14 0EG.
Tel: 01403 700063.
e-mail: info@fishersfarmpark.co.uk
web: www.fishersfarmpark.co.uk
Opening hours: From 10am to 5pm every day
except Christmas and Boxing Day.
Admission: Adults £7.75-£10.75. Children
(3-16) £7.25-£10.25. Children (to 2 yrs)
£4.00-£7.00. Seniors £6.25-£9.25.

Directions: Signposted from all main roads
approaching Wisborough Green. Off the A272.
Giant Spiders Web frame, pony rides, shire
horse and pony demonstrations. Adventure
play equipment, quad bikes, trampolines,
electric cars and tractors. Diggers, kites, outside
games, table football and garden machinery.
Farmers Grill in the park, hot food, snacks,
drinks and ice creams. Restaurant and tuck
shop. Animal adoption, family visits, birthday
parties, group visits and membership schemes.

BRIGHTON

Black Rock Lido
A place to visit for solace
Marine Drive, Brighton, East Sussex.
web: http://www.mybrightonandhove.org.uk
/black_rock_lido-personal.htm
Opening hours: Open beach.

Exposed section of famous "elephant beds". Full
of bones of mammoth, woolly rhino. All facilities
at the Marina. Birdwatching and sealife.

Booth Museum of Natural History
Fascinating place. A must! Over 525,000 insects and other animals – all dead!
194 Dyke Road, Brighton,
East Sussex, BN1 5AA.
Tel: 01273 292777. **Fax:** 01273 292778.
e-mail: boothmuseum@brighton-hove.gov.uk
web: www.virtualmuseum.info
Contact: D C Legg.
Opening hours: Monday, Tuesday,
Wednesday, Friday and Saturday, 10am to 5pm.
Thursday, closed. Sunday, 2pm to 5pm.
Admission: Free.

Specialises in birds, skeletons, geology.

CHICHESTER

Chichester Canal
Canal with very interesting sights along its banks
Chichester, West Sussex.
Opening hours: Open waterway.

Narrowboat rides, rowing boats, canoeing, angling, strolling, wild flowers, painting, bird watching and cycling.

Weald & Downland Open Air Museum
Traditional breed farm animals
Singleton, Chichester, West Sussex, PO18 0EU.
Tel: 01243 811348. **Fax:** 01243 811475.
e-mail: office@wealddown.co.uk
web: www.wealddown.co.uk
Contact: Cathy Clark.
Opening hours: April to October daily, 10.30am to 6pm. November to 21 December daily, 10.30am to 4pm. Plus daily for 'A Sussex Christmas', 26 December to 1 January 2007, 10.30am to 4pm. 3 Janurary to 18 February 2007, Wednesday, Saturday and Sunday only 10.30am to 4pm. 19 February to 31 March daily, 10.30am to 4pm.
Admission: Adults £7.95. Children £4.25. Seniors £6.95. Family £21.95 (2+3). under 5s free.

Directions: Midway between Chichester and Midhurst on A286.

CRAWLEY

Tulleys Farm
Adventure park with working farm
Turners Hill Road, Turners Hill, Crawley,
West Sussex, RH10 4PE.
Tel: 01342 718472. **Fax:** 01342 718473.
e-mail: shop@tulleysfarm.com
web: www.tulleysfarm.com
Opening hours: 9am to 5pm, seasonal hours.

Directions: Located between East Grinstead and Crawley. Accessible from the B2110. Many family activities available, festivals, parties and Christmas specials. Farm shop and tea room. Seasonal events throughout the year. Goats, rabbits, pigs and other farm animals. Dogs must be on leads, call before visiting.

FOREST ROW

Ashdown Forest Llama Park
A fabulous llama place in a great setting award-winning llamas and alpacas
Wych Cross, Forest Row,
East Sussex, RH18 5JN.
Tel: 01825 712040. **Fax:** 01825 713698.
e-mail: info@llamapark.co.uk
web: www.llamapark.co.uk
Contact: Linda Johnson.
Opening hours: Daily, 10am to 5pm.
Admission: Adults £4.50. Concessions £3.75.

Directions: On the A22, 3 miles south of Forest Row.

DID YOU KNOW?
Chickens were domesticated before cats.

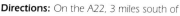

HAILSHAM

Knockhatch Adventure Park
Birds of prey and other fabulous animals
Hempstead Lane, Hailsham,
East Sussex, BN27 3PR.
Tel: 01323 442051. **Fax:** 01323 863035.
e-mail: knockhatch@aol.com
web: www.knockhatch.com
Contact: Colin Jaggers.
Opening hours: Daily, 10am to 5.30pm.
Admission: Adults £7.25. Children £6.25.
Family £25.00. Concessions £5.25.

Directions: Off A22 west of Hailsham.

HOVE

Hove Lagoon
**The lagoons and swans are a
great attraction**
The Kingsway, Hove, East Sussex, BN3 4LX.
Tel: 01273 292974.
Opening hours: Open park.

Directions: Follow A259 coast road towards Hove.
Children's playground, paddling pool, cafe and
toilets. Watersports centre.

LANCING

Coombes Farm Tours
**Working farm with 800 sheep and 90 beef
cows set on 1,000 acres**
Church Farm, Coombes, Lancing,
West Sussex, BN15 0RS.
Tel: 01273 452028.
e-mail: berty@churchfarm.fsworld.co.uk
web: www.coombes.co.uk
Contact: Jenny Passmore.
Opening hours: Check website for times as
they differ throughout the year.
Admission: Adults £5.00. Children £4.00.

Directions: Off A27 at Lancing College, 2 miles
on the left.

LEWES

Blackberry Farm
**Working farm open to the public.
Lovely place for children and adults.
Lots of animals**
Blackberry Farm, Whitesmith, Nr Lewes,
East Sussex, BN8 6JD.
Tel: 01825 872912. **Fax:** 01825 873082.
e-mail: info@blackberry-farm.co.uk
web: www.blackberry-farm.co.uk
Contact: Rebecca Foxley or Lee Lidbetter.
Opening hours: Daily, 10am to 5pm.
Admission: Adults £5.00. Children (3-15) £4.00.
Seniors £3.50. Children under 2, Free.

Directions: On A22, 5 miles south of Uckfield.

The Farmyard
**Suffolk Punch cart horse, donkeys and
Shetland ponies**
The Farmyard, Whitesmith, Lewes,
East Sussex, BN8 6JB.
Tel: 01825 872317.
web: www.the-farmyard.co.uk
Contact: Jenny Cottingham.
Opening hours: Monday to Friday, 2pm
to 5pm. Saturdays and bank holidays, 10am to
5pm. Sunday, closed.
Admission: Adults £3.00. Children £2.30.
Under 3 years free. Seniors £2.50.

Directions: Between Uckfield and Hailsham on
A22 Whitesmith Crossroads.

*A hamster
can put half its
weight in food into
its cheek pouches.*

DIRECTORY

LITTLEHAMPTON

Look and Sea Visitor Centre
Visitor centre
63-65 Surrey Street, Littlehampton,
West Sussex, BN17 5AW.
Tel: 01903 718984. **Fax:** 01903 718036.
e-mail: info@lookandsea.co.uk
web: www.lookandsea.co.uk
Opening hours: May to October, 10am
to 5pm. November to March, 11am to 4pm
Monday to Friday.
Admission: Check for up-to-date prices.

Directions: In Surrey Street near the river.
Meet the Old Boxgrove Man and discover how
big the Iguanodon dinosaur was who roamed
nearby 65 million years ago. Get your hands on
fossils and check out the views over the
harbour and Climping beach. Coffee shop and
gift shop. See website for details of events.

NEWHAVEN

Newhaven Fort
**Historic visitor attraction on stunning
10-acre site. Dogs welcome on a lead**
Newhaven, East Sussex, BN9 9DS,
Tel: 01273 517622.
e-mail: info@newhavenfort.org.uk
web: www.newhavenfort.org.uk
Opening hours: March to October, 10.30am
to 6pm. Weekends during November, 10.30am
to 4pm.
Admission: Adults £5.50. Children £3.60.
Seniors £4.60. Family £16.50.

Directions: Situated between Brighton and
Eastbourne on the A259 coast road and linked
to Lewes on the A27.
Cafe and toilets. Many special events
throughout the year (see website for further
details). Exhibitions and displays. Stunning
cliff-top views.

OVINGDEAN

Ovingdean Cliffs
**Chalk cliffs with amazing views over the
coast and Brighton**
Ovingdean, East Sussex.
Opening hours: Open park.

Directions: Along the coast road from
Brighton towards Peacehaven.
Lovely walks. Site of Special Scientific Interest.
Cafe. Birdwatching area (fulmar, gulls, stock
dove, peregrine falcon).

SHOREHAM

Widewater Lagoon
Wonderful lagoon with herons and swans
Shoreham Beach, Shoreham, West Sussex.
web: www.adur.gov.uk
Opening hours: Open lagoon.

Directions: North-west of Shoreham Beach
Herons, swans and wildfowl.

WOODINGDEAN

Newmarket Hill
A place to visit
Newmarket Hill, Woodingdean,
Brighton, Sussex.
Opening hours: Open nature reserve.

Directions: Follow Warren Road then Felmer
Road to Woodingdean.
Facilities in Woodingdean only. Nature reserve is
Special Site of Scientific Interest. Red-footed
Falcons and rare insects.

DIRECTORY

ANGMERING

Roundstone Kennels and Cattery
Kennels and cattery including
grooming parlour
Roundstone Lane, Angmering,
West Sussex, BN16 4AT.
Tel: 01903 850231.
Contact: Linda Clarke.
Opening hours: Daily, 8am to 6pm.

ARUNDEL

New Carlton Boarding Kennels
Animal sanctuary as well
as kennels and cattery
Ford Road, Ford, Arundel,
West Sussex, BN18 0BH.
Tel: 01903 883116.
web: www.clympingdogsanctuary.co.uk
Opening hours: Monday to Saturday. 10am
to 3pm. Sunday. 10am to 1pm.
Admission: £1 donation towards sanctuary
would be very welcome.

Directions: Turn off the A260 into Ford Road.
Shop on site as well as animal sanctuary. Toilets
and shop. Special events throughout the year,
see website for details.

BECKLEY

Manor House Cattery
Boarding for cats only
The Old Museum, Horseshoe Lane,
Beckley, Rye, East Sussex, TN31 6SD.
Tel: 01797 260253.
e-mail: manorhousecats@btconnect.com
web: www.manorhousecattery.co.uk
Contact: Bill Knight.

BATTLE

Bunny Breaks
Rabbit & guinea pig hotel
Gray's Cottages, Battle Hill, Battle,
East Sussex, TN33 0BS.
Tel: 01424 774102. **Fax:** 01424 774102.
e-mail: bunnybreaks@yahoo.co.uk
web: www.bunnybreaks.tripod.com
Fees: £1.50 per day or £8.00 per week per run.
Leave your rabbits and guinea pigs in safe
hands while you're away on holiday at our
rabbit and guinea pig hotel. They will be well
cared for and will have a very pleasant time
here. All rabbits must have been innoculated
against Myxomatosis and Haem viral disease at
least one month prior to their holiday.

BRIGHTON

A Pets Life
Dog walking service,
animal boarding and pet sitter
128 Whitehawk Way, Brighton,
East Sussex, BN2 5QJ.
Tel: 07932 239508.
e-mail: apetslife@hotmail.co.uk
Contact: Lorraine Ridley.

Opening hours: By arrangement.
Board any animal. A lovely and friendly service
available. Please do not hesitate to call.

BROAD OAK, BREDE

Beacon House Boarding Cattery
Cattery only
Beacon House, Udimore Road, Broad Oak,
Brede, Rye, East Sussex, TN31 6BX.
Tel: 01424 882326.
Contact: Jane Winnard.
Opening hours: Daily, 9.30 to 12.30.
Weekdays only, 4pm to 6pm.

Directions: On B2089 between Broad Oak
and Rye.
Garden access for wheelchairs. Deliveries and
collections of animals can be arranged for a
small charge.

Rohese Cattery
**Exclusive cattery set in 2.5 acres of
countryside. Luxury insulated pine cabins**
Rosewood, Furnace Lane, Broad Oak, Rye,
East Sussex, TN31 6ES.
Tel: 01424 882129. **Fax:** 01424 882129.
web: www.rohese.com
Contact: Mrs Swatton.
Opening hours: Monday to Saturday,
8.30am to 5pm. Sundays and bank holidays,
9am to 12noon.

Directions: Off A28 Tenterden-Hastings Road.
As you leave Broad Oak towards Northiam,
Furnace Lane is on the right and they are
about a quarter of mile down the lane.
The cattery resembles a little village with its
charming pine chalets, all heated with runs and
scratching post. Music to soothe the cats and
a wind and rain break to protect the cats from
the elements. Grooming a plus. Viewings
welcome after 10am.

CATSFIELD

Battle Oaks Boarding Cattery
Cattery only
Powdermill Lane, Catsfield, Battle,
East Sussex, TN33 0SZ.
Tel: 01424 892302.
Contact: Mrs Stephanie Fox.

CRAWLEY DOWN

Glenwood Boarding Cattery
Cattery only
Cuttinglye Road, Crawley Down,
West Sussex, RH10 4LR.
Tel: 01342 712370.
Contact: John Bingham.
Opening hours: Daily, 9.30am to 4.30pm.

Directions: Off Hophurst Hill.

CROWBOROUGH

Ashdown Cattery
Cats only
2 Spring Cats, London Road, Crowborough,
East Sussex, TN6 1NT.
Tel: 01892 662197. **Fax:** 01892 655559.
e-mail: sdaw898523@aol.com
Contact: Mrs S Dawkins.

Directions: Between Crowborough and
Groombridge. Seven miles from Tunbridge
Wells.

Did you know? Pigeons can count.

HAILSHAM

Lindey Lodge
Kennels and Cattery
Hempsted Lane West, Hailsham,
East Sussex, BN27 3PR.
Tel: 01323 842049.
e-mail: lindeylodgekennels@yahoo.co.uk
Contact: D Spellnam.
Opening hours: Sunday and Thursday, 9am to 11am. Monday, Tuesday, Wednesday, Friday and Saturday, 9am to 1pm and 2.30pm to 6pm.

Direction: Off A22 Eastbourne to London Road. South of Boship Roundabout.

Marshfoot Cattery
Boarding and grooming available
145 Marshfoot Lane, Hailsham,
East Sussex, BN27 2RD.
Tel: 01323 841204.
e-mail: marshfootcattery@aol.co.uk
web: www.marshfootcattery.co.uk
Contact: Mr T Minton.
Opening hours: Monday to Saturday, 10am to 1pm and 4pm to 6pm. Sunday, 10am to 1pm.

Directions: Off Hailsham High Street, into Vicarage Road or Lane to Marshfoot Lane.

HAMBROOK

Amberley Boarding Kennels
Caters for all dogs, young, old and on medication. Separate gardens for each dog. Set in approximately 7.5 acres
Woodmancote Lane, Hambrook,
West Sussex, PO18 8UL.
Tel: 01243 573671.
Contact: Derek Bhowmick-Shepherd.
Opening hours:
Summer, 9am to 12 noon and 2pm to 4pm.
Winter, 9am to 12 noon and 2pm to 3pm.
Sunday and bank holidays, 10am to 12 noon.

Directions: 6 miles west of Chichester, 3 miles east of Emsworth, 1 mile from A259.

HORAM

Tall Pines Boarding Kennel & Cattery
Kennels and cattery
Tall Pines, Swansbrook Lane, Horam,
East Sussex, TN21 0LD.
Tel: 01825 872522. **Fax:** 01825 872522.
web: www.tallpineskennels.co.uk
Contact: David Marshall.
Opening hours: By arrangement.

HORSHAM

St Andrews Farm Kennels
Quarantine kennels. Fabulous boarding kennels with lots of tender loving care
Brooks Green, Horsham,
West Sussex, RH13 0JW.
Tel: 01403 741248. **Fax:** 01403 741769.
e-mail: pets@standrewskennels.co.uk
web: www.kennelsgb.com
Contact: Annie Silver.
Opening hours:
Quarantine – Tuesday, Thursday and Saturday, 2pm to 4pm. **Kennels** – Monday to Saturday, 9am to 4.30pm. Sunday, 10am to 11am.

Dogs and cats.

www.animalloversguides.co.uk

IDEN, RYE

Iden Boarding Kennels
Dogs and cats, set in natural meadow and woodlands. Linked to Mallydams Wildlife Rescue as rehab point
Coldharbour Lane, Iden, Rye,
East Sussex, TN35 4NA.
Tel: 01797 280384.
Contact: James or Bernie Fiddimore.
Opening hours: Weekdays, 10am to 6pm
Sundays,10am to 1pm.

 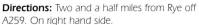

Directions: Two and a half miles from Rye off A259. On right hand side.

IFOLD, BILLINGSHURST

Rabbitmotel
Luxury accommodation for rabbits and guinea pigs
Dale Farm, The Lane, Ifold, Billingshurst,
West Sussex, RH14 0UL.
Tel: 01403 752211.
e-mail: admin@rabbitmotel.co.uk
web: www.rabbitmotel.co.uk
Contact: Anita Jefferies.
Directions: Surrey / Sussex borders in village of Ifold.

LEWES

Small Pets' Hotel
Pets hotel for small animals
35 Evelyn Road, Lewes, East Sussex, BN7 2SS.
Tel: 01273 476559.
e-mail: smallpetshotel@yahoo.com
Contact: Claire Meehan.
Opening hours: By appointment.

Directions: Landport Estate, Lewes.
Specialise in small animals.

LOWFIELD HEATH, CRAWLEY

Gatwick Kennels and Cattery
Specialises in geratric and post-op nursing care in beautiful lakeside cabins
Poles Lane, Lowfield Heath, Crawley,
West Sussex, RH11 0PY.
Tel: 01293 546546. **Fax:** 01293 546546.
Contact: Angela Rixon.
Opening hours: Daily by arrangement.

Directions: Adjacent to Gatwick Airport.
Parking for clients only.

PEACEHAVEN

Benwick Kennels and Cattery
Boards dogs, cats, small mammals and birds. They breed Irish wolfhounds and West Highland terriers
Maple Road, Peacehaven,
East Sussex, BN10 8UT.
Tel: 01273 587809. **Fax:** 01273 580400.
Contact: Linda McMillan.
Opening hours:
For viewing kennels, 10am to 3pm.

Directions: On A259 between Newhaven and Peacehaven.

DIRECTORY

RINGMER

Dart Vale Boarding Cattery Ltd
Cattery only
Laughton Road, Ringmer, Lewes,
East Sussex, BN8 5NH.
Tel: 01273 814722. **Fax:** 01273 812568.
e-mail: cattery@dartvale.net
web: www.dartvalecattery.co.uk
Contact: Sheila Tiller.
Opening hours: Weekdays, 9am to 11am and
4.30pm to 6.30pm. Weekends, 9am to 11am
and 4.30pm to 5.30pm.

Directions: On B2124 east of Ringmer. Map
on website.

UCKFIELD

Meadowside Boarding Kennels
**Established 16 years. Licensed by
the local authority**
High Cross Farm, Eastbourne Road, Uckfield,
East Sussex, TN22 5QW.
Tel: 01825 840674.
Contact: M J Chattaway.
Opening hours: Weekdays, 9am to 12noon
Other times by appointment.
Fees: Price list available.

Directions: Two and a half miles south
of Uckfield down Eastbourne Road.
All dogs given individual attention.
Reasonable charges.

Did you know?

*Cows have
seven stomachs.*

Pals4Pets
Home boarding service for dogs
The Old Dairy, New Road, Uckfield,
East Sussex, TN22 5TG.
Tel: 01825 749777. **Fax:** 01825 749777.
e-mail: lyn@pals4petsuk.com
web: www.pals4petsuk.com
Contact: Lyn Buckingham.
Opening hours: By appointment.

Directions: See website for directions.
An established, professional company whose
structure makes it unique. Peace of mind
knowing your pet is being looked after.
Dog boarding in private homes, cat feeding,
small animal and bird care. We have licensed
home-boarders throughout Sussex.

UPPER DICKER, HAILSHAM

Martlets Cattery
Cattery only
Martlets, Coldharbour Road, Upper Dicker,
Hailsham, East Sussex, BN27 3QA.
Tel: 01323 844023.
e-mail: info@martletscattery.com
web: www.martletscattery.com
Contact: Lisa.
Opening hours: Monday to Saturday, 2.30pm
to 6.30pm.

Directions: On A22 Boship Roundabout, north
onto A22 towards Uckfield. Take first left into
Coldharbour Road and about a mile on the left-
hand side is the cattery, opposite cricket ground
Tours on request by appointment. Specialises in
cats, takes cats on medication, elderly cats and
difficult to handle cats.

WADHURST

Browside Cattery
Luxury purpose built rooms. Fully licensed
Moseham, Wadhurst, East Sussex, TN5 6NA.
Tel: 01892 783038.
web: www.browsidecattery.co.uk
Contact: Malcolm Perry.
Opening hours: By appointment.

Directions: Half a mile outside Wadhurst on
the Ticehurst Road (B2099).

WASHINGTON

Old Clayton Kennels and Catteries
Dogs exercised four times a day.
Grooming, shop sales and dog rescue
Storrington Road, Washington,
West Sussex, RH20 4AG.
Tel: 01903 742930.
e-mail: clayton@coppy.supanet.com
web: www.oldclayton.storringtonsussex.co.uk
Contact: Yvonne Copp.
Opening hours: 9am to 1pm. 2pm to 6pm.

Coffee machine on site.

*A horse can't
see the end
of its nose.*

WESTFIELD

Whitelands Kennels
All animals boarded
Westfield Lane, Westfield,
East Sussex, TN35 4SB.
Tel: 01424 754287.   **Fax:** 01424 754287.
Contact: Sarah Croucher.
Opening hours: Visiting, 9am to 12noon
Customers, 8am to 12noon and 4.30pm
to 5.30pm.

Directions: Ten minutes from Hastings on
the A28.
Animals boarded from fish, birds, reptiles to
cats and dogs.

DIRECTORY

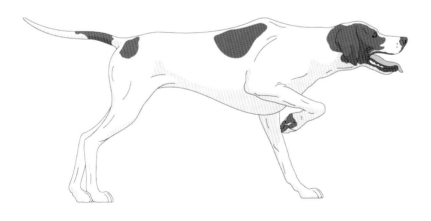

ASHBURNHAM, BATTLE

Brownbread Horse Rescue

Over 100 equines. Horse rescue.
Conducted walks around the 80 acres
Brownbread Street, Ashburnham, Battle,
East Sussex, TN33 9NX.
Tel: 01424 892381.
e-mail: tony.brownbread@tesco.net
web: www.brownbread_rescue.250free.com
Contact: Tony Smith.
Opening hours: By arrangement.
Admission: No admission charges, but
donations welcome.

Directions: 5 miles west of Battle off the A271.

COODEN, BEXHILL

Canine Concern

Tested dogs, cats and rabbits to visit
hospitals, nursing homes, care homes and
lonely people
c/o Miss K E Bendien, 'Ravopi', Elsted Road,
Cooden, Bexhill, East Sussex, TN39 3BG.
Tel: 01424 843661.
Contact: Miss Bendien.
Opening hours: By arrangement.

A loving, well-trained animal to visit the sick or
elderly and make their day.

HASTINGS

Hastings Animal Concern

Care and advice for rescue issues
96b All Saints Street, Hastings,
East Sussex, TN34 3BE.
Tel: 01424 430425.
e-mail: animalconcernse@aol.com
web: www.animalconcern2001.co.uk
Contact: Marchien Kuiper.

KINGSFOLD

Care for the Wild International

We raise funds to support the protection
of wildlife throughout the world
The Granary, Tickfold Farm, Kingsfold,
West Sussex, RH12 3SE.
Tel: 01306 627900. **Fax:** 01306 627901.
e-mail: info@careforthewild.com
web: www.careforthewild.com
Contact: B Jameson.

LOWER WILLINGDON

Hearing Dogs for Deaf People

Training dogs from rescue centres to alert
severely deaf people
117 Anderida Road, Lower Willingdon,
Eastbourne, East Sussex, BN22 0QE.
Tel: 01323 508932. **Fax:** 01323 508932.
e-mail: sue.pellow@hearing-dogs.co.uk
web: www.hearing-dogs.co.uk
Contact: Sue Pellow.
Opening hours:
Monday to Friday, 9am to 5pm.
Directions: on A22, A27 or A259.

WORTHING

Worthing and District Cats Protection

Cats rescue and rehoming
35 Rowlands Road, Worthing,
West Sussex, BN11 3JJ.
Tel: 01903 200332.
e-mail:
shop.worthingcatsprotection@btinternet.com
web: www.worthingcatsprotection.org.uk
Contact: Rod Austin.
Shop opening hours: Monday to Saturday,
10am to 4pm.
Directions to shop: Corner of Rowlands Road
and Montague Street; just west of town centre
Various events throughout the year. Garden
party in August. Please phone to enquire.
Dogs welcome but must be on a lead.

DIRECTORY

BURGESS HILL

Mid Sussex Happy Breed Dog Rescue
Dog Rescue Society
PO Box 126, Burgess Hill,
West Sussex, RH15 0SL.
Tel: 01444 239005. **Fax:** 01444 239005.
e-mail: linda@happybreed.co.uk
web: www.happybreed.co.uk
Contact: Linda Thurlow.
Opening hours: By appointment only as we
use boarding kennels and foster homes as we
do not own our own kennels.
Also rehome dogs.

CROWBOROUGH

Deerhound Club
**Friendly atmosphere where people share
common interest and attend dog shows**
Woodleight Ghyll Road, Crowborough,
East Sussex, TN6 1SU.
Tel: 01892 662842.
e-mail: secretary@deerhound.co.uk
web: www.deerhound.co.uk
Admission: Membership fees applicable.

Directions: Different locations throughout the
year. Please call to enquire.
Animal breed show and many other events
throughout the year. Club pedigree book for
members. Deerhound dogs welcome.

EASTBOURNE

Eastbourne and District Pond-keeping Club
Pond keeping club, fish and amphibians
61 Manvers Road, Eastbourne, BN20 8HH.
Tel: 01323 231369.
e-mail: brian@bdale.co.uk
web: www.pondclub.co.uk
Contact: Brian Dale.
Opening hours: Open last Friday of every.
month to the public, 7.30am to 10pm
Membership available and price list.

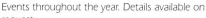

Events throughout the year. Details available on
request.

**A cuban
land crab can
outrun a horse.**

HAYWARDS HEATH

Mid Sussex Badger Protection Group
Badger protection group. Talks available
Centenary Hall, St Wilfrids Way,
Haywards Heath, West Sussex.
Tel: 07910 198720 (Hotline 24-hour).
Contact: Mrs J Spooner.
Opening hours: 2nd Tuesday of February,
March, April, May, September, October,
November and December, 8pm to 10pm for
meetings.
Admission: £3 non members. £1 members.

Directions: Behind Orchard Shopping Centre.
Various events throughout the year. Details
available. This group gives advice on anything
to do with badgers.

HORSHAM

Horsham and District Canine Society
Dog shows
Rikita Golden Retrievers, 6 Lambs Farm Close,
Horsham, West Sussex. RH12 4JZ.
Tel: 01403 257363.
e-mail: anne.rikita@tiscali.co.uk
Contact: Anne Bowden.

Two open dog shows a year held at South of
England Show Ground Ardingly.

Rabbit Welfare Association
**All the things you need to know about
rabbits. Great educational association**
PO Box 346, Horsham, West Sussex, RH13 5WL.
Tel: 01403 267658.
e-mail: hq@rabbitwelfare.co.uk
web: www.rabbitwelfare.co.uk
Contact: Anne Mitchell.
Opening hours: 10am to 8pm on phone only.

A female
kangaroo is
called a 'flyer'.

LEWES

Southern Bernese Mountain Dog Club
**For dogs - social, dog training, education,
shows and making friends**
Scrapers, Chiddingly, Lewes,
East Sussex, BN8 6HQ.
Tel: 01825 872251.
Contact: Irene Soper.
web: www.sbmdc.co.uk
Call to enquire about a membership fee.

Many benefits of a membership. Two open
shows and one championship show per year.
Working and fun weekend. Christmas party
and meetings. Two magazines and a yearbook
published yearly for members.

Sussex Chelonian Society
Tortoises, turtles and terrapins
PO Box 1191, Lewes, East Sussex, BN7 1QJ.
Tel: 01273 475680. **Fax:** 01273 488582.
e-mail:
sussexcheloniansociety@chelonia.fsnet.co,uk
web: www.chelonia.fsnet.co.uk
Contact: Sheila Kay.
Opening hours: Not open to public.
Members can visit every first Sunday morning
of the month, 10am to 12noon.

Private house, so limited facilities.

DIRECTORY

NEWHAVEN

South Downs Badger Protection Society
General public enquiries and advice.
Development projects
71 Court Farm Road, Newhaven,
East Sussex, BN9 9DY.
Contact: Graham Amy.
Opening hours: 9am to 5pm.

Lips of the hippo are almost two feet wide.

ST LEONARDS ON SEA

Hastings Badger Protection Society
Protects badgers by helping injured,
building setts, education and
conservation. A lovely society
304 Bexhill Road, St Leonards on Sea,
East Sussex, TN38 8AL.
Tel: 01424 439168.
e-mail: djwise304@aol.com
Contact: Don Wise.
Opening hours: By appointment only
because of protected species on site.
Admission: Free (donations gratefully accepted.)

Directions: available on phone.
Open days throughout the year. School
educational events. Badgers and native wildlife.
There is disabled access to the wildlife reserves.

WEST CHILTINGTON

West Chiltington Cavaliers
Care and socialisation of Cavaliers and
their owners and all those who love
the breed
Kelmscott, The Hawthorns, West Chiltington,
West Sussex, RH20 2QH.
Tel: 01798 813474.
Contact: Janette Wright.
Fees: Membership prices available on request.

Directions: Between A24 and A29. Half-way
between Horsham and Worthing between
Storrington and Pulborough.
Care and socialisation of Cavaliers and their
owners. Tea and coffee available on club nights
Christmas and birthday party. Seaside and
country walks and talks by professionals such
as vets, vet nurses, groomers, dog wardens
and hydrotherapists.

DIRECTORY

AMBERLEY

Amberley Wild Brooks
Country walk and nature reserve
Amberley, West Sussex.
Nearest postcode BN18 9NT.
Tel: 01273 494777.
web: www.sussexwt.org.uk

Directions: Access from Wey South path only,
which is located through the middle of the
Brooks Farm from Hog Lane in Amberley village.
Lovely country walks with the possibility of
sighting Bewicks swans, dragonflies and
wetland wildlife. Dogs must be on leads.

ARLINGTON

Arlington Bluebell Walk & Farm Trail
Many species of birds and wildlife.
Lovely nature park
Bates Green Farm, Tye Hill Road, Arlington,
Polegate, East Sussex, BN26 6SH.
Tel: 01323 485152.
e-mail: jmccutchan@nlconnect.co.uk
web: www.bluebellwalk.co.uk
Contact: Carolyn and John.
Opening hours: Daily, 10am to 5pm.
Please ring to check season opening times.
Admission: Adults £2.50. Children £1.00.
Seniors £2.00. Family £6.00.

Directions: 5 miles north west of Polegate,
midway between A22 and A27.
Wildlife, insects, flora and fauna. Many species
of birds to see. Dogs must be on leads.

Gorillas have fingerprints.

ARUNDEL

The Wildfowl and Wetlands Centre
A must-see! Fabulous place. Almost
certainly see kingfishers.
WWT Wetlands Centre, Mill Road, Arundel,
West Sussex, BN18 9PB.
Tel: 01903 883355. **Fax:** 01903 884834.
e-mail: info@arundel.wwt.org.uk
web: www.wwt.org.uk/arundel
Contact: Geoff Squire.
Opening hours: Summer, 9.30am to 5.30pm
Winter ,9.30am to 4.30pm.
Admission: Adults £5.95. Children £3.75.
Concessions £4.75.

Directions: On the A27 between Chichester
and Worthing. The WWT Centre is three-
quarters of a mile outside of town, next to river
and clearly signposted.
Wild and captive birds. Restaurant, gift shop,
toilets and disabled toilets. Birds, wildfowl,
Kingfishers and New Zealand blue ducks. Guide
dogs welcome.

BATTLE

Powerdmill Wood
Nature reserve with wildlife walks
Powdermill Wood, Battle, East Sussex.
Nearest postcode TN33 0SY.
Tel: 01273 494777.
web: www.sussexwt.org.uk
Opening hours: Open park.

Directions: Located off the B2095 towards
Powdermills Hotel.
Wildlife and beautiful setting. Plants such as
marsh marigold, tussock sedge, golden
saxifrage can be found here.

www.animalloversguides.co.uk

BEXHILL-ON-SEA

Gillham Wood
Small but beautiful woodland
Withyham Road, Bexhill-on-Sea, East Sussex.
Nearest postcode TN39 3BA.
web: www.sussexwt.org.uk
Opening hours: Open park.

Directions: Accessible via the B2182 (Cooden Drive). Many access points, the easiest being Withyham Road which runs across the southern border.
Many woodland birds. Dogs must be on leads.

Hooe Common
Nature reserve with wildlife walks
Bexhill, East Sussex.
Nearest postcode TN33 9HT.
web: www.sussexwt.org.uk
Opening hours: Open park.

Directions: Public footpaths begin in Hooe village opposite the telephone kiosk and cross a field to enter the reserve.
Variety of warblers. Many plant species. Dogs must be on leads.

BRIGHTON

Beacon Hill
Nature reserve with park for all the family
Brighton, East Sussex.
Opening hours: Open park.

Directions: Longhill Road (Ovingdean) or Nevill Road (Rottingdean). Between Rottingdean and Ovingdean about half a mile north of A259 coast road.
Old dry dew pond. No facilities available. Chalk grassland, Skylark butterflies (The pride of Sussex cowslip and marbled white and common blue butterflies)

Bevendean Down
Nature reserve with park for all the family
Brighton, East Sussex.
Opening hours: Open park.

Directions: Accessed by footpaths off the Avenue and Heath Hill Avenue.
Rich in invertebrate fauna, dew pond and horse paddocks. Chalk grassland.

Chattri Downs War Memorial
Nature reserve with park for all the family
Brighton, East Sussex.
Opening hours: Open park.

Directions: North of Brighton, between Patcham and Pyecombe. Take Braypool Lane, turnoff from A27, near the junction with the A23. Turn right onto the lane to Lower Standean Farm.
Popular local beauty spot, visit the Chattri Memorial (dedicated to the Indian solders who died in WWI). Sparrowhawk, little owl, green woodpecker, hen harrier and long-eared owl. Sussex Border Path and North Brighton Countryside Trail pass through.

Male monkeys go bald.

Falmer Conservation Area
Conservation / farm area
Falmer, Nr Brighton, East Sussex.
Opening hours: Open conservation area.

Directions: Follow A27 eastwards from Brighton.
Pond located within the Sussex Downs Area.

The South Downs
Nature reserve with beautiful
scenery and wildlife
The South Downs, Brighton, East Sussex.
Opening hours: Open reserve.

Directions: Off the A286 onto local roads,
near Charlton.
National park and area of outstanding natural
beauty. Prehistoric ridge with layers of chalk.
Grazing sheep, farmland, chalkland and local
wildlife.

Whitehawk Hill
Whitehawk Camp (a Neolithic enclosure
and ancient monument)
Brighton, East Sussex.
Opening hours: Open park.

Directions: Access via Warren Road, at top of
Manor Hill. Off Donald Road to the south.
Brighton Racecourse to the west, Whitehawk
housing estate to the east and Kemp Town to
the south.
No facilities available. Adonis and chalkhill
butterfies and Whitehawk soldier beetle.

Wild Park
Woodland, dew pond, largest nature
reserve in Brighton
Ditchling Road, Brighton, East Sussex.
Opening hours: Open park.

Directions: Access via Lewes Road
(Moulsecoomb area). Just off A27 Lewes Road or
off Ditchling Road towards London junction.
Woodland, dew pond. Cafe, toilets, sports
grounds, golf course and mountain bike tracks.
Arable and grazing fields attract seed-eating
birds, chalk grassland fauna.

BURGESS HILL

Bedelands Farm Nature Reserve
Nature reserve with pond wildlife
including wildfowl, plants and insects
Off Maple Drive, Burgess Hill, West Sussex.
web: www.burgesshill.gov.uk
Opening hours: Open reserve.

Directions: Bedelands Farm Nature Reserve is
situated on the northern edge of Burgess Hill
and access is from the playing fields next to
Burgess Hill Town Football Club, off Maple
Drive, and from Coopers Close. Other entry
points are from a footpath near Valeb.
The site is owned by Mid Sussex District
Council and the Friends of Bedelands Farm
Nature Reserve help maintain it.
The Nature Reserve consists of ancient
meadows, woodland, hedgerows and ponds,
covering 80 acres.

CHICHESTER

Cooksbridge Meadow
Country walk and nature reserve
Nr Henley Common, Chichester, West Sussex.
Tel: 01273 492630. **Fax:** 01273 494500.
web: www.sussexwt.org.uk

Directions: North of Henley Common, near to
Courts Furniture Store.
Woodland birds, peace and quiet. Dogs must
be on leads.

Levin Down
Nature reserve with wildlife walks
Nr Charlton, Chichester, West Sussex.
Nearest postcode PO18 0JG.
web: www.sussexwt.org.uk
Opening hours: Open park.

Directions: Chichester is accessible via the A285,
A27, A259 and the B2166. There is a parking
layby at the crossroads in Charlton and a
footpath leading across the field to the reserve.
Many butterfly species, including Duke of
Burgundy, brown and green hairstreaks.
Chalkland scenery and plants. Warblers and
finches. Dogs must be on leads.

CROWBOROUGH

Old Lodge
*Nature reserve with beautiful
scenery and wildlife*
Nr Kings Standing, Crowborough, East Sussex.
Nearest postcode TN22 3JD.
web: www.sussexwt.org.uk
Opening hours: Open park.

Directions: Located east of Kings Standing,
accessible off the B2026. There is a small car park.
Set in the Ashdown Forest. Nightjar, redstart,
woodcock, tree pipit, stonechat and alder.

DITCHLING

Stoneywish Nature Reserve
*Lovely nature walk with farm animals,
gardens and ponds*
Spatham Lane, Ditchling, East Sussex, BN6 8XH.
Tel: 01273 843498.
Web: www.stoneywish.com
Contact: Rosemary Alford.
Opening hours: Daily, March to November,
9.30am to 5pm. November to March, 9.30am
to 4pm.
Admission: Adults £3.75. Children £2.75.
Seniors £2.75. Under 3s free. Wheelchair
concessions.

Directions: Quarter of a mile off the B2116
on the east side of Ditchling.
Nature walk, play and picnic area, farm
animals, gardens and exhibitions. Tea room,
garden gift shop and toilets. Farm animals,
herons, woodpeckers and wild birds. Guide
dogs welcome.

ERIDGE

Eridge Rocks
*Beautiful location and scenery. Peaceful
and tranquil*
North-east of Eridge train station,
Eridge, East Sussex.
Nearest postcode TN3 9JU.
web: www.sussexwt.org.uk
Opening hours: Open park.

Directions: Entrance to private road off the A26
situated next to church and small printing works.
Rare wildlife and plants.

DIRECTORY

FAIRWARP

Brickfield Meadow
Country walk and nature reserve
Fairwarp, East Sussex.
Nearest postcode TN22 3BT.
Tel: 01273 494777.
web: www.sussexwt.org.uk
Opening hours: Open nature reserve.

Directions: Located 400 metres from
Fairwarp. Cars may be parked in the village.
Large variety of flowers and ancient fauna.
Ancient natural setting. Dogs must be on
leads.

FOREST ROW

Ashdown Forest
Outstanding natural beauty
The Ashdown Forest Centre, Wych Cross,
Forest Row, East Sussex, RH18 5JP.
Tel: 01342 823583.
e-mail: conservators@ashdownforest.org
web: www.ashdownforest.org
Opening hours: Open park.

Directions: 3 miles south-east of East
Grinstead. Just south of Forest Row. The forest
is on both sides of A22.
Rich in wildlife with many activities all year.
Rare wildlife, including marsh gentian, dartford
warbler, silver studded blue butterfly and
nightjar. Winnie the Pooh walk route and
Pooh Bridge.

HASTINGS

Filsham Reedbed
Nature reserve with wildlife walks
Hastings, East Sussex.
Nearest postcode TN38 8DY.
web: www.sussexwt.org.uk
Opening hours: Open park.

Directions: Footpath runs alongside Combe
Haven River, from the Bulverhythe Recreation
Ground, just off A259 in St Leonards. Footbridge
located over the river.
Reed warblers, water rail, teal, reed bunting and
other bird species. Variety of amphibians and
specialist moths. Dogs must be on leads.

Marline Valley
Nature reserve with wildlife walks
Near High Beech, Hastings, East Sussex.
Nearest postcode TN38 9NY.
web: www.sussexwt.org.uk
Opening hours: Open park.

Directions: Located east of Hollington off the
B2092. The easiest way to the park is via
Napier Road or nearby and cross over
Queensway to access one of the footpaths.
Many species of plants, including coppice,
bluebell, wild garlic, mosses and ferns.
nightingales and warblers. Dogs must be on
leads.

*Ants (and man)
are the only
animals that wage
war in battle formations.*

HAYWARDS HEATH

Newbury Pond
Nature reserve with wildlife walks
Nr Cuckfield, Haywards Heath, West Sussex.
Nearest postcode RH17 5LL.
web: www.sussexwt.org.uk
Opening hours: Open park.

Directions: Accessible from the A272 and the B2184. Possible to park at the end of Newbury Land, close to the pond. Parking also available by the church.
Delightful pond and area of marshy woodland. Many pondlife species and recently planted meadow. Dogs must be on leads.

HEATHFIELD

Selwyns Wood
Country walk and nature reserve
Heathfield, East Sussex.
Nearest postcode TN21 0LY.
Tel: 01273 494777.
web: www.sussexwt.org.uk

Directions: Access point marked with the Trust sign at entrance to a track near Fir Grove, next to White Lodge House.
Woodpeckers and other birds. Woodland species include cuckoo, heather, rowan, wood ant and bluebell. Dogs must be on leads.

HENFIELD

Sussex Wildlife Trust
All native wildlife
Woodsmill, Henfield, West Sussex, BN5 9SD.
Tel: 01273 492630. **Fax:** 01273 494500.
e-mail: enquiries@sussexwt.org.uk
web: www.sussexwt.org.uk
Contact: Sarah Hince.
Opening hours: Open all year except Christmas week.
Admission: Free.

Directions: 1 mile south of Henfield and half a mile north of Small Dole.
Nature reserve with woods, lake and meadow. Events throughout the year. See website for details or phone for enquiries. All native wildlife.

Woods Mill
Nature reserve with lake and waterbed
Horn Lane, Henfield, West Sussex.
Opening hours: Open nature reserve.

Directions: A2037 north of Small Dole.
Lake and waterbed. Main building is in Water Mill. School visits and education programmes. nightingales, woodpeckers, turtle doves, warblers and grey wagtail.

DIRECTORY

A male kangaroo is called a 'boomer'.

HORSHAM

Warnham Nature Reserve
Nature reserve with wildlife walks
Warnham Nature Reserve, Warnham Road,
Horsham, West Sussex, RH12 2RA.
Tel: 01403 256890.
e-mail: leisure@horsham.gov.uk
web: www.horsham.gov.uk
Opening hours: Daily, 10am to 6pm.
Admission: A low-cost fee allows access to
reserve features.

Directions: North-west of Horsham on the
B2237 (just off A24). Reserve is a 20-30
minute walk from Horsham town centre.
Variety of wildlife, plants, birds in a beautful
setting. Visitor centre and cafe. School parties.
Kingfisher, ancient woodlands, dragonflies,
woodpeckers, Warblers.

HOVE

St Andrew's Church
Guided walks
St Andrews Church, Waterloo Street,
Hove, East Sussex.
Tel: 01273 326491.
Contact: Michael Robin.
Opening hours: Tuesday to Saturday, 11am
to 4pm. Ring to arrange.
Admission: Free but donation to Church
Conservation Trust would be welcome.

Directions: On seafront, Waterloo Street is
opposite the Peace Statue.
Beautiful stained glass and late Georgian
marble monuments. Refreshments nearby.
Check answerphone for current events. Dogs
are welcome on the walks. Custodian Michael
Robins always leaves a dog bowl in porch so
the owners can allow their dogs to drink after
a walk on the beach.

LANCING

Lancing Ring Nature Reserve
Nature reserve with chalky grassland
Lancing, West Sussex.
Tel: 01273 625242.
web: www.adur.gov.uk
Opening hours: Open reserve.

Directions: See website for map.
Local wildlife.

LEWES

Mount Caburn
Nature reserve with beautiful
scenery and wildlife
Nr Lewes, East Sussex.
Tel: 01273 476595.
Opening hours: Open park.

Directions: Southern edge of an isolated tract of
downland 3km from Lewes. Access is from
Glynde village by the footpath opposite the shop
or along the path opposite Glynde Place.
The Caburn is one of the best preserved and
most important hill-forts in Sussex, dating from
the late Bronze Age. The warmth of the south-
facing slopes allows many plants to thrive.
From July, chalkhill blue butterflies appear in
great numbers, feeding on marjoram. The
scarce, day-flying Forester Moth with its
metallic green colours.

www.animalloversguides.co.uk

DIRECTORY

Railway Land Local Nature Reserve
Nature reserve with woodland, pond and garden
Nr Lewes town centre, Lewes, East Sussex.
web: www.mmhistory.gov.uk
Contact: Annabelle Kennedy.
Opening hours: Open reserve.

Woodland, pond and Victorian garden. Birds, marsh frogs, insects and flora. Annabelle Kennedy can be contacted at the Council Offices in Southover House in Lewes.

LITTLEHAMPTON

Arun Dunes and Sea Nature Trail
Nature trail and wildlife walk
Visitor Centre, 63-65 Surrey Street, Littlehampton,West Sussex.
Tel: 01903 718984.
web: www.naturecoast.org.uk
Opening hours: Open reserve.

Directions: Situated near Littlehampton train station off the B2140.
1.5 mile wildlife walk from Littlehampton, seeing river, saltmarsh, sand dunes, shingle and marine habitats. Facilities available in Littlehampton. Sandpipers, eels, spider crabs and dog fish.

West Beach Local Nature Reserve
Nature reserve with beautiful scenery and wildlife
Littlehampton, West Sussex.
Tel: 01903 718984.
e-mail: daphne.fisher@arun.gov.uk
web: www.arun.gov.uk
Opening hours: Call to enquire about tours.

Directions: Call visitor centre on number above.
Aquatic and terestrial oganisms. Marine vertebrates and birds. Local wildlife habitats, sand dunes and sea.

MILL HILL

Mill Hill
Nature reserve with beautiful scenery and wildlife.
Mill Hill, East Sussex.
Tel: 01273 625242.
web: www.adur.gov.uk
Opening hours: Open reserve.

Directions: East of Stone Cross.
Views across the Adur Valley. Wild flowers and butterflies, especially the rare Adonis blue butterfly. 500 metres of easy access trail for the disabled.

NEWHAVEN

Sussex Amphibian and Reptile Group
Conservation of indigenous herpertofauna – frogs, lizards, toads, newts, snakes and turtles
c/o 7 Gibbon Road, Newhaven, East Sussex, BN9 9EW.
Tel: 01273 515762.
e-mail: d.harris8@btinternet.com
Contact: David Harris.

PETWORTH

Burton & Chingford Ponds
Nature reserve with pond wildlife, including wildfowl, plants and insects
Petworth, East Sussex.
Nearest postcode GU28 0JR.
Tel: 01273 492630. **Fax:** 01273 494500.
web: www.sussexwt.org.uk

Directions: Located between Burton Hill and Crouch Farm.
Pond wildlife including wildfowl, plants and insects. Dragonflies, marsh orchids and tussock sedge. Dogs must be on leads. Parking is limited. Surfaced and unsurfaced footpaths.

DIRECTORY

Ebernoe Common and Butcherland
National nature reserve
with ancient woodland
Nr Petworth, West Sussex.
Nearest postcode GU28 9JY.
web: www.sussexwt.org.uk
Opening hours: Open park.

Many dormice and bats. Nightingales, fritillary butterflies. Dogs must be on leads.

The Mens
Nature reserve with woodland
Crimbourne, Petworth, West Sussex.
Opening hours: Open park.

Directions: Off the A272.
A woodland reverting to natural state with a wild, untamed feel. Near cycle network. 160 hectares so a compass is advisable.

POLEGATE

Arlington Reservoir
Conservation area with dog-walking park
Berwick, Nr Polegate, East Sussex.
Tel: 01323 870810.
e-mail: contactcentre@southeastwater.co.uk
web: www.southeastwater.co.uk
Opening hours: Open reservoir.

Directions: Approximately half a mile off the A27 Lewes to Eastbourne Road. Signposted to Berwick.
Beautiful settings with nature trail. Toilets, car park and several picnic areas.

PULBOROUGH

Pulborough Brooks
Superb nature reserve set in the heart of the beautiful Arun Valley. A must-see!
Wiggonholt, Pulborough, West Sussex, RH20 2EL.
Tel: 01798 875851. **Fax:** 01798 873816.
e-mail: pulborough.brooks@rspb.org.uk
web: www.rspb.org.uk
Contact: N Andrews.
Opening hours: Daily, 10am to 5pm.
Admission: Free for RSPB Members.
Adults £3.50. Children £1.00. Family £7.00.
Concessions. £2.50.

Directions: On A283 between Pulborough and Storrington.
Nature trail with viewpoints and hides.
Tearoom, shop, play area and toilets.
See events leaflet on arrival. Electric buggy provided for the disabled.

Waltham Brooks
Nature reserve!
Off Main Road to Pulborough,
Pulborough, West Sussex.
Opening hours: Open Park.

Directions: Car park at Greatham Bridge.
Wildfowl including teal, redshank, snipe,
lapwing and marsh plant. Grazing marsh with
a large open water area important for birds.
43 hectare.

RYE

Castle Water, Rye Harbour
**Lovely to visit. Bird watching all year with
unusual insects**
Rye Harbour Nature Reserve,
East Sussex, TN36 4LU.
web: www.wildrye.info
Opening hours: Open all times. Information
centre open 10am to 5pm (Summer).

Directions: South-east of Rye, signposted off
the A259 Winchelsea to Rye road.
Bird watching, including rare birds. Car park,
toilets, information centre and bird watching
hides. Notice board on
www.yates.clara.net/noticeboard. Frequent sights
of rare breeds of birds. Dogs must be on leads.

Flatropers Wood
Nature reserve with wildlife walks
Rye, East Sussex.
Nearest postcode TN31 6TH.
web: www.sussexwt.org.uk
Opening hours: Open park.

Directions: Access from Bixley Lane which joins
the A268 2km west of Peasmarsh.
Woodland flowers and plants. Variety of trees.
Woodpeckers, newts and beetles. Dogs must be
on leads.

SEAFORD

Seaford Head Nature Reserve
Beautiful scenery with local wildlife
West of Cuckmere Haven, Seaford, East Sussex.
Tel: 01323 871095.
Opening hours: Open reserve.

Directions: Within the Sussex Downs, between
Seaford and Beachy Head.
Vegetable shingle bark, flowers and beautiful cliffs.
Mammals and reptiles, birds, insects, Chalkhill
Blue Butterflies and bee-wolf.

Seven Sisters Country Park
**Beautiful wildlife, exhibitions, educational
tours, walled garden and restaurant**
Sussex Downs Conservation,
Exceat, Seaford, East Sussex, BN25 4AD.
Tel: 01323 870280. **Fax:** 01323 871070.
e-mail: sevensisters@southdowns-aont.gov.uk
web: www.sevensisters.org.uk
Contact: Katherine.
Opening hours: See website.

Directions: Situated at Exceat just off A259
between Eastbourne and Seaford.
Visitor centre, toilets and restaurant. School
parties and educational tours. Educational centre
ideal for dog walkers and cyclists. Interesting
history. Dogs must be on leads.

DIRECTORY

DID YOU KNOW?
*Butterflies shiver
in the cold.*

Conservation

SIDLESHAM

Pagham Harbour
Nature reserve with wildlife walks
The Ferry, Selsey Road, Sidlesham,
Chichester, West Sussex, PO20 7NE.
Tel: 01243 641508.
web: www.sussexwt.org.uk
Opening hours: Open park.

Huge variety of wildfowl and waders. Wildlife
hospital to the east. Visitor centre. Saltmarsh,
mudflats, copses, farmland, lagoons, reedbeds
and shingle beaches. Southern marsh orchid can
be seen here. Most of the 1450-acre reserve a
Site of Special Scientific Interest. Dogs must be on
leads.

SOUTH MALLING

Malling Downs
Country walk and nature reserve
Small entrance at Wheatsheaf Garden,
Opposite petrol station, South Malling,
East Sussex, Nearest postcode BN8 5AA.
Tel: 01273 494777.
web: www.sussexwt.org.uk
Opening hours: Open nature reserve.

Directions: Head east from Lewes Town
centre, take small entrance at Wheatsheaf
Gardens opposite petrol station.
Wonderful views with a variety of fauna and a
variety of wildlife. Many butterfly species
including Chalkhill Blue and Adonis. Grazing at
sometimes of the year. Dogs must be on leads.

SOUTHWATER

Southwater Country Park
Wildlife area and beautiful setting
Southwater Country Park, Cripplegate Lane,
Southwater, West Sussex, RH13 7UN.
Tel: 01403 215263.
e-mail: leisure@horsham.gov.uk
web: www.horsham.gov.uk
Opening hours: Daily, 8am to dusk.

Directions: Located in the southern part of
the village of Southwater, off Cripplegate Lane.
Cripplegate Lane is off the main Worthing
Road.
Recreational activities such as orienteering and
canoeing. Visitor centre, toilets and cafe are
open weekends and school holidays. Lizards,
kingfishers, nightingales and various dragonflies
and butterflies.

STEDHAM

Iping and Stedham Commons
Beautiful scenery with many plant species
Stedham, West Sussex.
Nearest postcode GU29 0PB.
Tel: 01273 492630. **Fax:** 01273 494500.
web: www.sussexwt.org.uk
Opening hours: Open park.

Directions: Midhurst is accessible via the A286 or
the A272. There is a large car park on the Elsted
Road just off the A272. Birds including warblers
and wood lark. Many insect varieties. Dogs must
be on leads.

DID YOU KNOW? To show anger, a gorilla curls its fingers.

DIRECTORY

The temperature of a newly laid hen's egg is 105 degrees F.

WADHURST

Bewl Water
Lovely nature reserve and reservoir with beautiful views
Clapham Lane, Nr Wadhurst, East Sussex.
Nearest postcode TN5 7LH.
Tel: 01273 492630. **Fax:** 01273 494500.
Visitor centre on reservoirs, northern side.
01892 890661.
web: www.sussexwt.org.uk
Opening hours: Open nature reserve.

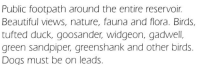

Public footpath around the entire reservoir. Beautiful views, nature, fauna and flora. Birds, tufted duck, goosander, widgeon, gadwell, green sandpiper, greenshank and other birds. Dogs must be on leads.

WEST STOKE

Kingley Vale
Fabulous nature reserve and yew forest. gamekeeper's lodge
West Stoke House Farm, West Stoke, Chichester, West Sussex, PO18 9BN.
Tel: 01243 557353. **Fax:** 01243 557353.
e-mail: dave.mercer@english-nature.org.uk
web: www.english-nature.org.uk
Contact: Dave Mercer.
Opening hours: Open nature reserve.
Admission: Free admission.

Directions: Take the A286 out of Chichester. At mid Lavant take the left turn to West Stoke, the carpark is sign posted National Nature Reserve. Fallow deer, roe deer, badgers, stoats, rabbits, mice, buzzards. Dogs must be on leads.

WESTMESTON

Ditchling Beacon
Country walk and nature reserve
Access from National Trust Car Park
Westmeston, East Sussex, BN6 8XG.
Tel: 01273 494777.
web: www.sussexwt.org.uk
Opening hours: Open nature reserve.

Directions: See website for details. Chalkhill Blue butterflies. Beautiful grassland flowers. The road through the reserve is too dangerous for pedestrians on foot.

DIRECTORY

BATTLE

1066 Country Walk
Country walk and nature trail
Battle Tourist Information Centre,
Battle Abbey Gatehouse, High Street,
Battle, East Sussex, TN33 0AD.
Tel: 01424 773721. **Fax:** 01424 773436.
e-mail: battletic@rother.gov.uk
web: www.1066country.com
Opening hours: Open country.

Directions: Just off junction of A2100 and
Marley Lane.
Stunning countryside between Rye and Battle.
Information centres at Rye and Battle. Many
events throughout the year. See website for
details. Many species of plants and wildlife.
Dogs must be on leads.

Buckwell Farm
**Country walk with views of the
High Weald landscape**
Buckwell Farm, Nr Battle, East Sussex.
Opening hours: Open park.

Directions: The 2km circular walk connects
with a public right of way to take you through
a characteristic High Weald landscape which is
being sensitively managed for the benefit of
wildlife. Hedgerows are being restored through
a programme of copicing and replanting and
arable land is being reverted to species-rich
grassland using seed from neighbouring flower-
rich meadows. Please keep to the marked path
and keep dogs on leads.

BEXHILL

Broad Oak Park
Open park with allotments
Broad Oak Park, Broad Oak Lane,
Bexhill, East Sussex.
Tel/contact: Rother District Council
web: www.rother.gov.uk
Opening hours: Open park.

Directions: See website for directions.
Allotments, open space and woodland.
Horse rides available.

Egerton Park
Lovely park with pretty lakes
Egerton Park, Egerton Road,
Bexhill, East Sussex.
Tel/contact: Rother District Council
web: www.rother.gov.uk
Opening hours: Open park.

Directions: Start at Sackville Road in town
centre and head towards seafront. Egerton
Road is on the right hand side but Egerton Park
is on the left. Play area, bowls, five-a-side
football, tennis, putting, boating lake, yacht
pond, swans and ducks.

Galley Hill Park
**Take your dog and children – wonderful
views across the sea**
Galley Hill Park, East Parade,
Bexhill, East Sussex.
Tel/contact: Rother District Council.
web: www.rother.gov.uk
Opening hours: Open park.

Directions: Along the seafront towards
Hastings, up on the hill.
Play area. Basketball hoop. Skateboard ramps.
Cafe a short walk from park.

www.animalloversguides.co.uk

DIRECTORY

BILLINGSHURST

The Wey and Arun Canal Trust
Canal restoration and wildlife walk
The Granary, Flitchfold Farm, Loxwood,
Billingshurst, West Sussex, RH14 0RJ.
Tel: 01403 752403. **Fax:** 01403 753991.
e-mail: pr@wact.org.uk
web: www.weyandarun.co.uk
Contact: Sally Schupke.
Opening hours: Daily, 9am to 9pm

Directions: The public trip boat operates from
the landing stage at the Onslow Arms on the
B2133 in Loxwood.
Scenic towpath along the Surrey/Sussex border.
Refreshments available at the canalside pub.
Small boats rally in May. Heritage open days in
September and special boat trips Christmas,
Boxing Day and Easter. Dogs and horses are
very welcome to use the wide and restored
towpath. Boat trips cost £4.00 per person.

BLACKBOYS

Brownings Farm
Wildlife walk!
Blackboys, East Sussex.
Tel: 020 7238 6907.
web: www.defra.gov.uk
Opening hours: Open park but best to visit
spring, summer and autumn.

Directions: Accessible off the B2102 towards
Blackboys. East of Hollow Lane.
Picnic areas and linking paths. Range of
birds, mammals and insects. Dogs must be
on leads.

BOGNOR REGIS

Hotham Park
*Lovely park to walk your dog and
take the children*
Hotham Way, Bognor Regis, West Sussex.
Opening hours: Open park.

Picnic area, play area, mini railway, tennis
courts, boating lake, putting green and pond.
Cafe and toilets. Crows and wood pigeons,
blackbirds, tits, sparrows, starlings, robins and
wrens. Squirrels by the millions, rabbits, foxes
and fish in the pond. Many sweet pea trees in
the park and a rose garden.

Marine Park Gardens
*Lovely park to walk your dog and
take the children*
Marine Drive West, Bognor Regis, West Sussex.
Tel: 01243 820245.
web: http://bognor-regis.co.uk
Opening hours: Open park.

Directions: On the seafront.
Road train from pier will take you to the park.
Bedding displays, putting green and fountain.

BRIGHTON

Devil's Dyke
National Trust open space
Devil's Dyke Road, Brighton,
East Sussex, BN6 9DY.
Tel: 01273 834830.
Opening hours: Open park.

Deepest dry valley in the world. Horse riding trails Facilities are in the local pub.

Dyke Road Park
Park with lots to do as well
as walk your dog
Dyke Road Park, Dyke Road, Brighton,
East Sussex, BN3 6EH.
Opening hours: Open park.

Directions: Opposite the Booth Museum. Bowling, tennis, playground and football pitch. Cafe and toilets.

East Brighton Park
Fun for all the family park
Wilson Avenue, Brighton, East Sussex.
Tel: 01273 292059.
Opening hours: Open park.

Directions: Behind Brighton Marina. Wide open space to contemplate wildlife. Cafe, tennis, football, cricket, playground, small dog-free area, caravan grounds. Local wildlife.

Easthill Park
Park with fun for all the family
Easthill Way, Brighton, East Sussex.
Tel: 01273 292216.
Opening hours: Open park.

Directions: Between Easthill Way and Fairfield Gardens in Portslade. At the edge of Portslade village.
Cafe, toilet and picnic area. Green Flag Award. Green woodpecker and swift.

Hollingbury Park
Park with lots to do as well
as walk your dog
Ditchling Road, Brighton, East Sussex, BN1 7HS.
Opening hours: Open park.

Directions: Between A23 and A27. Golf club, toilets and cafe.

Preston Park
Brighton's first and largest planned park
Preston Road (A23), Brighton, East Sussex.
Tel: 01273 292060.
Opening hours: Open park.

Directions: On eastern side of the London to Brighton Road (A23). Preston Drive to the north and Preston Park Avenue to the east. Opposite the western side is the Rock Garden. Two cafes, children's playground, toilet, lawn bowls, tennis, cricket, football, skating, cycle track and skateboarding. Phone for details of events. Green Flag Award.

DID YOU KNOW

The bullfrog's skin turns dark 12 hours before rain.

Queen's Park
Family fun park
Between West Drive and East Drive,
Brighton, East Sussex.
Tel: 01273 293193.
Opening hours: Open park.

Directions: Signposted from seafront and junction of Eastern Road and Egremont Place. Lake with cascades, ducks and a fountain. Cafe, toilet, disabled toilet, scented garden, tennis, bowls and lake. Wildlife garden with workshops run by Council.

Stanmer Park
Recreation and wildlife facility
English Heritage (Grade II-listed site)
Brighton, East Sussex.
Tel: 01273 292060.
Opening hours: Open park.

Directions: West of Sussex University Campus, off A27 Lewes Road.
Grade II-listed stable complex. Pasture land and pond.

The Level
Park with fun for all the family
Ditchling Road, Brighton, East Sussex.
Opening hours: Open park.

Directions: Between Ditchling Road and Lewes Road, near St Peter's Church. Centre of town by the Open Market.
Cafe, playground, sand pit, paddling pool, skateboard run, cycling.

Undercliff Walk, Saltdean
Wonderful walk with rock pools
Undercliff Walk, Brighton, East Sussex.
Opening hours: Open walkway.

Directions: Follow the path from Brighton Marina towards Saltdean.
The rock pools are alive with various sea creatures. Cafe and toilet.

Withdean Woods
Woodlands surrounded by urban development along London/Brighton railway line
Withdean Road, Brighton, East Sussex.
Opening hours: Open park.

Directions: Access from Withdean Road and Eldred Avenue. South of Withdean Stadium and west of the Deneway.
Local nature reserve. No facilities available. Diverse woodland bird community and native fauna and flora. Great spotted woodpecker, tawny owl and goldcrest.

CHICHESTER

Chichester Harbour
Dog walking harbour with wildlife
Harbour Office, Itchenor, Chichester,
West Sussex, PO20 7AW.
Tel: 01243 512301.
e-mail: harbourmaster@conservancy.co.uk
web: www.conservancy.co.uk
Opening hours: Open harbour.
Admission: Some facilities will charge.

Directions: Located north of B2179 towards West Wittering.
Area of outstanding natural beauty, nature walks, boating, wildlife. Visitor information, toilets, shop and cafe. Wading birds, mud creatures, sea wildlife, herons and gulls.

DIRECTORY

Earnley Butterflies and Gardens
Walk among tropical butterflies and exotic birds
133 Almodington Lane, Earnley, Chichester, West Sussex, PO20 7JR.
Tel: 01243 512637.
Opening hours:
March to October, 10am to 6pm.
Admission: Call to enquire.

Wander through a maze of 17 covered theme gardens, with a free competition for kids. See the artefacts from the shipwrecked HMS Hazardous, sunk in 1706. Refreshments, picnic and play area, crazy golf and gift shop.

West Dean Gardens
Beautiful gardens and open landscape with wildlife
West Dean, Chichester, West Sussex.
Tel: 01243 811301. **Fax:** 01243 811342.
e-mail: gardens@westdean.org.uk/site/gardens
web: www.westdean.org.uk
Opening hours: March to October, 10.30am to 5pm, daily. November to February, 10.30am to 4pm, Wednesday to Sunday. Christmas and New Year: Closed 24th December to 3rd January.
Admission: March to October: Adults £6.00. Children £2.50. November to February: Adults £3.00. Children £1.25.

Directions: Accessible from the A286 southwards to Chichester. Take the A27 from the West.
Visitor centre. Licensed restaurant. Several events hosted annually. Victorian glasshouses. Walled kitchen garden. Guide dogs allowed.

CRAWLEY

Buchan Country Park
Wide variety of birds, reptiles, deer and foxes
Horsham Road, Crawley,
West Sussex, RH11 9HQ.
Tel: 01293 542088. **Fax:** 01293 513811.
e-mail: buchanpark@westsussex.gov.uk
web: www.westsussex.gov.uk
Contact: Simon Rowledge.
Opening hours: Summer, 8am to 8pm. Winter, 8am to 6pm.

Directions: Access from westbound A2220 Horsham Road from Crawley.
Haven for quiet recreation and nature study. Also has a visitor centre. Events throughout the year. See website or park itself for adverts. Wide variety of birds, dragonflies, reptiles, deer and foxes.

CROWBOROUGH

The Cuckoo Trail
Nature trail
Wealden District Council, Crowborough, East Sussex, TN6 1BR.
Tel: 01273 481637.
e-mail: countryside.management@eastsussex.gov.uk
web: www.eastsussex.gov.uk
Opening hours: Open trail.

Directions: Situated from Eridge to Polegate, passing through Heathfield, Horam, Hellingly and Hailsham.
Dog walking, horse riding, cycling and wildlife. Accommodation, toilets, information centre, shops, cafe and pub. Wildlife in a beautiful setting.

DIRECTORY

EAST GRINSTEAD

Forest Way Country Park
30 acres of beautiful countryside
Nr East Grinstead, East Sussex.
Tel: 01273 481000. **Fax:** 01273 481261.
web: www.eastsussex.gov.uk
Opening hours: Open park.

Directions: Near the B2110 between Forest
Row in the East.
Horse riding and cycling allowed. Swallows,
badgers and foxes.

EAST HOATHLY

Crouches Farm
Network of bridle paths and a vast range
of countryside and insects to view
Crouches Farm, East Hoathly, East Sussex.
Tel: 01825 840242.
web: www.defra.gov.uk
Opening hours: Open access.

Call for specific locations permitted for
bridlepaths. Bridlepaths and views of
countryside. Permissive routes for horse riders.

FONTWELL

Denmans Garden
Walled garden, gravel stream,
ponds and wildlife
Denmans Lane, Fontwell, Nr Arundel,
West Sussex, BN18 0SU.
Tel: 01243 542808. **Fax:** 01243 544064.
e-mail: denmans@denmans-garden.co.uk
web: www.denmans-garden.co.uk
Opening hours: 9am to 5pm.
Admission: Adults £3.95. Children (4-16)
£2.25. Seniors £3.45.

Directions: Situated off the A27 (westbound)
between Chichester and Arundel. Adjacent to
Fontwell Racecourse.
Garden cafe and plant centre. Cafe and toilets.
Courses, functions and evening visits. Guide
dogs welcome.

FRANT

Eridge Park
Walk along the edge of Eridge Old Park –
views of deer and other wildlife
Eridge, Nr Frant, East Sussex.
Tel: 020 7238 5909.
web: www.defra.gov.uk
Opening hours: Open park.

Directions: Small circular route available
through Whitehill Wood and Saxonbury Wood.
Lovely walks. Eridge Old Park is reputed to be
one of the oldest and largest deer parks in
England. Dogs must be on leads.

DIRECTORY

DIRECTORY

HASTINGS

Alexandra Park
109-acre park with wildlife, trees and duck pond
Lower Park Road, Hastings, East Sussex.
Tel: 01424 781066. **Fax:** 01424 781769.
e-mail: hbc@hastings.gov.uk
web: www.hastings.gov.uk
Opening hours: Open park.

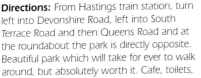

Directions: From Hastings train station, turn left into Devonshire Road, left into South Terrace Road and then Queens Road and at the roundabout the park is directly opposite. Beautiful park which will take for ever to walk around, but absolutely worth it. Cafe, toilets, tennis courts, bandstand, fishery and boating lake. Ducks, bird species, squirrels and fish. The best burger and chips overlooking a lovely park.

HAYWARDS HEATH

Borde Hill Garden
Fabulous heritage garden with lots going on including sculptures
Borde Hill Garden, Balcombe Road, Haywards Heath, West Sussex, RH16 1XP.
Tel: 01444 450326. **Fax:** 01444 440427.
e-mail: info@bordehill.co.uk
web: www.bordehill.co.uk
Contact: Sarah Brook.
Opening hours: April 1st to 31st October daily, 10am to 6pm.
Admission: Adults £6.00. Children £5.00. Concessions £3.50.

Directions: Leave the A23 at Junction 10a, follow the B2036 to Cuckfield and turn left into Ardingly Road. At the T-Junction, turn left and Borde Hill is 300 metres on the left. Botannical collection of plants. Tea rooms, restaurant and toilets. Heritage garden set within 200 acres of spectacular parkland. Stunning views and magical woodland and lakeside walks. Dogs must be on leads.

Nymans Gardens
Rare, beautiful plans, rose garden and woodland walks
Staplefield Road, Handcross, Haywards Heath, West Sussex, RH17 6EB.
Tel: 01444 405250. **Fax:** 01444 400253.
e-mail: nymans@nationaltrust.org.uk
web: www.nationaltrust.org.uk
Opening hours: February to October: Wednesday to Sunday, 11am to 6pm and bank holidays
Admission: Adults £7.00. Children £3.50. Family £17.50.

Restaurant, shop and plant sales area. See website for details of events. Local wildlife. Rok garden, sunken garden, topiary, lakes and cascades.

HORSHAM

Horsham Park
Lovely park for all the family, with wildlife too
Park House, North Street, Horsham, West Sussex.
Tel: 01403 215256.
e-mail: leisure@horsham.gov.uk
web: www.horsham.gov.uk
Opening hours: Open park.

Directions: North of the town's main shopping area, on the way to the train station. Lakes, trees and colourful flowerbeds. Cafe, tennis courts, children's play area and bowls green. Family fun days and concerts. See website. Wildlife in a beautiful setting.

Leechpool and Owlbeech Woods

Ancient woodland of 53 acres
Leechpool and Owlbeech Woods
Harwood Road, Horsham, West Sussex.
Tel: 01403 731218.
e-mail: leisure@horsham.gov.uk
web: www.horsham.gov.uk
Opening hours: Open woodland.

Directions: To the east of Horsham off the Harwood Road (B2195).
Rare selection of flora and fauna.

HOVE

Hove Park

Fun for all the family park
Old Shoreham Road, Hove, East Sussex.
Tel: 01273 292974.
Opening hours: Tuesday to Saturday, 10am to 5pm. Sunday, 2pm to 5pm.

Directions: On the A270 - entrance opposite the Goldstone Retail Park.
Twelve tennis courts, bowling green, basketball court, children's playground, cafe, miniature steam railway. The Goldstone - a huge rock dug up in 1900 is believed to be a sacred Druid stone. Parking in residential area.

The shark is the only marine animal that doesn't sleep at all.

St Ann's Well Gardens

A really beautiful and quiet park which has something for everyone
Davigdor Road, Hove, East Sussex.
Tel: 01273 292974.
Opening hours: Open park.

Directions: Half a mile from Hove seafront, northwards.
Chalybeate (iron bearing) spring. Also a ley line to the South Downs. Scented garden, cafe, toilets, tennis, bowls, playground and conservation areas. Green Flag Award. Fish pond with biological filter system. Many friendly squirrels.

IDEN

Barons Grange and Moat Farm

Beautiful views, bridle path leads to views of Walland & Romney Marsh
Barons Grange, Nr Iden, East Sussex.
Tel: 020 7238 6907.
web: www.defra.gov.uk

Directions: Access is available off the B2082 under the River Rother.
Rich in frog wildlife - the 'frog' chorus is particularly loud in June. Dogs must be on leads. Layby at new bridge provides excellent parking.

LEWES

Landport Brooks

Wildlife Walk!
Offham Road, Lewes, East Sussex.
Tel: 020 7238 6907.
web: www.defra.gov.uk
Opening hours: Open park.

Directions: Access is via Offham Road (A2029). Turn at the sign of the "Tally Ho" pub.
Rich in wildlife, particularly ditch flora and fauna. Dogs must be on leads.

DIRECTORY

Lewes Brooks
Wildlife walk!
Nr Mountfield Road, Lewes, East Sussex.
Tel: 020 7238 6907.
web: www.defra.gov.uk
Opening hours: Open park.

Directions: Access points situated near Priory School playing fields and near the Southgraham junction off the A26/A27 roundabout.
Restored areas of natural beauty, rich in wildlife. Grazing cattle and wildlife. Dogs must be on leads.

LITTLEHAMPTON

Brookfield Park
Lovely park to walk your dog and take the children
Brookfield Park, Worthing Road, Littlehampton, West Sussex.
Opening hours: Open park.

Woodland, grassland, wild flowers, pond, cycleway, footpath, play area, football area, basketball area and around 8,000 trees.

Marina Gardens
Lovely park to walk your dog and take the children
St Catherines Road, Littlehampton, West Sussex.
Opening hours: Open park.

Mewsbrook Park
Lovely park to walk your dog and take the children
Sea Road, Littlehampton, West Sussex.
Opening hours: Open park.

Boating lake, mini railway, shelters, play areas for children, cafe and the Ruby Gardens conservation area.

MIDHURST

Cowdray Leisure
Badger watching. Guided wildlife awareness. School trips catered for.
The Estate Office, Easebourne, Midhurst, West Sussex, GU29 0AQ.
Tel: 01730 812423. **Fax:** 01730 817962.
e-mail: leisure@cowdray.co.uk
web: www.cowdray.co.uk
Contact: Darron Carver.
Opening hours: By appointment only.
Admission: £70 for an outing.
Maximum of four in group.

Directions: 1 mile north of Midhurst on the A272.
Guided walks and badger watching. Toilets and refreshments in golf club. Most indigenous mammals and birds, flora and fauna.

PETWORTH

Petworth House and Park
Beautiful park in Victorian setting
Petworth, West Sussex, GU28 0AE.
Tel: 01798 342207. **Fax:** 01798 342963.
e-mail: petworth@nationaltrust.org.uk
web: www.nationaltrust.org.uk
Opening hours: Open most of the year. See website for more details.
Admission: Adults £7.50. Children £4.00. Family £19.00.

Directions: Located north off the A285. Wildlife, beautiful landscapes and family attractions.
House, shop, restaurant, park and pleasure ground. Open-air concerts. Set in a deer park. Introductory talks.

PRESTON

Blakers Park
Lovely park for all the family
Cleveland Road, Preston Drove and
Southdown Road, East Sussex.
Tel: 01273 293080.
Opening hours: Open park.

Directions: Follow directions to Five Ways,
Ditchling Road, then down to Preston Drove.
Clocktower (miniature copy of Big Ben).
Cafe, toilets, tennis court, playground and
clocktower.

ROTTINGDEAN

Kipling Gardens
*Park with rose garden, herb garden
and wild garden*
The Elms, Rottingdean, West Sussex.
Tel: 01273 292059.
Opening hours: Open park.

Directions: Opposite North End House.
Replica of Victorian walled garden. Birds.

RYE

Camber Sands
*Dog walking park with fun for
all the family*
Camber, Near Rye, East Sussex.
Tel: 01797 225207.
web: www.eastsussex.gov.uk
Opening hours: Open beach.

Directions: Camber is situated three miles east
of Rye. Signposted off the A259.
Dog walking, horse riding and cycling in
beautiful setting. Car park and toilets Sealife
and dune animals and birds. Dogs can be
walked in marked zones only.

SOUTH CHAILEY

Hewenstreet Circuit
*Lovely walk with views of
the South Downs*
South Chailey, East Sussex.

Directions: A275 Lewes Road at Hewenstreet.
8km walk with lovely views. Dogs must be on
leads.

DIRECTORY

UCKFIELD

Heaven Farm

Nature trail with oast house, campsite, ancient woodland, wallabies and deer
Furners Green, Uckfield, East Sussex, TN22 3RG.
Tel: 01825 790226. **Fax:** 01825 790881.
e-mail: butler@enterprises@farmline.com
web: www.heavenfarm.co.uk
Contact: John Butler.
Opening hours: March to October, 10am to 5.30pm.
Admission: Camping charges.

Directions: From Brighton, follow A23 north bound to Bolney Junction, follow A272 through Haywards Heath to Chailey, turn left at mini roundabout along A275, then 4 miles on the left. Nature trail and wildlife. Located on the Greenwich Meridian Line. Tea rooms, campsite, toilets, museum and gift shop. Wallabies and deer.

Ouse Banks

Pleasant walk through waterside meadows
Leading into Lewes Road, Uckfield, East Sussex.
Tel: 020 7238 5909.
web: www.defra.gov.uk
Opening hours: Open park.

Wilderness Wood

62 acres with lots of paths and trails. Highly recommended but must keep dog under control
Wilderness Wood, Hadlow Down,
Nr Uckfield, East Sussex.
Tel: 01825 830509. **Fax:** 01825 830977.
e-mail: enquiries@wildernesswood.co.uk
web: www.wildernesswood.co.uk
Contact: Anne Yarrow.
Opening hours: Daily, 10am to 5.30pm.
Admission: Adults £3.15. Children (3-15) £1.90. Under 3s, free. Family £9. Concessions £2.65. Season tickets available and reduced rates from November to February.

Directions: 5 miles north east of Uckfield, in Hadlow Down Village on south side of main A272.
Exhibition throughout the year. Tea room garden with local produce, picnic area and bbq places, play area, gift shop, garden furniture and products including bird boxes, tables and feeders. Please see website or phone for details of events – includes Working Horses Day in March.

WANNOCK

Crane Down

Views of Polegate Windmill and across the Cuckmere
Nr Wannock, East Sussex.
Tel: 020 7238 6907.
web: www.defra.gov.uk
Opening hours: Open park.

Directions: South of Folkington, near Filching Quarry. Path accessible via Mill Way Road next to Cornmill Gardens. Rich in wildlife. Dogs must be on leads.

BATTLE

Battle Dog Training School
Superb training school. Highly
recommended – the author and her dog
went along. Lovely classes
11 Stream Farm Cottages, Battle,
East Sussex, TN33 0HH.
Tel: 01424 774089.
e-mail: gusssit@hotmail.com
Contact: Marianne Van Gils.
Classes: Tuesday and Wednesday evenings,
Thursday mornings.
Fees: Prices available per course.

Directions: St Mary's Church Hall.

*An octopus
really does turn
white with fear.*

BILLINGSHURST

Little Brockhurst Farm Canine Centre
Canine centre. Founder members of
hydrotherapy association
Little Brockhurst Farm, Lordings Road,
Billingshurst, West Sussex, RH14 9JE.
Tel: 01403 784516. **Fax:** 01403 78516.
e-mail: hydrotherapy@littlebrockhurst.com
web: www.littlebrockhurst.com
Contact: Lindsay Williams.
Opening hours:
Monday to Sunday, 9am to 5pm.
Fees: Price list available.

Directions: On B2133, midway between
A272/ A29 at Adversane.
Occasional open days. Contact to find out
Qualified behaviourist.

FELPHAM, BOGNOR REGIS

Bognor Regis and District Dog Training Club
Obedience Training
Felpham Village Hall, Vicarage Lane, Felpham,
Bognor Regis, West Sussex, PO22 7DZ.
Tel: 01243 860083.
e-mail: hilarypepper@aol.com
web: www.bognordogclub.co.uk
Contact: Mrs H Sykes.
Classes: Thursday and Friday, 6.30am to 10am
- according to ability.
Fees: £15 per term (12-13 weeks).
£2.00 membership. £2.50 for family.

Directions: Felpham Village is just east of
Bognor Regis.
Dogs are the main attraction. Shows, rambles
and Christmas parties for dogs and owners.

HAILSHAM

Just Minis Agility Club
Just Minis dog agility under 15
c/o 61 Hawkswood Drive, Hailsham,
East Sussex, BN27 1UP.
Tel: 01323 441583.
e-mail: harlie@tiscali.com
Contact: Denise Welsh.
Classes: Wednesday evenings, 8 to 9pm.
Fees: £4.00 per hour.

Directions: Off A22, opposite Michelham
Priory.
Annual Agility Show.

HEATHFIELD

Weald Agility Society
Dog agility classes
c/o Haverbrack, Cade Street, Heathfield,
East Sussex, TN21 9DA.
Tel: 01435 863221.
Contact: Deanna Bane.

DIRECTORY

LANCING

Lancing Canine Obedience Group
Trains puppies, juniors and advanced classes. Also gives nutrition, behaviour and grooming advice
114 First Avenue, Lancing, Sussex, BN15 9QE.
Tel: 01903 762600.
e-mail: lancingcanineobediencegroup
@btopenworld.com
web:
www.geocities.com/dogtraining2/index.html
Contact: Brenda and Sara Redford.
Opening hours: Saturday, 12 to 4pm.
Fees: Nine-week courses with scale of fees available.

Classes held at a local village hall. Directions given on enrolment for course.

MERSTON, CHICHESTER

Westergate Dog Training
Outdoor dog training, pet obedience. Member of the British Institute of Professional Dog Trainers
4, Merston Cottages, Marsh Lane, Merston, Chichester, West Sussex, PO20 1ED.
Tel: 01243 536231.
e-mail: dustydogtraining@btinternet.com
Contact: Dusty Benson.
Classes: Saturday, 9.30am or by appointment.

All breeds catered for from 12 weeks of age. Reward-based motivational training.

PEASMARSH

D.I.T.T.O. - Barbara Pointer MBIPDT
Dog training and behaviourist
Tel: 01797 230687. **Fax:** 01797 230687.
web: www.dittodogclub.co.uk
Contact: Barbara Pointer.
Classes: By appointment.

SEAFORD

Seaford and District Dog Training Club
Training all levels of the kennel club good citizen scheme
4 Kingsmead Close, Seaford,
East Sussex, BN25 2EY.
Tel: 01323 899032.
e-mail: sddtclub@btinternet.com
Contact: Diane Costanzo.
Classes: Thursdays, 6.30pm to 9.45pm.
Admission: £1.50 per class plus £5.00 annual subs.

Directions: Training takes place in Queens Hall (Drill Hall), Broad Street, Seaford. Toilets on first floor. Monthly walks in forest. Summer BBQ and dog's Christmas party. Dog obedience training.

WOODMANCOTE, Nr Henfield

W Wrighting
Training of racing greyhounds and rehoming retired greyhounds
Albourne Kennels, Wheatsheaf Road, Woodmancote, Nr Henfield,
West Sussex, BN5 9BD.
Tel: 01273 492722. **Fax:** 01273 492722.
e-mail: wasama@ntlword.com
Contact: W Wrighting.
Classes: Sundays, 10am to 3pm.

Directions: South of Henfield on Albourne Road. Every Sunday events, please ring. Only greyhounds allowed.

Reindeer have six stomachs.

ARLINGTON

Pet Behaviour Centre
Member of the Association of Pet
Behaviour Counsellors. Referred by vets
The Old School, Arlington, Nr. Polegate,
East Sussex, BN26 6SE.
Tel: 01323 870558. **Fax:** 01323 870558.
e-mail: inga@petbehaviour.co.uk
web: www.petbehaviour.co.uk
Contact: Inga Mackellar MSc, CCAB.
Specialises in cats and dogs.

BERWICK

Berwick Obedience
Happy well established classes with kind
reward methods
Berwick, East Sussex.
Tel: 01435 830265.
Contact: Diane Jones.
Fees: Seven-week courses available. Prices to
be discussed.

Directions: On the A22.
Dog shows, dog walks and demonstration
team. Specialises in dogs.

BEXHILL-ON-SEA

Naturally Pets
Animal behaviour consultants, dogs
and cats
Sunnylea, Watermill Lane, Bexhill on Sea,
East Sussex, TN39 5JB.
Tel: 01424 830551. **Fax:** 01424 830551.
e-mail: rosemary@naturallypets.co.uk
web: www.petbehaviour.net
Contact: Rosemary.
Opening hours: 24-hour.

Specialises in dogs, cats and equine.

EASTBOURNE

South East Dog Services
Canine Training and Behaviour Consultants
39 Cunningham Drive, Eastbourne,
East Sussex, BN21 6BL.
Tel: 01323 735458.
e-mail: wendy@southeastdog.freeserve.co.uk
web: www.southeastdog.freeserve.co.uk
Contact: Wendy Hanson.

Specialises in puppies.

FELPHAM

Canine Advise
Agility, obedience and behaviour
modification for dogs
7 Outerwyke Road, Felpham, Bognor Regis,
West Sussex, PO22 8HX.
Tel: 01243 869011.
e-mail: john@canineadvise.co.uk
web: www.canineadvise.co.uk
Contact: John Sharwood.
Admission: Hourly rate for training.

DIRECTORY

HOLLINGBURY

Companion Animal Behaviour Services
One-to-one dog training
153 Denton Drive, Hollingbury, Brighton,
West Sussex, BN1 8DL.
Tel: 01273 559399.
e-mail: tanyaj35@hotmail.com
Contact: Tanya Jeffery.
One-to-one dog training by appointment.
Charges discussed with client directly.

A penguin can swim faster than a salmon.

SHOREHAM-BY-SEA

Taking The Lead
Pet training. Vet referrals only
16 Mill Hill Close, Shoreham-by-Sea,
West Sussex, BN43 5TP.
Tel: 01273 463554.
e-mail: gill@takingthelead.co.uk
web: www.takingthelead.co.uk
Contact: Gill White/ John White.
Opening hours: By appointment only.

Directions: Between Brighton and Worthing.

ST LEONARDS ON SEA

Keith Bing MBIPDT
Trainer and behaviourist
4 Sandwich Drive, St Leonards on Sea,
East Sussex, TN38 0XJ.
Tel: 01424 720475.
e-mail: dogmankeith@aol.com
Contact: Keith Bing.
Opening hours: Phone between 8am to 7pm.

Specialises in dog behaviour.

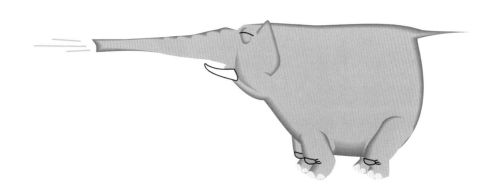

BEXHILL-ON-SEA

The Stable Door
Equine tack shop
3 Collington Mansions, Collington Avenue,
Bexhill-on-Sea, East Sussex, TN39 3PU.
Tel: 01424 216657.
Contact: Katy Rushton
Opening hours: Monday to Saturday, 9.30am
to 5pm. Sunday and Wednesday, closed.

Various special events and sale days
throughout the year.

BURGESS HILL

Bodle Bros Ltd
Agricultural and equestrian store
Southdown Store, Cuckfield Road,
Burgess Hill, West Sussex, RH15 8RE.
Tel: 01444 247757.   **Fax:** 01444 870953.
e-mail: info@bodlebros.co.uk
web: www.bodlebros.co.uk
Opening hours: Monday to Friday, 8.00am to
5.30pm. Saturday, 8.00am to 12.30pm.

Track Right Equestrian shop within the store,
equine wormers. Toilets. Staff will load car.
Various special offers all the time. Trained,
helpful, friendly staff.

T C Tack and Things
3 Valebridge Road, Burgess Hill,
West Sussex, RH15 0RA.
Tel: 01444 230709.   **Fax:** 01444 230709.
Contact: T Carter.
Opening hours: Monday to Friday, 9.30am
to 5.30pm. Saturday, 9.30am to 2.30pm.

Toilets in park across the road.

CHICHESTER

Goodwood Racecourse
Goodwood, Chichester, West Sussex, PO18 0PS.
Tel: 01243 755022.   **Fax:** 01243 755025.
e-mail: racing@goodwood.co.uk
web: www.goodwood.co.uk/horseracing
Opening hours: 11.30 mornings, 4.30
afternoons.

Directions: A3 from London and A27 from
Brigton and Southampton. Look for tourist
signs towards racecourse.
Horse racing. Bars, eateries and toilets. Many
events throughout the year. See website for
more details. Family days.

FIVE OAKS

Redmire Stables and Buildings Ltd
Stable Manufacturers
Five Oaks Sawmill, Haven Road, Five Oaks,
West Sussex, RH14 9BD.
Tel: 01403 785508.   **Fax:** 01403 785333.
e-mail: enquiries@redmire.co.uk
web: www.redmire.co.uk
Contact: Andy Leaver.
Opening hours: Showsite open Monday
to Friday, 8am to 5.30pm and on Saturday,
8am to 12.30pm.
Directions: Between Slinfold and Billingshurst,
just off the A29. 8 miles from Horsham.

DIRECTORY

HOVE

Stable Horses
Natural horsemanship centre
4 Shirley Street, Hove, East Sussex, BN3 3WJ.
Tel: 01273 727785.
e-mail: philip.sharp@ntlworld.com
Contact: Philip Sharp.
Opening hours: By appointment.

Directions: The farms are situated in Shoreham. Ring for directions.

LAUGHTON

The Rug Doctor
Washing and repairing of horse rugs
Lewes Road, Laughton, East Sussex.
Tel: 01323 811313.
e-mail: horserugdoctor@aol.com
Opening hours: Please call.

Please call before visiting. Tack, girths and most non-leather equine equipment. Do not do leather repairs.

LEWES

The Equine Warehouse
Equine and agricultural
The Depot, Spring Gardens, Lewes, East Sussex, BN7 2PT.
Tel: 01273 483399. **Fax:** 01825 721141.
e-mail: nick@farmcare.uk.com
web: www.farmcare.uk.com
Opening hours: Monday to Saturday, 9.30 to 5.30pm. Sunday, 10am to 12 noon.

Windmill Lodge Stables
Equine horse transport in emergencies
Windmill Lodge Stables, Spital Road, Lewes, East Sussex, BN7 1LS.
Tel: 01273 477124.
Opening hours: By appointment.

MARESFIELD

Flight Equestrian Services Ltd
Online shop with over 790 products
26 The Paddock, Maresfield, Uckfield, East Sussex, TN22 2HQ.
Tel: 01825 766262.
e-mail: enquiries@flightequestrian.com
web: www.flightequestrian.com
Opening hours: Call before visiting.

Directions: Located just off crossroads, between A272 and A22. Take exit towards Maresfield.
Clothing and equipment. Tack, supplements, horse equipment, riding gear, yard equipment and horse care.

DITCHLING

Gospels Farm Livery Stables
Small private livery yard
Gospels Farm, Beacon Road, Ditchling,
East Sussex, BN6 8XB.
Tel: 01273 843128.
Opening hours: Not open to public.

GOLDEN CROSS, Nr Hailsham

Golden Cross Equestrian Centre
Liveries – hunter and schooling as well as
individual packages
Chalvington Road, Golden Cross,
East Sussex, BN27 3SS.
Tel: 01825 873022.
e-mail: goldencross@equestrian.co.uk
web: www.equestrian.co.uk/goldencross
Opening hours: By appointment.

Directions: Located on the A22 with good
access from the M23 and M25.
Full, part competition. Toilets, spectators'
gallery, function room and cafe. Regular
affiliated and unaffiliated show jumping and
dressage events. We host many pony and
riding clubs. We host lectures, demos and
clinics.

LEWES

Lower Stoneham Livery & Stud
Livery farm with great atmosphere
Lower Stoneham Farm, Uckfield Road, Lewes,
East Sussex, BN7 5JN.
Tel: 07801 079332.
Opening hours: By appointment.

Large stalls, grazing all year, great atmosphere.
Rescued horses and horses available on loan.

NUTLEY

Pippingford Manor Liveries
Livery yard favours holistic approach
Millbrook Hill, Nutley, East Sussex, TN22 3HW.
Tel: 07803 195311.
e-mail: mail@dwaygood.fsnet.co.uk
web: www.animal-aromatherapy.co.uk
Contact: Deborah Waygood.

Parking by appointment only.

STORRINGTON

Fryern Home Farm Livery
Equine and livery
Fryern Home Farm Stables
Fryern Park, Storrington,
West Sussex, RH20 4BQ.
Tel: 01903 744216.

WHYDOWN, BEXHILL-ON-SEA

Greystud
Equine and livery and dressage.
High standard of care for horses
Whydown Road, Whydown, Bexhill-on-Sea,
East Sussex, TN39 4RB.
Tel: 01424 846123.
Contact: Emma Staples.
Opening hours: Private livery yard.
Ring to arrange.

Directions: Past Turkey Road, located on right-
hand side just after Whydown.
Sometimes hosts clinics for clients.

A typical
polar bear
lives 25 years.

ALBOURNE

Albourne Equestrian Centre
Horse riding school and livery yard
Albourne Equestrian Centre, Henfield Road,
Albourne, West Sussex, BN6 9DE.
Tel: 01273 832989. **Fax:** 01273 833392.
e-mail:
megan@albourneequestriancentre.co.uk
web: www.albourneequestriancentre.co.uk
Contact: Megan Hughes.
Opening hours: 8am to 6pm.
Admission: Price list available.

Shows and clinic throughout the year.

BEXHILL-ON-SEA

Pebsham Riding School
Riding school for the disabled -
approved centre
Pebsham Lane, Bexhill-on-Sea,
East Sussex, TN40 2RZ.
Tel: 01424 732637.
Contact: A Rodriguez.
Opening hours: Book in advance.
Fees: Prices of lessons to be discussed.

Stable yard, indoor school and toilet.

BURGESS HILL

Ditchling Common Riding School
Floodlit indoor school, outside
showjumping, liveries and dressage
Burgess Hill, West Sussex, RH15 0SE.
Tel: 01444 871900.
e-mail: office@ditchlingcommonstud.co.uk
web: www.ditchlingcommonstud.co.uk
Opening hours: Tuesday to Friday, 10am to
1pm and 2pm to 6.30pm. Saturday and Sunday,
9am to 1pm and 2pm to 5.30pm. Monday,
closed.

Directions: From M23/A23, head south
towards Brighton. Take Hickstead exit onto
A2300. Head towards Ditchling Common.
Also do courses, shows, weddings, dressage.
Please see website for more details. Skill at arms,
retreats, camps, BHS exams and horse hire.

CROWBOROUGH

Orchid Riding Centre
Riding centre that teaches children
Walshes Road, Crowborough,
East Sussex, TN6 3RE.
Tel: 01892 652020.
Contact: Nigel Patty.
Opening hours: Tuesday to Saturday, 6.30am
to late
Admission: Phone for details.

Directions: Near Jarvis Brook Street.
Equine disciplines, competing and breeding.

IDEN, Nr Rye

Grove Farm Riding School
Tuition and hacking in local countryside
Grove Farm, Grove Lane, Iden, Nr Rye,
East Sussex, TN31 7PY.
Tel: 01797 280362.
e-mail: lmathews@tesco.net
Contact: Louise.
Opening hours: Seven days a week.
Fees: Prices available for lessons.

Directions: Two miles from Rye.
Pony days for children five years and older.

LEWES

Hamsey Riding School
Indoor riding school with quality horses
Hope in the Valley, Brighton Road, Lewes,
East Sussex, BN7 3JH.
Tel: 01273 477120.
Opening hours: 8.30am to 5pm.

Hacking facilities, beautiful settings.

NEWICK

Mitchels Wood Farm Equestrian Centre
Serious riding school
for children between eight and 14
Newick, Lewes, East Sussex, BN8 4NH.
Tel: 01825 722296. **Fax:** 01825 724010.
e-mail: seona@mitchelswoodfarm.com
web: www.mitchelswoodfarm.com
Opening hours: 8.30am to 6pm.

Directions: Accessible from the A272 towards
North Chailey. Follow Lewes Road leading into
Station Road.
BHS approved. Toilets and tea. Activity days,
ladies' mornings and children's events. Pony
club and camps, liveries and loans, clothing
and equipment. Dogs allowed, but please ring
before coming.

NUTLEY

Ashdown Riding Stables
Lower Misbourne Farm
Nutley, East Sussex, TN22 3LN.
Tel: 01825 712516.
Opening hours: Call before visiting.

Directions: Off the A22
Specialise in hacking. No riding lessons!

DIRECTORY

255

Equine - Saddle & Harness Makers

CROWBOROUGH

Acre Feeds and Saddlery Ltd
Saddlery supplies
Unit 8, Beacon Business Park,
Farningham Road, Crowborough,
East Sussex, TN6 2GD.
Tel: 01892 669660.
Opening hours: 8.30am to 5.30pm.

Saddlery and outdoor clothing.

DITCHLING

Dragonfly Saddlery
We have a wide range of horse riding, dressage and eventing and much more
2 South Street, Ditchling,
East Sussex, BN6 8UQ.
Tel: 01273 844606.
e-mail: sales@dragonflysaddlery.co.uk
web: www.dragonflysaddlery.co.uk
Opening hours: 24-hour shopping online.

Directions: Located off the B2122 leading east to Lewes Road.
Show jumping, pony club and riding club equipment. Public are welcome to visit shop during business hours. Please call to enquire. Member of the Society of Master Saddlers.

EAST HOATHLY

Something Different
Saddlery supplies
Village Works, Unit 3 & 4, 4 London Road,
East Hoathly, East Sussex, BN8 6QA.
Tel: 01825 840086.
Opening hours: 9am to 5pm.

Second hand clothing. Rug cleaning and repairs. Buy and sell second-hand riding clothes and equipment.

POLEGATE

Polegate Saddlery
Horse and rider wear
Station Road, Polegate, East Sussex, BN26 6AS.
Tel: 01323 483382. **Fax:** 01323 484575.
Contact: Mrs J Streeter.
Opening hours: Monday, Tuesday, Wednesday, Friday and Saturday, 9.15am to 5.30pm. Thursday and Sunday, closed.

PUNNETT'S TOWN

Farthing Saddlery
Makes harnesses and saddles
South West View, Punnetts Town,
Nr Heathfield, East Sussex, TN21 9DE.
Tel: 01435 830440. **Fax:** 01435 831626.
e-mail: farthings_42@msn.com
web: www.farthingssaddlery.co.uk
Contact: Jackie Winchester.
Opening hours: Monday to Friday, 10am to 6pm. Saturday, 9am to 1pm. Wednesday, closed.

Directions: From Upper Greenwoods Lane, 200 yards from Punnetts Town Primary School. Off the Battle Road B2096.

UCKFIELD

Sian Saddlery
Saddlery retail and workshop
Vulcan House Farm, Coopers Green, Buxted,
Uckfield, East Sussex, TN22 4AT.
Tel: 01825 732636.
Contact: Sian Mitchell.
Opening hours: Monday to Saturday, 9am to 5pm.

Directions: On the A272 400 yards east of Coopers Green crossroads.

DIRECTORY

DUDDLESWELL

Hobgoblins Stud
Artificial insemination and breeding centre
Duddleswell, Ashdown Forest,
East Sussex, TN22 3BH.
Tel: 01825 713631.
e-mail: info@hobgoblins-stud.com
web: www.hobgoblins-stud.com
Directions: Next to Duddleswell Tea Rooms.

HAYWARDS HEATH

Anglo European Studbook
Horses and breeding
PO Box 630, Haywards Heath,
West Sussex, RH16 1QD.
Tel: 01444 484840. **Fax:** 01444 484844.
e-mail: info@angloeuropeanstudbook.info
web: www.angloeuropeanstudbook.info
Contact: Susie Thompson.
Opening hours:
Monday to Friday, 9am to 5pm.

Various shows around the UK. Please phone
before visiting.

LEWES

Chailey Stud
**Show jumping training centre with indoor
school and solarium**
Station Road, North Chailey, Lewes,
East Sussex, BN8 4HE.
Tel: 01825 722866.
e-mail: chaileystud@hotmail.com
web: www.chaileystud.com
Opening hours: Call before visiting.

Directions: Located on the A272 between
North Chailey and Newick.
Breed and produce, international show
jumpers. Training for horse and rider. Showers
and toilets available. Stallions, show jumping
horses. Call before bringing dog please.

DIRECTORY

ASHINGTON

Vickathea Animal Grooming
Caring expert staff
London Road, Ashington, West Sussex, RH20 3JR.
Tel: 01903 893790.
Contact: Kathie Kirk.
Opening hours: 10am to 4pm, or by arrangement.

Directions: Off the A24 on main road to Ashington.

BECKLEY

Mucky Pups
Dogs only welcome
High Cottage, Beckley, East Sussex.
Tel: 01797 260223.
Contact: Vicky Wilcox.
Opening hours: 9am to 2pm.

BRIGHTON

Doggy Fashion
Grooming parlour and boutique
1 Grafton Street, Kemptown, Brighton,
East Sussex, BN2 1AQ.
Tel: 01273 684711. **Fax:** 01273 684711.
e-mail: info@doggyfashion.co.uk
web: www.doggyfashion.co.uk
Contact: Rupert Elliot.
Opening hours: Tuesday to Sunday, 9am to 5pm.

Just dogs allowed.

CROWBOROUGH

Crowborough Grooming
Grooming parlour. All breeds welcome
11 Springfield Close, Crowborough,
East Sussex, BN6 2PN.
Tel: 01892 611830.
e-mail: tessa.harley.chick@hotmail.com
Opening hours: Flexible hours. Call to arrange.

Kind and caring approach. Your pet will feel the difference and you will see the difference! City and Guilds qualified.

Dashing Dogs
All breeds of dogs welcome
66 East Beeches Road, Crowborough,
East Sussex, TN6 2AZ.
Tel: 01892 669226.
e-mail: campbell.heather@tiscali.co.uk
Contact: Heather Campbell.

Karen's Dog Parlour
Dogs only welcome
Sunrise Cottage, Queens Road, Crowborough,
East Sussex, TN6 1PT.
Tel: 01892 663210.
Contact: Karen Dier.
Opening hours: Monday to Friday, 9am to 5pm. Wednesday, half day. Saturday, morning only.

DID YOU KNOW

The elephant is the only mammal with four knees.

EAST GRINSTEAD

Erard's Dog Salon

Willing to advise on all aspects of grooming

96 Railway Approach, East Grinstead,
West Sussex, RH19 1BP.
Tel: 01342 321885.
Contact: Pam Evans.
Opening hours: Monday to Wednesday and Friday, 8am to 5pm. Saturday, 9am to 12 noon.

Dogs only. Regular grooming plan available.
Practical styling to owner's requirements.
Quality work at a reasonable price.

EAST PRESTON

K9 Clips

Dogs only welcome

2 South Strand Parade, Willowhayne Crescent,
East Preston, West Sussex, BN16 1NR.
Tel: 01903 850919.
Contact: Juliet Davis.
Opening hours: Monday to Friday, 9am to 5pm.

Directions: Shops at south end of East Preston, behind village green.

Sally's Dog Grooming

Grooming parlour for dogs

2 South Strand Parade, East Preston,
West Sussex, BN16 1NR.
Tel: 01903 776800.
Contact: Sally Webb.
Opening hours: Monday to Friday, 9am to 5pm.

Grooming parlour for dogs. Local beaches for walking. Cafes and toilets in local village.

EAST WITTERING

Canine Clips

Dog and cat grooming, 12 years experience. Dog Groomer of the Year 1997

4 Stocks Lane, East Wittering, Chichester,
West Sussex, PO20 8BS.
Tel: 01243 671444.
Contact: Ms Bowles.
Opening hours:
Wednesday and Sunday, 9am to 4pm.

EASTBOURNE

Champooch Studios

Dogs and cats grooming

27 Firle Road, Eastbourne,
East Sussex, BN22 8EE.
Tel: 01323 438999.
Web: www.champooch.co.uk
Contact: Mr Chris Warry.
Tuesday to Friday, 9am to 6pm
Saturday, 9am to 2pm.

HASTINGS

Luxicote Poodles Specialist Dog Groomer

Established 35 years. Poodle specialist, breeder and judge

82 Vicarage Road, Hastings,
East Sussex, TN34 3LY.
Tel: 01424 428692.
Contact: Fay Hughes.
Opening hours: By arrangement.

Directions: Between Mount Pleasant Road and Priory Road.

HAYWARDS HEATH

The Dog Scene
Grooming studio
6 Climping Close, Haywards Heath,
West Sussex, RH16 4DY.
Tel: 01444 454398.
e-mail: allison@tal2000.wanadoo.co.uk
Contact: Allison Talmage.
Opening hours: Monday to Saturday,
9am to 6pm.

Directions: Walking distance from town centre
Dogs allowed only for grooming.

HEATHFIELD

J & J Pets
All breeds catered for
23 Ridgeway Close, Heathfield,
East Sussex, TN21 8NS.
Tel: 01435 866544.
e-mail: jackienjane@aol.com
web: www.jjpetservices.co.uk
Contact: Jackie Plant.

Directions: Off Mutton Hall Lane.

HORSHAM

A Cut Above
Mobile grooming service
27 Swann Way, Horsham, Sussex, RH12 3NQ.
Tel: 01403 272184.
Contact: Victoria James.
Opening hours:
Monday to Saturday, 9am to 5pm.
Fees: Prices available.

Hand stripping.

HOVE

Avon's Dog Grooming
Dog and cat groomers
Unit 1, Lion Mews, Richardson Road, Hove,
West Sussex, BN3 5RA.
Tel: 01273 771779.
Contact: Avon Gobeil.
Opening hours: Monday, closed. Tuesday,
9.30am to 5pm. Wednesday, 9.30am to 5pm.
Thursday, closed. Friday, 9.30am to 5pm.
Saturday, 9am to 1pm.

MIDHURST

Posh Dogs
All breeds taken for grooming and training
Cocking Causeway, Midhurst, West Sussex.
Tel: 01730 816167.
e-mail: lynette@poshdogs.fsnet.co.uk
Contact: Lynette Irwin.
Hours: By appointment.

All breeds taken.

SEAFORD

Raggy's Dog Grooming
Friendly, caring atmosphere
Sutton Parade, Alfriston Road, Seaford,
East Sussex, BN25 3PX.
Tel: 01323 893476.
Opening hours: 10am to 5pm

Directions: Situated just off Eastbourne Road
in Seaford.
All dogs washed and groomed.

DIRECTORY

SOMPTING

Four Paws Dog Grooming
Caters for most breeds of dogs
34 Sedbury Road, Sompting,
West Sussex, BN15 0LL.
Tel: 01903 521499.
e-mail: sarahj@fourpaws.wanadoo.co.uk
Contact: Mrs S Jukes.
Admission: Price list available.

Directions: From North Lancing, along
Manor Road, Meadowview Road. Left into
Halewick Lane. Right by pub, first right into
Sedbury Road.
Does local deliveries and collection of animals.

ST LEONARDS ON SEA

Designer Dogs
Dogs only welcome
6 Harrow Lane, St Leonards on Sea,
East Sussex, TN37 7JR.
Tel: 01424 752113.
e-mail: judyholtuk@hotmail.com
Contact: Judy Holt.

*Tigers walk
on their toes.*

TWINEHAM

Groomingdales
Groomers and shop
Hillmans Farm, Bolney Chapel Road, Twineham,
West Sussex, RH17 5NN.
Tel: 01444 881810.
Contact: Michelle Bourne.
Opening hours: Tuesday, 11am to 5.30pm.
Wednesday, 1pm to 5.30pm. Thursday, 11am
to 5.30pm. Saturday, 9.30am to 4pm.

Directions: 2 minutes from A272 between
Horsham and Haywards Heath.

UPPER BEEDING

Handsome Hounds
Dog grooming salon
4 Hyde Square, Upper Beeding,
West Sussex, BN44 3JE.
Tel: 01903 810061.
Contact: Sharon Smith.
Opening hours: Monday to Friday, 9.30 to
2.30pm, Friday, closed. Saturday, open all day.

Directions: BP Garage on the right. Right at
roundabout.

DIRECTORY

Hotels and B&Bs

BARNHAM

Saxby Bed and Breakfast
Near to Arundel, Dogs welcome
Yapton Road, Barnham, West Sussex, PO22 0B6.
Tel: 01243 552996.
e-mail: saxby-bandb@tiscali.co.uk
web: www.saxbybandb.co.uk
Contact: Lin Hotston.
Opening hours: By appointment.
Rates: Price list available.

COUNTY OAK, CRAWLEY

Ibis Hotel London Gatwick
Three miles from Gatwick.
Dogs are always welcome
London Road, County Oak, Crawley,
West Sussex, RH10 9GY.
Tel: 01293 590300. **Fax:** 01293 590310.
e-mail: H1889@access.com
web: www.ibishotel.com
Contact: Candan Erdeviren.
Opening hours: 24-hour.
Rates: Room prices available on request.

Directions: 3 miles from Gatwick Airport. 10 miles from Crawley town centre. Parking free for hotel guests.

Fleas spend 95% of their time OFF your dog.

FITTLEWORTH

Farthings
Lovely vegetarian bed and breakfast. Dogs are very welcome. Step out the back gate into woodlands and meadows
Wyncombe Close, Fittleworth, Pulborough, West Sussex, RH20 1HW.
Tel: 01798 865495.
e-mail: pat.parsons@clara.co.uk
Contact: Pat Parsons.
Opening hours: Ring to discuss.
Rates: Prices available.

FONTWELL

Woodacre
Dogs welcome. Handy to travel to Arundel
Arundel Road, Fontwell, Walberton, West Sussex, BN18 0QP.
Tel: 01243 814301. **Fax:** 01243 814344.
e-mail: wacrebb@aol.com
web: www.woodacre.co.uk
Contact: Vicki Richards.
Fees: Prices available.

Directions: On A27 for 3 miles, take left slip road to Fontwell Village. Turn immediate left again, Woodacre is first house on the right.

DIRECTORY

PETWORTH

The Stag Inn
Old 17th century pub with stone floor.
Dogs welcomed
Balls Cross, Petworth, West Sussex, GU28 9JP.
Tel: 01403 820241.
Contact: H B Hippleston.
Opening hours: Monday to Saturday, 11am to 3pm and 6pm to 11pm. Sunday, 12 noon to 3pm and 7pm to 10.30pm.

Directions: North from Petworth, turn right to Kirdford and about 2 miles on the left is the Stag Inn.

WORTHING

Manor Guest House
Pet friendly guest house, especially dogs
100 Broadwater Road, Worthing,
West Sussex, BN14 8AN.
Tel: 01903 236028.
e-mail: stay@manorworthing.com
web: www.manorworthing.com
Contact: S Colbourne.
Opening hours: All year round.
Rates: Price list available.

Directions: Located on A24 on the outskirts of Worthing Town Centre.
Licensed restaurant for lunches and evening food. Toilets and gardens. Ground-floor en suite available for disabled persons.

DIRECTORY

DIRECTORY

HORSHAM

Oak Leaves Pet Crematorium
Calming, soothing place to say farewell to
a loved pet
Brooks Green, Horsham,
West Sussex, RH13 0JW.
Tel: 01403 741112. **Fax:** 01403 741769.
e-mail: info@oakleaves.net
web: www.oakleaves.net
Contact: Annie Silver.
Opening hours: By appointment.
Fees: Price list available.

Individual and communal cremation memorials
and caskets. Remembrance room and gardens
of remembrance.

NINFIELD

Happy Hunting Grounds
A really lovely spot for your animals'
resting place. Beautiful walks and tranquil
lake - 22 acres
Little Park Farm, Hooe Road (B2095),
Russells Green, Ninfield, East Sussex, TN33 9EH.
Tel: 01424 892396.
e-mail: tas1@tesco.net
web: www.pet-rest.net
Contact: Tas Cornwell.
Opening hours: 24 hours a day for
emergencies. Open daylight hours.
Admission: Donations gratefully accepted for
grounds walks.

Directions: Situated on the B2095 between
Pevensey Marsh Road and Herstmonceux to
Bexhill Road.
Blessings – see press or website for details
when applicable. All pets accepted. No bitches
in season permitted on the walks.

RINGMER

Kent and Sussex Horse Cremations
Horse crematorium
Diplocks Yard, Bishops Lane,
Ringmer, East Sussex, BN8 5LD.
Tel: 01273 812313.
Opening hours: By appointment.

Birds are the only animals with hollow bones.

www.animalloversguides.co.uk

BEXHILL-ON-SEA

Bow Wow
Pet sitting and dog walking service
Amherst Road, Bexhill-on-Sea,
East Sussex, TN40 1QJ.
Tel: 01424 218706. **Fax:** 01424 218706.
e-mail: alison.hoyle@onetel.net
Contact: Alison.
Costs: £5 per walk (one full hour min.) £10 per
day pet sitting, £15 per 24 hours pet sitting.

Pet Sitting and dog walking service by dog-
loving lady, RSPCA trained. We promise to spoil
them as much as you do ... if not more! Bring
your dog to us in our loving caring family
home. Dogs must be child- and dog-friendly to
be accepted.

BRIGHTON

Animal Carers of Sussex
Quality care for beloved pets!
13 Denmark Terrace, Brighton,
East Sussex, BN1 3AN.
Tel: 01273 711055.
e-mail: info@animalcarers.co.uk
web: www.animalcarers.co.uk
Contact: Karla.
Opening hours: Operate seven days a week
Costs: Daycare from £15 per day. Boarding
from £25 per day. Holiday/feeding services from
£10 per hour. Pet tax from £10. Exact prices on
enquiry.

Walks and runs, Day care and boarding in our
homes, training augmentation, feeding service,
pet taxi, hutch and cage cleans, basic
grooming, holiday services. Speciality dogs all
ages, shapes and sizes! Walked and trained
individually or small groups if requested and
agreed by owners concerned. All domestic pets
cared for.

Runners
Dog walkers and animal service
32 Bates Road, Brighton, East Sussex, BN1 6PG.
Tel: 01273 500064.
e-mail: runners-laura@hotmail.co.uk
Contact: Laura West.
Opening hours: Monday to Saturday,
3 walks per day. All-day care also available.
Fees: Prices on request.

DURRINGTON

Pet Sitting Service
**Dogs that stay are part of the family. We visit
homes and feed birds, goldfish and rabbits**
68 Greenland Road, Durrington, Worthing,
West Sussex, BN13 2RN.
Tel: 01903 260851.
e-mail: dianaspetsitting@aol.com
Contact: Diana Hewett.
Opening hours: By arrangement.
Fees: Prices on request.

Directions: Off Durrington Lane, which is off
the A27.

EASTBOURNE

Promise Pets
Dog walking, shopping for you and your pet
33 Green Way, Eastbourne,
East Sussex, BN20 8UG.
Tel: 07816 605146.
Contact: Erin

Dog walking, shopping for you and your pet,
feeding and general care for pets. Home sitting
and cuddles and basic grooming.

DIRECTORY

Pet Minding

HARTFIELD

Pet Patrol 365
Specialises in domestic pets, livestock and poultry. Domestic pet tax and one-to-one dog walking
Hartfield, East Sussex.
Tel: 01892 771498.
e-mail: zita@petpatrol365.co.uk
web: www.petpatrol365.co.uk
Contact: Zita Robinson.
Opening hours: By arrangement, 365 days a year.

Puppy and elderly dog care. Equine support. 20 plus years' experience, pre-visit free of charge, vet and owner references, reliable and police checked, competitive rates, general and equine liability insurance.

HASTINGS

Animal Home Carers
Service of pet sitting in pets' own homes
Flat 1, 3 Robertson Terrace, Hastings,
East Sussex, TN34 1JE.
Tel: 01424 439110.
Contact: Jacqueline Terry.
Opening hours: By arrangement.
Fees: Charges vary with number of pets and type of pet.

Directions: Near town centre on the seafront.

HASSOCKS

Sandie Stevens
Pet sitting service for cats and small animals
55 The Quadrant, Hassocks,
West Sussex, BN6 8BS.
Tel: 01273-843736.
e-mail: sandie_stevens@hotmail.com
Contact: Sandie Stevens.

HAYWARDS HEATH

Supreme Pet Care
Dog walking, pet boarding, pet/house sitting, pet feeding, pet taxi service
43a Haywards Road, Haywards Heath,
West Sussex, RH16 4HX.
Tel: 07913 371403. **Fax:** 01444 410661.
e-mail: caroline@woolgar43.freeserve.co.uk
Contact: Caroline Woolgar.
Opening hours: By arrangement.
Fees: Price list available.

Directions: Off main town centre at Haywards Heath.

HORSHAM

Noah's Ark
Dog walking service and pet at home care
41 Greenfields Road, Horsham,
West Sussex, RH12 4JL.
Tel: 01403 276163.
e-mail: jane.a.lee@btinternet.com
web: www.weRnoahsark.co.uk
Contact: Jane Lee.
Opening hours: Monday to Friday.

Dog walking service, dog creche and pet at home care.

HOVE

Pets Stay Home
Ideal for those who prefer their rescued or elderly cats to enjoy home comforts while mum and dad are away
14 Stonecroft Close, Hove,
East Sussex, BN3 8BP.
Tel: 01273 261956.
e-mail: petsstayhome@ntlworld.com
web: www.petsstayhome.co.uk
Contact: Kathy Janio.
Opening hours: By arrangement, phone between 9am and 6pm.

HUNSTON, CHICHESTER

Holidays Animal Care
Home from home for pets
5 Heath Close, Hunston, Chichester,
West Sussex, PO20 1PL.
Tel: 01243 775267.
Contact: Hazel Yates.
Opening hours: By arrangement.
Fees: Prices available on request.

Directions: Near Chichester Golf Club.

LEWES

Woof! Dog Walking and Petcare
**Dog walking, day boarding and
cat feeding**
Lewes, East Sussex.
Tel: 01273 470993.
Contact: Charlotte Homewood.
Opening hours: 9am to 6pm by
arrangement.

Covers a five mile radius.

NORTHIAM

Doggy Daycare
An alternative to traditional kennels
3 Garden Cottages, Staplecross Road,
Northiam, East Sussex, TN31 6JL.
Tel: 01580 830114.
e-mail: kate@doggydaycare.wanadoo.co.uk
Contact: Kate.
Opening hours: By arrangement.
Fees: £10 per day boarding, discount offered
for more than one dog from the same family.
£6 per hour dog walking.

All sizes of dogs welcome.

PARTRIDGE GREEN

Di's Pet Sitting
Pet boarding, dog walking and house sitting
38 St Michael's Way, Partridge Green,
West Sussex, RH13 8LB.
Tel: 01403 711972.
e-mail: di@dispetsitting.co.uk
Contact: Di Holman.
Opening hours: By arrangement.
Fees: Prices available on request.

PEASMARSH

Mari French
Pet sitting service
Cobweb, Barrets Hill, Peasmarsh,
East Sussex, TN31 6YJ.
Tel: 01797 230833.
e-mail: marzrye@aol.com
Contact: Mari French.
Opening hours: By appointment.

Home service for pet sitting. All animals
cared for.

PORTSLADE

Barkies
Give dogs full hour's walk and fully insured
33 Rowan Close, Portslade,
East Sussex, BN41 2PT.
Tel: 01273 270816.
e-mail: clare@barkies.co.uk
web: www.barkies.co.uk
Contact: Clare House.

Fully insured dog walking. Walk dogs five days
a week. Feed dogs seven days a week.

DIRECTORY

Pet Minding

DIRECTORY

SALTDEAN

Animal Sitter
Caring for pets in their own homes
4 Withyham Avenue, Saltdean,
East Sussex, BN2 8LF.
Tel: 01273 304676.
Contact: Joy Page.
Opening hours: By arrangement.

Also for the special needs of animals with medical conditions.

ST LEONARDS ON SEA

Pets Home Alone
House and pet sitting. Specialises in horses
82 Bulverhythe Road, St Leonards on Sea,
East Sussex, TN38 8AE.
Tel: 07734 357345.
e-mail: petshomealone@fsmail.net
Contact: Sally Ash.
Opening hours: By arrangement.

WILMINGTON

Dogs on the Downs
Dog walking service
4 Ades Field, Wilmington, Polegate,
East Sussex, BN26 5SH.
Tel: 01323 871121.
e-mail: cathycrez@aol.com
Opening hours: Mornings, afternoons and evenings.

Dog walking in Eastbourne and Hailsham.

WORTHING

K9 Goodcare
Dog walking service
7 Cranmer Road, Worthing,
West Sussex, BN13 1AH.
Tel: 01903 203708.
web: www.k9goodcare.co.uk
Contact: Nikki.
Opening hours: Monday to Friday, by arrangement.

Directions: Near West Worthing Station
Various offers available.

BRIGHTON

Diamond Edge Ltd
Wide range of top-quality grooming equipment
126 Gloucester Road, Brighton,
East Sussex, BN1 4BU.
Tel: 01273 605922. **Fax:** 01273 625074.
e-mail: diamondedge@btclick.com
web: www.diamondedgeltd.com
Contact: David Noakes.
Opening hours: Monday to Thursday, 8.30am to 5pm. Friday, 8.30am to 4pm.

Directions: Near St Peter's Church, Brighton Pavilion.
Top quality grooming equipment for sale. Toilets available on request

A snapping turtle never snaps in the water.

MIDHURST

Jet Set Pets
Pet relocating agency
14 Heatherwood, Midhurst
West Sussex GU29 9LH.
Tel: 0788 400 3038. **Fax:** 01730 815 822.
e-mail: supportteam@jetsetpets.co.uk
web: www.jetsetpets.co.uk
Contact: Gill July.
Opening hours: Monday to Saturday 9am to 6pm. 24-hour assistance when travelling.
We **export** pets to Amsterdam, Austria, Barbados, Bulgaria, Canada, Dominican Republic, Florida, France, Greece, Ireland, Italy, Jersey, Malta, Mexico, Portugal, Spain, Switzerland and Turkey. We also **import** pets from Spain, Portugal, Tenerife, Jersey and Cyprus.

DIRECTORY

BATTLE

Senlac Vets
Veterinary care. Mixed practice
Mount Street, Battle, East Sussex, TN33 0EG.
Tel: 01424 772148. **Fax:** 01424 777321.
Contact: Beshlie.
Opening hours: Monday to Friday, 8.30am
to 7pm. Saturday, 9am to 1pm.

Puppy parties by arrangement.

BEXHILL-ON-SEA

Claremont Veterinary Group Ltd
Veterinary Care
8 Wainwright Road, Bexhill-on-Sea,
East Sussex, TN39 3UR.
Tel: 01424 222835. **Fax:** 01424 217080.
Contact: Stephen White.
Opening hours: By appointment. Weekdays,
8am to 7pm. Saturday, 9am to 5.30pm.

Directions: Near police station.
Occasional events, please ring to enquire.

BOGNOR REGIS

Downland Veterinary Hospital
Veterinary hospital and care for cats, dogs
and family pets
118 Victoria Drive, Bognor Regis,
West Sussex, PO21 2EJ.
Tel: 01243 841111. **Fax:** 01243 860285.
Web: www.downlandvets.co.uk
Contact: Paul Tucker.
Opening hours: 8.30am to 6.30pm, by
appointment.

Directions: From roundabout at junction of
A259 and A29.
Facilities only for clients.

BRIGHTON

St Francis Veterinary Surgery
Veterinary care
40 Norfolk Square, Brighton,
East Sussex, BN1 2PE.
Tel: 01273 770800. **Fax:** 01273 747186.
e-mail: st.francis@virgin.net
web: www.saintfrancis.co.uk
Contact: Mr S Van Vuuren.
Opening hours: Monday to Friday, 8am
to 6.30pm. Saturday, 8am to 12noon.

PDSA
Veterinary care and charity
Robertson Road, Brighton,
East Sussex, BN1 5NL.
Tel: 01273 566595.
Contact: J Gravestock.
Opening hours:
Monday to Friday, 9am to 6pm.

Directions: Off South Road which leaves A23
near Preston Park.
Hosts an open day on Wednesday afternoon in
October half-term.

BURGESS HILL

Cootes Veterinary Clinic
Veterinary care
Gatehouse Lane, Burgess Hill,
West Sussex, RH15 9XD.
Tel: 01444 242434. **Fax:** 01444 242464.
web: www.cootes.org.uk
Contact: Ros Norledge.
Opening hours: Monday to Friday, 8.30am to
7pm. Saturday, 8.30am to 1pm.

www.animalloversguides.co.uk

CROWBOROUGH

Dier & Johnston Veterinary Surgeons
Vets for small animals
The Well House Veterinary Clinic
Crowborough, East Sussex, TN6 2SE.
Tel: 01892 653088. **Fax:** 01892 669799.
Contact: Gayle Barrett.
Opening hours: Monday to Friday, 8.30am
to 7pm. Saturday, 8.30am to 4pm.

EAST DEAN

St Annes Veterinary Group
Veterinary care for small animals
15 Downland Way, East Dean,
East Sussex, BN20 0HR.
Tel: 01323 422062. **Fax:** 01323 738060.
web: www.eastbournevet.co.uk
Contact: Jim Dash.
Opening hours:
Monday to Friday, 2pm to 3pm.

Directions: In the East Dean shopping area.

EAST GRINSTEAD

East Grinstead Veterinary Hospital
Puppy parties for registered clients
Maypole Road, East Grinstead,
West Sussex, RH19 1HL.
Tel: 01342 323072. **Fax:** 01342 317659.
Contact: Richard Cunnington.
Opening hours: Monday to Friday, 8am to
6pm. Saturday, 8.30am to 12noon. Sunday,
10am to 2pm. Also by appointment.

Directions: Off A22 in East Grinstead (opposite
Homebase).

Equine Veterinary Services International Ltd
Equine vet
PO Box 314, East Grinstead,
West Sussex, RH19 1GB.
Tel: 01342 300008. **Fax:** 01342 301034.
Contact: Mary McGinness.
Opening hours: Monday to Friday, 8.30
to 6pm. 24-hour emergency service.

Directions: please ring.

Portland Road Veterinary Surgery
Veterinary care
27 Portland Road, East Grinstead,
West Sussex, RH19 4EB.
Tel: 01342 327799.
e-mail: welcome@portlandvets.co.uk
web: www.portlandvets.co.uk
Contact: Sarah Pearce.
Opening hours: Monday to Friday, 8.30am to
7pm. Saturday, 9am to 12noon.

EASTBOURNE

St Annes Veterinary Group
Veterinary care for small animals
6 St Anne's Road, Eastbourne,
East Sussex, BN21 2DJ.
Tel: 01323 640011. **Fax:** 01323 738060.
web: www.eastbournevet.co.uk
Contact: Jim Dash.
Opening hours: Monday to Friday, 8am
to 7pm. Saturday, 8am to 5pm. Sunday, 10am
to 12noon.

Directions: Off The Avenue in Eastbourne.

DIRECTORY

FOREST ROW

Forest Lodge Veterinary Centre Ltd
Advanced pet health counsellor
Station Road, Forest Row,
East Sussex, RH18 5DW.
Tel: 01342 824452. **Fax:** 01342 826088.
Contact: Maria Sitford.
Opening hours: Monday to Friday, 8.30am
to 6.30. Saturday, 8.30am to 2pm.

HAILSHAM

Highcroft Vet Group
Small animals, exotics, large animals
and equine
25 London Road, Hailsham,
East Sussex, BN27 3BN.
Tel: 01323 841666.
Opening hours: Monday to Friday, 8am
to 6.30pm. Saturday, 9am to 12noon.
24-hour emergency service.

Directions: On main road, near Caffyns.

HAYWARDS HEATH

Oathall Veterinary Group
Veterinary care for small animals
30 Oathall Road, Haywards Heath,
West Sussex, RH16 3EQ.
Tel: 01444 440224. **Fax:** 01444 459187.
Contact: Karen Puzio.
Opening hours: 8am to 8pm and 24-hour
emergency service on own premises, using
own nurses and vets.

Directions: Oathall Road runs between The
Sussex roundabout at the east side of the main
street to the roundabout, towards Linfield village.
Events very occasionally. Please ring for details.
Small animals only. Car park for clients only.

The Mewes Veterinary Clinic
Treating pets as friends
4 Haywards Road, Haywards Heath,
West Sussex, RH16 4HT.
Tel: 01444 456886. **Fax:** 01444 413481.
Contact: Nikki Etherton.
Opening hours: Monday to Thursday, 8.30am
to 7.30pm. Friday, 8.30am to 6.30pm. Saturday,
9am to 12.30pm.

Directions: Just off South Road, main
shopping street, next to public car park.

HORAM

Downwood Veterinary Centre
Specialises in reptiles and birds
High Street, Horam, Heathfield,
East Sussex, TN21 0EJ.
Tel: 01435 812152. **Fax:** 01435 813927.
Contact: Julie Harding.
Opening hours: Monday to Friday, 9am
to 11.30am and 2pm to 6.30pm. Saturday,
9am to 11.30am for collections.

Car park at end of high street for free parking.

HORSHAM

Farthings Veterinary Group
Tends to all species
Guildford Road, Horsham,
West Sussex, RH12 1TS.
Tel: 01403 252900. **Fax:** 01403 261986.
e-mail: vets@farthingsvets.co.uk
Contact: R Keddie.
Opening hours: Monday to Friday, 9am to
6.30pm. Saturday, 9am to 12noon. 24 hour
emergency cover.

Directions: A264 from Horsham. Adjacent
to A24.

HOVE

Acorn
Homeopathic vet also works here
177 Hangleton Way, Hove,
East Sussex, BN3 8EY.
Tel: 01273 430301. **Fax:** 01273 430308.
web: www.acorn-vets.co.uk
Contact: Jo Hawkins.
Opening hours: By appointment between,
8am and 6pm.

Directions: On the A27. Ring for more details.

Wilbury Veterinary Surgery
Orthopaedic referral practice
20 Wilbury Avenue, Hove,
East Sussex, BN3 6HR.
Tel: 01273 737924. **Fax:** 01273 701845.
web: www.wilburyvets.co.uk
Contact: Peter Haggis and Anne Greenwood.
Opening hours: 8.30am to 6.30pm.
24-hour emergency service.

Some events throughout the year.
Phone for more details.

HURSTPIERPOINT

Heath Veterinary Clinic
Tends to all small animals
9 High Street, Hurstpierpoint,
West Sussex, BN6 9TT.
Tel: 01273 832968. **Fax:** 01273 831174.
e-mail: heathvets@aol.com
Contact: Sarah Solomon.
Opening hours: By appointment.
24-hour emergency treatment.

Directions: On the high street, near the church.

LANGNEY

St Annes Veterinary Group
Veterinary care for small animals
1 Anstrim Court, Pembury Road, Langney,
East Sussex, BN23 7LU.
Tel: 01323 763949. **Fax:** 01323 738060.
web: www.eastbournevet.co.uk
Contact: Jim Dash.
Opening hours: Monday to Friday, 9am to
11am and 5pm to 7pm. Saturday, 9am to 11am.

Directions: Off Langney Rise near Langney
Shopping Centre.

LEWES

Pet Doctors
Veterinary care
Unit 10, Cliffe Industrial Estate, South Street,
Lewes, East Sussex, BN8 6JL.
Tel: 01273 474857. **Fax:** 01273 474817.
web: www.petdoctors.co.uk
Contact: Grant Divall.
Opening hours: Monday to Friday, 9am
to 6.30pm. Saturday, 9am to 12noon.

Veterinary Surgeries

LITTLEHAMPTON

Fitzalan House Veterinary Group
Veterinary care
31 Fitzalan Road, Littlehampton,
West Sussex, BN17 5ET.
Tel: 01903 713806. **Fax:** 01903 716373.
web: www.fitzalanhouse.co.uk
Contact: Julie Saunderson.
Opening hours: Monday to Friday, 8.30am to 6.30pm. Saturday, 9am to 12.30pm.

Directlions: Approximately 250 metres north of seafront. Opposite the old Littlehampton Hospital.
Tends to all small animals.

LOWER WILLINGDON

St Annes Veterinary Group
Veterinary care for small animals
9 Gorringe Valley Road
Lower Willingdon, Eastbourne,
East Sussex, BN20 9SX.
Tel: 01323 487655. **Fax:** 01323 738060.
web: www.easbournevet.co.uk
Contact: Jim Dash.
Opening hours: Monday to Thursday, 9am to 10.30am. Monday to Friday, 2pm to 4pm.

Directions: Off the main Eastbourne to Polegate Road.

MIDHURST

Woodland Veterinary Hospital
Veterinary care for small animals
Woodland Vets, Grange Road, Midhurst,
West Sussex, GU29 9LT.
Tel: 01730 814321. **Fax:** 01730 817202.
e-mail: wagvet@btconnect.com
web: www.woodlandvethosp.co.uk
Contact: Ann Boxall.
Opening hours: Monday to Friday, 8am to 6.30pm. Saturday, 8am to 1pm.

Directions: Situated in Grange Centre car park.

NUTBOURNE

Priors Leaze Veterinary Clinic
Veterinary care – established 22 years
Priors Leaze Lane, Nutbourne, Nr Chichester,
West Sussex, PO18 8RH.
Tel: 01243 376000.
Contact: R W Kynoch.
Opening hours: Monday to Friday, 9.00am to 11.00am, 4.30pm to 7.00pm.

Directions: Call for directions.

PEACEHAVEN

Meridian Veterinary Practice
Veterinary care – small animal practice
11 Edith Avenue, Peacehaven,
East Sussex, BN10 8JB.
Tel: 01273 585386. **Fax:** 01273 580874.
e-mail: vets@meridianvets.co.uk
web: www.meridianvets.co.uk
Contact: Paula Borthwick.
Opening hours: Monday to Friday, 8am to 6pm. Saturday, 8am to 12noon.

Directhurs: Check website for details.

A dog's hearing and sense of smell are 300 times better than a human's.

PULBOROUGH

Arun Veterinary Group
Mixed practice. Homeopathy and
physiotherapy
121 Lower Street, Pulborough,
West Sussex, RH20 2BP.
Tel: 01798 872089. **Fax:** 01798 872080.
web: www.arunvetgroup.co.uk
Contact: Mr Gittings.
Opening hours: By appointment.

Directions: In the centre of Pulborough.

RINGMER

Cliffe Veterinary Group
Veterinary care
70 Springett Avenue, Ringmer,
East Sussex, BN8 5QX.
Tel: 01273 814590. **Fax:** 01273 815310.
Contact: Samantha Fleet.
Opening hours: Monday, Tuesday, Thursday,
Friday, 8.30am to 6pm. Wednesday, 8.30am to
1pm. Saturday, 9am to 11am.

RUSTINGTON

Companion Care
Veterinary care for pets at home
Barn Nursery Retail Park, New Road,
Rustington, West Sussex, BN16 3RT.
Tel: 01903 777670. **Fax:** 01903 856671.
Contact: Nicole Bailey.
Opening hours: Monday to Friday, 9am to 7pm.
Saturday, 9am to 6pm. Sunday, 10.30 to 3pm.

RYE

Cinque Ports Veterinary Associates
Veterinary care
Cinque Port Square, Rye,
East Sussex, TN31 7AN.
Tel: 01797 222265. **Fax:** 01797 224248.
Contact: Richard Williams.
Opening hours: By arrangement with
24-hour carer.

Directions: On the Kent/Sussex border.
Please call.

SEAFORD

Pet Doctors
Veterinary care for small animals
Brooklyn Road, Seaford,
East Sussex, BN25 2DU.
Tel: 01323 894568. **Fax:** 01323 491044.
web: www.petdoctors.co.uk
Contact: Helen Baldwin.
Opening hours: Monday to Friday, 8.30am
to 6.30pm. Saturday, 1.30pm to 3.30pm.

Customer and disabled toilet.

UCKFIELD

Henley House Veterinary Practice
Veterinary care for small animals
Henley House, 2 London Road, Uckfield,
East Sussex, TN22 1HY.
Tel: 01825 766099. **Fax:** 01825 769926.
Contact: Mr A DeVilliers.
Opening hours: Monday to Friday, 8.30am
to 6.30pm. Saturday, 8.30am to 12noon.

DIRECTORY

DID YOU KNOW? *Himalayan snow fleas freeze solid overnight, then thaw out in the morning.*

WARNHAM

Mayes & Scrine Equine Veterinary Practice
Veterinary care for horses
Dawes Farm, Bognor Road, Warnham,
Horsham, West Sussex, RH12 3SH.
Tel: 01306 628222. **Fax:** 01306 628379.
e-mail: office@equinevetpractice.co.uk
web: www.equinevetpractice.co.uk
Contact: Judy Scrine.
Opening hours: Monday to Friday, 8am to
5pm. Emergency service outside these hours.

Directions: Northlands Business Park, 2 miles
south of Ockley on A29.
Equine veterinary care. Has a stand at the
Cranleigh Show, August.

Westpoint Veterinary Services
Farm animal vets
Dawes Farm, Bognor Road, Warnham,
West Sussex, RH12 3SH.
Tel: 01306 628086. **Fax:** 01306 628080.
e-mail: maria.farino@westpointfarmvets.co.uk
web: www.westpointfarmvets.co.uk
Contact: Maria Farino.
Opening hours: Daily, 7.30am to 5.30pm.

Directions: Off A29 at Northlands Bus Park.

WEST MEADS

AlphaPet Veterinary Clinic
The Precinct, West Meads, Bognor Regis,
West Sussex, PO21 5SB.
Tel: 01243 842832. **Fax:** 01243 842669.
e-mail: info@alphapetvets.co.uk
web: www.alphapetvets.co.uk
Contact: S Eglen.
Opening hours: Monday to Friday.
Ring for appointment.

WORTH

A K Jones Birdvet
Treatment for birds only
The Cottage, Turnershill Road, Worth, Crawley,
West Sussex, RH10 4LY.
Tel: 01293 884629. **Fax:** 01293 885507.
e-mail: akjones@birdvet.co.uk
web: www.birdvet.co.uk
Contact: Alan Jones.
Opening hours: By appointment.

Directions: 1 mile from Junction 10 of M23.
See website for more details.

WORTHING

Grove Lodge Veterinary Group
Tends to all domestic animals and wildlife
Upper Brighton Road, Worthing,
West Sussex, BN14 9DL.
Tel: 01903 234866. **Fax:** 01903 233604.
e-mail: grovelodgevets@lineone.net
web: www.grove-lodge.co.uk
Contact: Lisa Bailey.
Opening hours: Monday to Sunday,
by appointment.

Directions: On A27 at Broadwater.
Special events throughout the year.
We also offer digital radiography, ultrasound
including doppler echocardiography,
electrocardiology, ultrasound dental treatment,
endoscopy and arthroscopy.

Heene Road Veterinary Practice Ltd
Companion animals only
206 Heene Road, Worthing,
West Sussex, BN11 4NT.
Tel: 01903 200187.
Contact: J Yeatts.
Opening hours: By appointment.

Worthing Animal Clinic
**Veterinary care that does acupuncture.
Also a charity**
30/32 Newland Road, Worthing,
West Sussex, BN11 1JR.
Tel: 01903 202248. **Fax:** 01903 537759.
e-mail: worthinganimal@tiscali.co.uk
web: www.worthinganimal.co.uk
Contact: J C Kirk.
Opening hours: Monday to Friday, 9.30am
to 11am and 2pm to 3.30pm.

Directions: 200 yards east of roundabout by
Teville Bridge.
Fully equipped veterinary clinic with qualified
vet and nurse. Occasional fund-raising events.

MOBILE UNIT

Westrow Equine Dental Service
**Mobile equine dental service that deals
with ponies, donkeys and horses**
Westrow House, Mobile Unit, Sussex.
Tel: 01825 732728. **Fax:** 01825 732025.
e-mail: dougvieweg@aol.com
Contact: Doug Vieweg.
Opening hours: Weekdays by arrangement.
Covers south east area. Horses, ponies and
donkeys.

DIRECTORY

CHIDDINGLY

The Mohair Centre
Nature trail with working farm
Brickfield Farm, Laughton Road,
Chiddingly, East Sussex, BN8 6JG.
Tel: 01825 872457. **Fax:** 01825 872460.
Opening hours: March to October. Please call for times.

Directions: Situated on the B2124 off the A22 between Hailsham and Lewes.
Children's farm with angora goats and other farm animals. Courses available. Toilets, educational facilities. Lambing in the spring and other events. Please call for details. Nature trail and spinning and weaving demonstrations.

No animal can make a louder noise than a lion.

EAST DEAN

Seven Sisters Sheep Centre
Largest collection of sheep breeds in the world – 47!
Birling Gap Road, East Dean, Nr Eastbourne, East Sussex, BN20 0AA.
Tel: 01323 423302. **Fax:** 01323 423302.
e-mail: sevensisters.sheepcentre@talk21.com
web: www.sheepcentre.co.uk
Contact: Terry Wigmore.
Opening hours: July to September, 2pm to 5pm on weekdays 11am to 5pm on weekends and school holidays. March to May, 2pm to 5pm on weekdays. Closed at weekend.
Admission: Adults £3.50. Chilldren (2-15) £2.50. Seniors and Concessions £3.00. Family £11.00 (2 plus 2).

Directions: 3 miles west of Eastbourne on the A259. In the village of East Dean, turn left towards sea and Birling Gap the centre is half a mile on the left.
Lambing time, shearing, sheep milking. Tea room, picnic area and toilets. No disabled toilets. Lambing and shearing and sheep milking. Sheep, horses, calves, goats, pigs, geese, ducks, chickens, rabbits, guinea pigs, chinchillas and ferrets.

DIRECTORY

Camels don't sweat and they don't pant either.

HORSHAM

Chesworth Farm
Working farm and nature trail
Chesworth Lane, Horsham, West Sussex.
Tel: 01403 731218.
e-mail: leisure@horsham.gov.uk
web: www.horsham.gov.uk
Opening hours: Open farm.

Directions: 10 to 15-minute walk from town centre to the north east Following the A281 off Queensway.
Woodland, bridle path, natural beauty and coppice woodland. Farm animals can be seen. Dogs must be on leads.

Holmbush Farm World
Farm animals, tractor rides and much more
Faygate, Nr Horsham, West Sussex, RH12 4SE.
Tel: 01293 851700.
e-mail: info@holmbushfarm.co.uk
web: www.holmbushfarm.co.uk
Opening hours: Daily, 10am to 5.30pm. March to November.
Admission: Adults £4.50. Children £4.00.

Directions: Situated between Crawley and Horsham off the A264.
Cow and goat milking, goat races and tractor rides. Tea room, toilets and gift shop. Farm animals with lambing in spring. Guide dogs allowed.

HURSTPIERPOINT

Washbrooks Farm
Working farm, open to the public
Brighton Road, Hurstpierpoint,
West Sussex, BN6 9EH.
Tel: 01273 832201.
e-mail: enquire@washbrooks.co.uk
web: www.washbrooks.co.uk
Opening hours: Daily, 9.30am to 5pm.
Admission: Adults £4.25. Children (3-14) £3.75. Seniors £3.75.

Directions: From Brighton, travel north up A23, turn off at B2117. Follow signs to Hurstpierpoint. From London, take the A23 south and turn off at B2118.
Rides, attractions and lovely walks. Tea rooms, picnic area, party rooms, playrooms and brook walk. Birthday parties available. Horses, sheep, ponies, pigs and all types of farm animals.

DIRECTORY

LEWES

Middle Farm

Open farm with cider shop and gift shop.
A great day out
Middle Farm, Firle, Lewes, East Sussex, BN8 6LJ.
Tel: 01323 811411. **Fax:** 01323 811622.
e-mail: info@middlefarm.com
web: www.middlefarm.com
Contact: Helen.
Opening hours: Daily. Summer, 9.30am to 6pm. Winter, 9.30am to 5pm.
Admission: Open farm costs £2.50.

Directions: Situated on the main A27 Lewes to Eastbourne Road between villages of Firle and Selmeston.
Plough Monday restaurant, Middle Farm shop, national collection of cider and perry. Gift shop. Lots to see and do. Restaurant, toilets, gift shop, cider and perry. See website for events throughout the year. Donkeys, chickens, ducks, pigs and Shire Horses. Watch Jersey cows being milked!

MIDHURST

Canine Partners

Training assistance for wheelchair users
Mill Lane, Heyshott, Nr Midhurst,
West Sussex, GU29 0ED.
Tel: 08456 580480. **Fax:** 08456 580481.
e-mail: info@caninepartners.co.uk
web: www.caninepartners.co.uk
Contact: Terry Knott.
Opening hours: 9am to 5pm.
By appointment.

Directions: 2 miles south of Midhurst off A286
Training of dogs. Local pub called the Unicorn nearby. Open days monthly. Ring for details. Labradors, retrievers, labradoodles, retroodles.

RYE

Farm World

Real working farm –
something for everyone
Beckley, Nr Rye, East Sussex.
Tel: 01797 260250. **Fax:** 01797 260347.
e-mail: enquiries@farmworldrye.co.uk
web: www.farmworldrye.co.uk
Opening hours: Tuesday to Saturday, 11am to 5.30pm, term time. Open daily during school holidays.
Admission: Adults £6.00. Children £5.00. Seniors £5.00.

Directions: A268 between the villages of Newenden and Beckley. Five miles from Rye town centre.
Family day out. Toilets and shops. Please check our website for events. Llamas, rare breeds of pigs, ponies, horses and lambs. Guide dogs welcome.

DIRECTORY

So how did you get on?

Answers to the crossword on page 188.

A					E	R	A		S	
R	O	A	R		C		P	R	E	Y
A			A		R		E		R	
C	E	N	T	A	U	R			V	
H				N					A	
N	I	G	H	T	I	N	G	A	L	E
I							O			M
D	O	E			D	A	P	P	L	E
	W		E				H			R
S	L	O	W				E			G
	S		E	I	D	E	R			E

Index

A

A Cut Above 260

A Pets Life 214

Acorn 273

Acre Feeds and Saddlery Ltd 256

Action for Animals Charity 174

acupuncture 112, 116, 192, 277

adders 140-1, 151

Aesop's fables 130

Albourne Equestrian Centre 254

Aldwick Pets 201

Alexandra Park 76, 242

Alfie Greys 205

alpacas 75

Alphapet Veterinary Clinic 276

alternative therapies 112-16, 192-3

Amberley Boarding Kennels 216

Amberley Wild Brooks 39, 224

amphibians

   charity 180

   conservation group 231

Anglo European Studbook 257

angora goats 68

Animal Aid 174

animal behaviourists 249-50

Animal Carers of Sussex 265

animal charities 174-83, 220

Animal Concerns 167

animal conservation 117-19

Animal Cruelty Investigation Group and the Animal Welfare Information Service 167

Animal Defenders 167

Animal Defenders International 167

Animal Fare 204

Animal Home Carers 266

Animal Park, The 206

animal sanctuaries 195-7

Animal Sitter 268

animal supplies 198-206

Animaline 154, 195

Animals in Distress Sanctuary 174

Animals in Mind (AIM) 174

anteaters 153

anthropomorphism 131

ants 99, 194, 228

aquatics 207-9, see also fish

arachnophobia 138-40

Arlington Bluebell Walk & Farm Trail 39, 224

Arlington Reservoir 40, 232

Arnolfini Marriage 130

aromatherapy 112, 116

art, animals in 130-1

artists, animal portraits 194

Arun Dunes and Sea Nature Trail 92, 231

Arun Veterinary Group 275

Arundel Boatyard and Riverside Tea Gardens 40, 210

Ashdown Cattery 215

Ashdown Forest 74, 228

Ashdown Forest Llama Park 75, 211

Ashdown Riding Stables 255

ass 131

assistance dogs 176, 177, 178, 180, 220, 280

Association of Chartered Physiotherapists in Animal Therapy 116

www.animalloversguides.co.uk

Association of Circus Proprietors 164
Association of Private Pet Cemeteries and
   Crematoria 185
aviary suppliers 206
Avon's Dog Grooming 260
Ayurveda 113

B

baboons 111
Badger Rescue 154
badgers
   protection and rescue 154, 156, 157,
   178, 222, 223
   where to see 95, 150-1
Barby Keel Animal Sanctuary 196
Barkies 267
Barnjet Shelter 154
Barons Grange and Moat Farm 86, 243
Bat Conservation Trust 180
bats 141
   rescue centres 157
   smallest 158
Battersea Dogs Home 180
Battle Dog Training School 247
Battle Oaks Boarding Cattery 215
Beacon Hill 50, 225
Beacon House Boarding Cattery 215
bears 205
beavers 84, 129
bed and breakfast 262-3
Bedelands Farm Nature Reserve 62, 226
bees 45, 76, 101

behaviourists 249-50
Bell Walk Pet Supplies 206
Benwick Kennels and Cattery 217
Bernese Mountain Dog Club,
   Southern 222
Berwick Obedience 249
Bevendean Down 50, 225
Bewick swans 39
Bewl Water 108, 235
Bichon Frise Rescue 196
Bing, Keith 250
Birdie Bread 132
Birdlife International 174
birds, see also specific birds
   aviary suppliers 206
   bones 264
   charities 174, 175, 179
   eyelids 150
   garden 117
   homemade treats 132-3
   indigenous 129
   of prey 75, 149
   places to visit 41, 99, 100, 104
   smallest 159
   songs 82
   specialist suppliers 200, 201, 202,
   205, 206
   specialist vets 272, 276
   talking 147
   wading, where to see 148-9
   where to see 148-50
bird's nest soup 60
Black Rock Lido 51, 210
Blackberry Farm 88, 212
Blakers Park 51, 245

blood sports 166
bloodhounds 124, 167
Blue Cross Adoption Centre 154
Blue Cross Equine Rescue 174
blue whale 158
bluebell walk 39, 224
boarding for animals 214-19
boating 40, 47, 63, 210
Bodle Bros Ltd 251
Bognor Regis and District Dog
    Training Club 247
Bonnie's News & Pet Supplies 199
Bonzo's Breakfast Bars 134
Booth Museum of Natural History 52, 211
Borde Hill Garden 78, 242
Border Collie Rescue 175
Border Collie Trust GB 174
Born Free Foundation 167
Bow Wow 265
Bowen Association 116
Bowen therapy 113
Brent Lodge Bird & Wildlife Trust 154, 175
Brickfield Meadow 74, 228
British Butterfly Conservation
    Society Ltd 180
British Chelonia Group 175
British Chiropractic Association 116
British Deer Society 180
British Hedgehog Preservation Society 175
British Herbal Medicine Association 116
British Herpatological Society 180
British Holistic Medical Association 116
British Horse Society 175
British Horseball Association 123
British Medical Acupuncture Society 116

British Ornithologists' Union 175
British Riding Clubs 125
Broad Oak Park 44, 236
Brook Hospital for Animals 175
Brookfield Park 92, 244
Brownbread Horse Rescue 154, 175, 220
Brownings Farm 48, 237
Browside Cattery 219
BTCV Green Gyms 142-3
Buchan Country Park 69, 240
Buckwell Farm 42, 236
Bulldog Rescue and Rehoming Service 196
bullfrog 238
Bunny Breaks 214
Burton & Chingford Ponds 97, 231
butterflies
    charity 180
    chocolate-smelling 118
    in language 48
    largest 159
    places to visit 64, 240
    shivering 233
buzzard 149

calves 48
Camber Sands 101, 245
camels 94, 110, 279
canals 47, 63, 211, 237
Canine Advise 249
Canine Clips 259
Canine Concern 175, 220

Canine Hydro Healing 193

Canine Lifeline UK 175

Canine Partners 280

Canine Partners for Independence 176

Captive Animals' Protection Society 167

Care for the Wild International 176, 220

Carrot Crunchies 135

cartoons 131

Castle Water, Rye Harbour 101, 233

Cat Action Trust 176

Cat and Kitten Rescue of Chandlers
   Ford 176

Cat and Rabbit Rescue Centre 154, 197

Cat Rescue 154, 196

catnip 90

cats

   boarding catteries 214-19

   charities 176, 177, 181, 182, 183, 220

   grooming 259, 260

   homemade treats 134, 135

   lapping 121

   oldest 158

   places to visit 100

   rescue 154, 155, 157, 196, 197

   suitability as pets for children 120

Cats Protection 154

Cats Protection League 176

Cavalier King Charles Spaniel club 223

Celia Hammond Animal Trust 154, 176

cemeteries for pets 100, 185, 264

Challey Stud 257

chameleons 169-70

Champooch Studios 259

charities 174-83, 220

Charity Animal Helpline 9

Chattri Downs War Memorial 52, 225

Cheese Chomps 134

chelonia groups 175, 222

Chesworth Farm 81, 279

Chichester Canal 63, 211

Chichester Harbour 63, 239

chickens 46, 48, 60, 107, 211

chimpanzees 111, 165

chinchilla 48, 66, 168

chipmunks 66, 75

chiropractic therapy 112-13, 116, 192

Chirpy Cookies 133

Cinque Ports Veterinary Associates 275

circuses 163-4

Claremont Veterinary Group Ltd 270

Cliffe Veterinary Group 275

clubs 221-3

Coakham Bloodhounds 124

coarse fishing 88, 208

cold water hosing 114

collared dove 127

Colour Therapy Healing 193

Companion Animal Behaviour Services 250

Companion Care 275

competition 166

complementary therapies 112-16, 192-3

composting 118

conservation 117-19, 142-3, 224-35

Cooksbridge Meadow 64, 227

Coombes Farm Tours 87, 212

Cootes Veterinary Clinic 270

corn snakes 171

cougar 159

Country Parks and Gardens 236-46

Court Lodge Farm Sanctuary 154

Cowdray Leisure 95, 244

cows 81, 90, 107, 203, 218

crabs 77, 207, 221

Crane Down 108, 246

craniosacral therapy 113

Crazy Cat's Chicken Chomps 134

cremation 185, 264

crocodiles 134

crossword puzzle 188

   solution 282

Crouches Farm 72, 241

Crowborough Grooming 258

Cuckoo Trail 70, 240

D

Dart Vale Boarding Cattery Ltd 218

Dashing Dogs 258

dating agency 27

David Shepherd Conservation

   Foundation 181

Dawg's Biscuit, The 200

deer

   charity 180

   places to visit 98, 106

Deerhound Club 221

degu 168

Denmans Garden 41, 241

Designer Dogs 261

Devil's Dyke 53, 238

Devotedly Discus Ltd 209

Diamond Edge Ltd 269

Diana Brimblecombe Animal Rescue

Centre 181

Dicker Aquatics 207

Dier & Johnston Veterinary Surgeons 271

Di's Pet Sitting 267

discus fish 209

Disney, Walt 131

Ditchling Beacon 71, 235

Ditchling Common Riding School 254

D.I.T.T.O. 248

Dog Dogs Bakery 198

Dog Scene, The 260

Doggy Daycare 267

Doggy Fashion 258

dogs

   agility clubs 247

   assistance dogs 176, 177, 178, 180,

   220, 280

   behaviourists 249-50

   boarding kennels 214-19

   charities 174, 175, 176, 177, 178, 179,

   180, 220

   clubs 221, 222, 223

   grooming 258-61

   homemade treats 133-5, 198, 200

   hydrotherapy 114, 193

   places to visit 100

   places to walk 236-46

   rescue 154, 156, 174, 175, 177, 178,

   180, 196, 221

   senses 274

   smallest 158

   suitability as pets for children 120

   training 186-7, 247-50

   walking services 265-8

   working 110-11

Dogs for Homing 176
Dogs for the Disabled 176
Dogs Home Battersea 180
Dogs on the Downs 268
Dogs Trust 176
Dogs Trust Rescue Centre 154
dolphins 152, 182
Donkey Sanctuary 181
donkeys
    in art 130-1
    charities 181
    dental service 277
    places to visit 75, 90, 107
    suitability as pets for children 121
dormouse 129
Downland Veterinary Hospital 270
Downwood Veterinary Centre 272
Dragonfly Saddlery 256
dragons 131
drug testing 111
Drusillas Park 38, 210
ducks 41, 44, 48, 76, 90, 93
duprasi 169
Dyke Road Park 53, 238

Easthill Park 54, 238
Ebernoe Common and Butcherland
    97, 232
Edinburgh Dog and Cat Home 176
Effects of Intemperance 130
Egerton Park 44, 236
elephants 110, 158, 258
Elite Pets 201
English Springer Spaniel Rescue 177
Enterprise Centre 198
equestrian pursuits 122-6
Equilibrium Therapy 193
equine services 251-7
equine studies 125-6
Equine Veterinary Services
    International Ltd 271
Equine Warehouse 252
Erard's Dog Salon 259
Eridge Park 73, 241
Eridge Rocks 73, 227
essential oils 112
Eurostar Travel 173
euthanasia 184
exotic pets 168-71

Earnley Butterflies and Gardens 64, 240
East Brighton Park 54, 238
East Grinstead Veterinary Hospital 271
East Hoathly Pet Centre 192
East Sussex Wildlife Rescue 155, 195
Eastbourne and District
    Pond-keeping Club 221

faith healing 113-14
Falmer Conservation Area 55, 225
farm animals 69, 71, 81, 86, 87
Farm World 102, 280
Farmyard, The 89, 212
farriers 124
Farthing Saddlery 256

www.animalloversguides.co.uk

Farthings 262

Farthings Veterinary Group 273

Fauna and Flora International 177

Feathers and Firs 202

Feline Advisory Bureau (FAB) 177

Feline Foster Cat Welfare Association 155

ferrets 48

Filsham Reedbed 76, 228

fish

    coarse fishing 88, 208

    divination 104

    getting drunk 201

    most poisonous 159

    slowest 159

    specialist suppliers 207, 209

    suitability as pets for children 121

    tree climbing 159

fish and chips 103

Fishers Farm Park 47, 210

Fitzalan House Veterinary Group 274

Flatropers Wood 102, 233

fleas 169, 262, 276

Flight Equestrian Service Ltd 252

Flopsy rabbit 136-7

Florida panther 159

Folly Wildlife Rescue 177, 197

food suppliers 198-200

Forest Lodge Veterinary Centre Ltd 272

Forest Way Country Park 72, 241

fossils 93

Foundation for Integrated Medicine 116

Four Paws Dog Grooming 261

Fox Project 155, 180

Foxhollow Animal Sanctuary 155

French, Mari 267

Fryern Home Farm Livery 253

Fur Feathers 'n' Fins 204

G

Galley Hill Park 45, 236

Garden Pride Garden Centre 202

gardening for wildlife 117-19

Gatwick Kennels and Cattery 217

gecko 169

geese 48

German Shepherd Dog Helpline 177

giant turtles 58

Gillham Wood 45, 225

giraffe 53, 158

Glenwood Boarding Cattery 215

glowworm 74

goats

    oldest 158

    places to visit 48, 68, 69, 75, 81, 107

Golden Cross Equestrian Centre 253

golden eagle 129

goldfish, oldest 158

Goodwood Racecourse 65, 251

Goofy's Garlic Biscuits 133-4

gorillas 63, 224, 234

Gospels Farm Livery Stables 253

Goughs 202

grass snake 140, 151

Great Dane Adoption Society 180

Great Dane Rescue 177

Greatwood Sanctuary 177

Greek mythology 131

Green Fields Rescue 177
Green Gyms 142-3
greenfly 43
grey squirrels 127
Greyhound Rescue West of England 177
greyhounds
    charities 177, 178
    racing 166
    training 248
Greystud 253
grooming
    equipment 269
    parlours and mobile 258-61
Groomingdales 261
Grove Farm Riding School 255
Grove Lodge Veterinary Group 277
Guide Dogs for the Blind Association 177
Guinea Pig Rescue Centre 155, 196
guinea pigs
    boarding 214, 217
    places to visit 48
    rescue 155, 177, 196

H

Hadlow College 125-6
Ham, space chimp 111
Hamsey Riding School 255
hamsters
    cheek pouches 212
    suitability as pets for children 121
Handsome Hounds 261
Happy Hunting Grounds 100, 264

hares 151
harness makers 256
Hastings Animal Concern 155, 178, 220
Hastings Badger Protection Society 156,
    178, 223
Hayden Feeds 198
Hearing Dogs for Deaf People 178, 220
Heath Veterinary Clinic 273
Heaven Farm 106, 246
hedgehog charity 175
Heene Road Veterinary Practice Ltd 277
Hells Bells Art & Illustration 194
Helpline 9
Hen Heaven 156
Henley House Veterinary Practice 275
hens' eggs 89, 235
herbal remedies 113, 116, 192
Hereford & Worcester Animal Rescue 178
herons 150
Hewenstreet Circuit 104, 245
Highcroft Vet Group 272
Hillside Animal Sanctuary 181
hippopotamus 56, 158, 223
hobby 149
Hobgoblins Stud 257
Holidays Animal Care 267
Holistic Healers Association 116
holistic healing 113-14, 116
Hollingbury Park 55, 238
Holmbush Farm World 81, 279
Home of Rest for Horses 178
homeopathy 114, 116, 192, 273, 275
honeybees 45
Hooe Common 46, 225
horned toad 86

www.animalloversguides.co.uk

horseball 123
horses
  bloodhound hunts 124
  Bowen therapy 113
  charities 174, 175, 177, 178, 179, 182, 183, 220
  college courses 125-6
  craniosacral therapy 113
  cremations 264
  dental service 277
  emergency transport 252
  endangered 124-5
  equilibrium therapy 193
  farriers 124
  harness makers 256
  horseball 123
  hosing 114
  hydrotherapy 114
  insurance 160
  livery stables 253
  natural horsemanship 252
  places to visit 47, 48, 67, 86, 89, 90, 100, 102, 107
  polocrosse 123
  pursuits 122-6
  racecourse 65, 251
  racing injuries 166
  rescue 107, 154, 157, 197, 220
  riding clubs 125
  riding schools 254-5
  rug washing and repair 252
  saddle fitting 126
  saddle makers 256
  seeing end of nose 219
  shiatsu 115, 192
  side saddle riding 122
  spas 114
  specialist vets 271, 276
  sports massage 113
  stable manufacturers 251
  stud farms 257
  suitability as pets for children 121
  supplies 251-2
  swimming 114
  tack shops 251
  talks, lectures and demonstrations 123
  tallest 158
  training 187
horseshoe crab 207
Horsham and District Canine Society 222
Horsham Park 82, 242
hosing 114
hot water hosing 114
hotels 262-3
Hotham Park 49, 237
Hove Lagoon 84, 212
Hove Park 84, 243
Humane Slaughter Association 181
Hurstwood Feeds Ltd 199
Husse 199
hydrotherapy 114, 193

I

Ibis Hotel London Gatwick 262
ice cream, for birds 132
ichthyomancy 104
Iden Boarding Kennels 217

IFAW 178
Ifield Park Animal & Country Centre 204
indigenous species 127-9
injured animals 153-7
insurance 160-2
Internal Arts 193
International Animal Rescue 156
International League for the Protection of
Horses 178
International Otter Survival Fund 178
International School of Animal
    Aromatics 116
invertebrates 39, 79, 171
Iping and Stedham Commons 95, 234

K9 Goodcare 268
kangaroos 157, 222, 229
Karen's Dog Parlour 258
Kent and Sussex Horse Cremations 264
Kent Target Polocrosse 123
kestrels 149
kinesiology 192
kingfishers 41, 83, 150
Kingley Vale 65, 235
kingsnakes 171
Kipling Gardens 56, 245
Kit Wilson Trust for Animal Welfare
    156, 195
Kitty Cat Loaf 134
Knockhatch Adventure Park 75, 212

J

J & J Pets 260
Jack, baboon 111
Jersey cows 90
Jet Set Pets 269
jird 168-9
John the Baptist 131
jokes 189
Jones, A. K., bird vet 276
Josie Tipler Animal Portraits 194
Just Minis Agility Club 247

K

K9 by Igloo Designs 201
K9 Clips 259

L

Labrador Rescue 156, 178
ladybirds 51
Lancing Canine Obedience Group 248
Lancing Ring Nature Reserve 87, 230
Landport Brooks 89, 243
lar gibbons 38
lawns 118
leeches 111
Leechpool and Owlbeech Woods 82, 243
leopard gecko 169
Level, The 59, 239
Levin Down 66, 227
Lewes Brooks 90, 244
Lguanodon dinosaur 93
Licky Liver Lumps 134
Lincolnshire Greyhound Trust 178

Lindey Lodge 216
lions 278
Little Brockhurst Farm Canine Centre 247
livery stables 253
Living World 200
lizards 66
llamas 75, 102, 107, 211
London Wildlife Trust 179
London Zoo 116
Look and Sea Visitor Centre 93, 213
Lord Whisky Animal Sanctuary 156
lost animals 153-7
Lower Stoneham Livery & Stud 253
Luxicote Poodles Specialist Dog Groomer 259
Lyndon-Dykes, K. 123

maggots 111
magnotherapy 114
Malling Downs 105, 234
Mallydams Wood Wildlife Sanctuary & Study Centre 156
Mammal Society 181
mammoth 51
Manor Guest House 263
Manor House Cattery 214
Marina Gardens 93, 244
marine life 58, 60, 77, 207, 208
Marine Park Gardens 49, 237
Marline Valley 77, 228
marsh frog 127

Marshfoot Cattery 216
Martlets Cattery 218
massage 113
Mayes & Scrine Equine Veterinary Practice 276
Mayhew Animal Home 181
McTimoney treatment 113
Meadowside Boarding Kennels 218
medicine, use of animals 111
Medusa 131
Mens, The 98, 232
Meridian Veterinary Practice 274
Mewes Veterinary Clinic, The 272
Mewsbrook Park 94, 244
Mid Sussex Badger Protection Group 156, 222
Mid Sussex Happy Breed Dog Rescue 221
Middle Farm 90, 280
Mill Hill 38, 231
Mitchels Wood Farm Equestrian Centre 255
Moggery, The 181
Mohair Centre 68, 278
moles 151
monkeys 225
Mount Caburn 91, 230
Mount Noddy 156
mountain lion 159
Mucky Pups 258
museums 52, 67, 211
mythology 131

N

National Animal Welfare Trust 179
National Association of Animal Therapists 116
National Federation of Reiki Practitioners 116
Native American Indians 144
Natural Animal Health 116
Naturally Pets 249
New Carlton Boarding Kennels 214
New Zealand Blue ducks 41
Newbury Pond 78, 229
Newhaven Fort 96, 213
Newick Aquatics 209
Newmarket Hill 56, 213
nightingales 149-50
Noah's Ark 66, 195, 266
Northiam DIY and Garden 204
Nymans Garden 79, 242

O

Oak Leaves Pet Crematorium 264
Oathall Veterinary Group 272
octopus 159, 247
Old Clayton Kennels and Catteries 219
Old Lodge 70, 227
ophidiophobia 138, 140-1
Orchid Riding Centre 254
Oscar Pet Foods 199, 200
osteopathy 115
ostrich 97
Otter Trust 181

otters
    charities 178, 181
    declining population 128
    where to see 148
Ouse Banks 106, 246
Ovingdean Cliffs 96, 213
owls 80, 108, 158

P

Pagham Harbour 67, 234
paintings
    animal portraits 194
    animals in 130-1
Pals4Pets 218
Pampermepet 201
Paradise Pets 205
parakeets 128
Parrot Line UK 182
parrots
    charities 182
    oldest 158
    specialist suppliers 202, 205
Passies Pond 88, 208
Paws & Claws Animal Rescue Service 156
Paws Animal Sanctuary 195
Paws for Kids 179
PDSA 156, 179, 270
Pebsham Riding School 254
penguins 250
People and Dogs Society (PADS) 179
People's Dispensary for Sick Animals
(PDSA) 156, 179, 270

performing animals 163-7
Performing Animals (Regulation)
   Act 1925, 163
Pet and Garden Warehouse, The 203
Pet Behaviour Centre 249
Pet Doctors 273, 275
Pet Food Shop, The 198
Pet Love 205
Pet Passports 172-3
Pet Patrol 365 266
Pet Pet Pet 203
Pet Pride 203
Pet Shop, The 204
pet shops 201-6
Pet Sitting Service 265
Pet Travel Scheme 172, 173
PETA UK 179
PETS 172, 173
pets
   cemeteries and crematoria 100,
      185, 264
   for children 120-1
   death 184-5
   exotic 168-71
   food suppliers 198-200
   homemade treats 132-5
   import and export 269
   insurance 160-2
   minding 265-8
   name questionnaire 25-6
   ownership 190
   passports 172-3
   relocation agency 269
   shops 201-6
   as therapy 111

training 186-7
unusual 168-71
Pets Corner 206
Pets Home Alone 268
Pets Stay Home 266
Pette Shoppe, The 205
Petworth House and Park 98, 244
phobias 138-41
physiotherapy 115, 116, 275
Pierpoint Pet Supplies 203
pigeons 215
pigs 48, 69, 75, 86, 90, 102, 107
Pippingford Manor Liveries 253
Pointer, Barbara 248
polar bears 253
Polegate Saddlery 256
polocrosse 123
Pond Restoration and Maintenance Ltd 208
Pondakoi Aquatics 207
ponds 117-18
   builders 209
   pond-keeping club 221
   restoration and maintenance 208
ponies
   dental service 277
   endangered 124-5
   oldest 158
   places to visit 47, 86, 88, 102
   suitability as pets for children 121
poodles, specialist groomer 259
porpoise 152
Portland Road Veterinary Surgery 271
portrait artists 194
Portslade Retreat Horse and Animal
   Rescue 157

Posh Dogs 260
Powdermill Wood 43, 224
predator attacks 154
Preston Park 57, 238
Priors Leaze Veterinary Clinic 274
Promise Pets 265
puffer fish 159
puffins 72
Pulborough Brooks 99, 232
pullets 46
puma 159
puzzles 188-9
   solution 282

Q

quarantine 172
   kennels 216
Queen's Park 57, 239

R

Rabbit Welfare Association 222
Rabbit Welfare Fund 182
Rabbitmotel 217
rabbits
   boarding 214, 217
   charities 182
   club 222
   indigenous 127
   nests 137

oldest 158
places to visit 48, 66, 69, 75
rescue 154, 177, 197
suitability as pets for children 120
training humans 136-7
Raggy's Dog Grooming 260
Railway Land Local Nature Reserve
   91, 231
Rare Breeds Survival Trust 124-5
rays 58
Raystede Centre for Animal Welfare Ltd
   100, 157, 182, 196
recipes 132-5
record breakers 158-9
red kites 129
red squirrels 127
red tiger 159
Redmire Stables and Buildings Ltd 251
Redwings Horse Sanctuary 179
Reef Aquatics 207
reiki 115, 116, 192, 193
reindeer 248
religious art 131
relocation agency 269
Repco Herpetological Supply 201
reptiles
   charity 180
   conservation group 231
   specialist supplier 201
   specialist vets 272
rescue centres 153-7
Research Council for Complementary
Medicine 116
Respect for Animals 167
rhinocerous 40

charities 179, 180
riding clubs 125
riding schools 254-5
Roger's Wildlife Rescue 197
Rohese Cattery 215
Rose Holistic Health 192
Roundstone Kennels and Cattery 214
Royal College of Veterinary Surgeons 116
royal python 171
Royal Society for the Protection
    of Birds 179
RSPCA 179
    Head Office 157
Rug Doctor, The 252
Runners 265

S

saddle
    fitting 126
    makers 256
Saddlers' Company 126
saints 131
Sally's Dog Grooming 259
sanctuaries 195-7
Save the Rhino International 179
Saxby Bed and Breakfast 262
scorpions 171
sea life 58, 60, 77, 207, 208
Seaford and District Dog Training Club 248
Seaford Aquatics 209
Seaford Head Nature Reserve 103, 233
seahorse 58, 77, 159

Seahorse Trust 182
Sealife Centre 58, 207
seals 152
Sebakwe Black Rhino Trust 180
Selwyns Wood 79, 229
Senlac Vets 270
serpents 131
Seven Sisters Country Park 103, 233
Seven Sisters Sheep Centre 48, 278
shark 58, 59, 77, 243
sheep 48, 58, 86, 87, 107, 278
shiatsu 115, 192
Shiatsu Society (UK) 116
Shire horse 47, 67, 90
Shoreline Pet Supplies 199
Siamese Cat Club Welfare Trust 182
Sian Saddlery 256
Side Saddle Association 122
sloth 158
Small Pets' Hotel 217
smooth snake 140
snails, edible 127
snakes
    adders 140-1, 151
    in art 131
    corn snake 171
    grass snake 140, 151
    indigenous 140-1
    kingsnake 171
    as pets 171
    phobia 138, 140-1
    places to visit 66
    royal python 171
    smooth snake 140
    where to see 151

snapping turtle 269

societies 221-3

Society of Homeopaths 116

Society of Master Saddlers 126

Something Different 256

South Downs 58, 226

South Downs Badger Protection Society
    157, 223

South East Dog Services 249

Southern Aviaries 206

Southern Bernese Mountain Dog Club 222

Southwater Country Park 105, 234

space travel 111

sparrowhawk 149

spas 114

sperm whale 159

spiders
    most venomous 159
    as pets 171
    phobia 138-40
    webs 110

spirit world 144-7

sports 166

sports massage 113

SPR Centre 198

Squirrel Rescue 157

squirrels 49, 76, 127

St Agnes 131

St Andrew's Church 85, 230

St Andrews Farm Kennels 216

St Annes Veterinary Group 271, 273, 274

St Ann's Well Gardens 85, 243

St Francis Veterinary Surgery 270

St Jerome 131

St John the Evangelist 131

Stable Door, The 251

Stable Horses 252

stable manufacturers 251

Stag Inn, The 263

Stanmer Park 59, 239

Stevens, Sandie 266

Steyning Pet Shop 206

stoat 119

Stoneywish Nature Reserve 71, 227

Stopham Pets 205

stud farms 257

Studio, The 194

Suffolk Horse Society 182

Suffolk Punch 89

Support Dogs 180

Supreme Pet Care 266

Sussex Amphibian and Reptile Group 231

Sussex Bat Hospital 157

Sussex Chelonian Society 222

Sussex Horse Rescue Trust 107, 157, 197

Sussex Wildlife Trust 80, 157, 229

swans 39, 44

swimming 114, 193

symbolism 130-1, 144-7

T

T C Tack and Things 251

Tabitha's Tuna Tasters 135

tack shops 251

Taking The Lead 250

Tall Pines Boarding Kennel & Cattery 216

Tammy's Pet Store 203

tarantulas 171
1066 Country Walk 42, 236
Therapaws 193
tigers 261
Tipler, Hayley, 194
Tipler, Josie 194
toad, horned 86
Tortoise Trust 182
tortoises
    as pets 170
    places to visit 66
Traffic 182
travel
    Pet Passports 172-3
    pet relocation service 269
treat recipes 132-5
tree frogs 170-1
tropical fish 207, 209
TTL Shop 206
Tulleys Farm 69, 211
tuna 55
turkeys 107
turtles
    giant 58
    snapping 269

U

Ultimate Animals 202
Undercliff Walk 60, 239
Underwater World 77, 208
unicorn 131
unusual pets 168-71

V

Vale Wildlife Rescue 182
Venus of Urbino 130
Veteran Horse Society 183
veterinary surgeries 270-7
Vickathea Animal Grooming 258

W

wallabies 106, 128
Waltham Brooks 99, 233
Warnham Animal Sanctuary 157
Warnham Nature Reserve 83, 230
Washbrooks Farm 86, 279
wasp nests 159
water vole 148
Weald Agility Society 247
Weald & Downland Open Air Museum
    67, 211
West Beach Local Nature Reserve 94, 231
West Chiltington Cavaliers 223
West Dean Gardens 68, 240
Westergate Dog Training 248
Westpoint Veterinary Services 276
Westrow Equine Dental Service 277
Wetnose Animal Campaign 183
Wey and Arun Canal Trust 47, 237
Whale and Dolphin Conservation Society 182
whales
    charity 182
    record breakers 158, 159

where to see 152

White Orchid, The 193

Whitehawk Hill 60, 226

Whitelands Kennels 219

Widewater Lagoon 104, 213

Wilbury Veterinary Surgery 273

Wild Park 61, 226

Wilderness Wood 107, 246

Wildfowl and Wetlands Centre 41, 224

Wildfowl and Wetlands Trust 183

wildlife

    charities 176, 177, 179, 182, 183, 220

    conservation 117-19

    rescue 153-7, 195, 197

    where to see 148-52

Wildlife Rescue 157

Wildlife Rescue Ambulance Service 183

Windmill Lodge Stables 252

Withdean Woods 61, 239

wolves 71, 128

Woodacre 262

Woodgreen Animal Shelters 183

Woodland Veterinary Hospital 274

Woods Mill 80, 229

Woof! Dog Walking and Petcare 267

woolly rhino 51

wordsearch 189

working animals 110-11, 278-80

World Parrot Trust 182

World Society for the Protection of Animals 183

Worshipful Company of Farriers 126

Worshipful Company of Loriners 126

Worshipful Company of Saddlers 126

Worthing and District Animal Rescue Service 157

Worthing and District Cat Protection 183, 220

Worthing Animal Clinic 183, 277

Worthing Cat Welfare Trust 157, 183

wound healing 111

Wrighting, W. 248

yak 89

zebra 64

Zoo Licensing Act 1981, 165

zoophobia 141

zoos 38, 116, 164-6, 210

The Animal Lovers' Guides Team would like to acknowledge and thank the following photographers for their contributions:

Ali Taylor, Alison Scott, Arjan Boer, Bill Sarver, Caroline Knight, Chris Potter, Christophe Libert, Cormac Scanlan, Daniel Nedelcu, Daniel West, Drusillas Zoo Park, Elke Rohn, Eridge Rocks by permission of www.southernSandstone.co.uk, Fran Roger, Gillian Townsend, Hugh Clark, Jack Kemp, Joanna Atkinson, John Evans, Kevin Walsh, Kieron Saunders, Kirsty Doherty, Luis Rock, Lynne Lancaster, Martin R.W, Mark V, Michael Bernpaintner, Michael Richert, Mike Jones, Nick Pye, Peter Zelei, Rebecca Kerton, Redster, Rico Jensen, Rob Waterhouse, Sarah Avayou, Skyro, Steve Cannon, Steve Knight, Susan McManus.

Back cover photograph and photograph on page 10 by titch photography of Bexhill-on-Sea.